7-7-65

Principles of Computation

PETER CALINGAERT

ADDISON-WESLEY PUBLISHING COMPANY, INC.

Reading, Massachusetts · *Palo Alto* · *London* · *Dallas* · *Atlanta*

This book is in the

ADDISON-WESLEY SERIES
IN COMPUTER SCIENCE AND INFORMATION PROCESSING

Consulting Editors
RICHARD S. VARGA AND EDWARD J. McCLUSKEY, JR.

Foreword

1316112

This book was developed from notes for a one-semester course which I introduced in 1962 at the Computation Laboratory of Harvard University. About half of the material was prepared specifically for that course, and half adapted from courses taught previously. The text is intended for freshmen and sophomores in the natural sciences, mathematics, engineering, and the quantitative social sciences. Students in the course for which the material was developed were expected to be taking concurrently, or to have already taken, the second half of the freshman mathematics course. The reader is assumed to have been introduced to differentiation and antidifferentiation, and to know how to integrate polynomials. Further knowledge of the calculus is not required. Taylor's series, in particular, is used in only two brief sections which may be omitted without loss of continuity.

In most textbooks on automatic computation it is customary to discuss minute details either of machine-language coding or of compiler use. The former requires the choice of an illustrative computer. The author is then caught between the Scylla of inventing a hypothetical computer and the Charybdis of using an existing machine. The first alternative is unreal and the second places on the reader the burden of obtaining access to a copy of the machine. On the other hand, although the introduction of a language such as COBOL or FORTRAN may give the reader a tool he can often use directly, it certainly isolates the student from the fundamental characteristics of a computer. Moreover, there is no more reason to incorporate in an academic course the details of computer programming than those of slide rule operation.

This book offers a basic introduction to the principles of computation, both digital and analog, both manual and automatic. Although considerable emphasis is placed on the use of automatic computers, the primary focus remains on the fundamentals of computation rather than on computers. The student is exposed to various techniques and devices for solving computational problems and is presented with elements of the relevant mathematical theory. The text is divided into four parts each followed by a collection of exercises.

With few exceptions, the exercises have been tested on homework assignments and examinations. I strongly urge that they be supplemented by laboratory exercises with digital and analog computing equipment, simple and complex. Because of widely varying facilities and student requirements, such exercises are better developed by the individual instructor than incorporated in the text.

Part I is entitled *Digital Computation*. The elements of computer programming are introduced in a variant of the Iverson notation, without reference to either an existing or a hypothetical machine. Emphasis is placed on problem preparation and on basic programming concepts, rather than on the development of programming skill. A historical introduction is included; computer-aided coding and the control of error are also discussed. The reader with access to an automatic computing system is expected to learn the details of its use, with or without the intermediary of a compiler, from sources appropriate to the system.

Part II, *Numbers*, starts from the assumption, lamentably too often true, that the student comprehends inadequately the decimal or any other system of representation. It develops the notion that all numbers of practical utility are rational. Representations, properties, and arithmetic of integer, rational, and complex numbers are introduced. An extensive section on error starts with the types, sources, and propagation of uncertainty, and continues with a treatment of selected topics from probability theory and large-sample statistics. The statistical material acquaints the student with some of the elementary methods of handling data, and is used to illustrate the importance of organizing computations with care.

Part III, *Analog Computation*, introduces alignment-chart nomograms as a tool for the graphical solution of algebraic equations. Graphical algebra is succeeded by graphical analysis, in the form of differentiation and integration. Differential equations are introduced by proceeding from the quadrature $dy/dx = f(x)$ to the problem $dy/dx = f(y)$ and the more general $dy/dx = f(x, y)$. Nowhere are analytic methods of solution used. Exposition of the direction field is followed by the introduction of analog computers. A brief physical explanation, independent of the remainder of the text, is provided of the circuital use of an operational amplifier. However, analog computer programming is developed without recourse to physical intuition or engineering background. Particular emphasis is laid on the scaling of both magnitude and time. Computer solutions of differential equations both linear and nonlinear, with constant or variable coefficients, are discussed.

Part IV, *Numerical Methods*, is essentially mathematical in content, and concerned with problem analysis. Because of the lack of a calculus prerequisite, a rigorous treatment of error is not attempted, although the importance of error terms is underscored. Theory and practice are developed in parallel for five important subjects. Iterative methods are derived for the solution of algebraic and transcendental equations. Topics in the theory of linear systems are illustrated with and proved by the use of Gauss elimination. Elementary polynomial theory, which provides a link to the complex numbers of Part II, covers evaluation and root extraction and leads to ordinate methods of interpolation. The interpolating polynomial unifies a presentation of numerical differentiation and quadrature. Differential equations, already discussed in Part III from the analog point of view, are treated numerically in the final chapter.

I could not have completed the book without the contributions of the many students who taught me, of the teaching assistants, Mr. H. James Herring in particular, who aided with the creation of exercises, and of several former colleagues. I was generously assisted by Professor Douglas P. Adams in preparing the section on graphical calculus, and much of Part IV was inspired by Dr. Robin Esch. To Dr. Kenneth E. Iverson and Professor Robert L. Ashenhurst I am indebted for careful reading of the manuscript. Of course, since I declined almost as many of their suggestions as I adopted, they cannot be held responsible for deficiencies in the final result. Especially helpful was the contribution of Professor Myron B Fiering, who risked the success of his course upon a classroom trial of the manuscript.

Poughkeepsie, N.Y.   P.C.
December, 1964

Contents

Part I

Digital Computation

Chapter 1

History of Digital Devices

1-1 ARITHMETIC MACHINES

Man's earliest aid in performing digital operations, other than his digits themselves, was probably small stones or pebbles. Indeed, our word *calculation* is derived from the Latin *calculus* for pebble. By piercing the stones and sliding them along strings or rods, man developed the line abacus about five thousand years ago. This device is still employed extensively in many parts of the world.

Further progress in digital devices did not occur until the seventeenth century. In 1617, three years after his invention of logarithms, Napier devised a set of sliding rods with numbers on them for use in multiplication. The rods constituted a mechanization of the multiplication table and were essentially different from the mechanization of logarithms embodied in the slide rule, which is due primarily to Oughtred (1632). Since the material of the rods was often bone, the device was commonly called *Napier's bones*. In 1642 Pascal built a machine to add and subtract, and in 1671 Leibniz started work on a machine to multiply and divide. Although the machine was completed in 1694, it did not prove practical. A century and more passed before Thomas de Colmar introduced in 1820 his *Arithmomètre*, the first commercial multiplying machine. The first practical key-driven adder was made in 1886 by Felt, who patented the *Comptometer* the following year. The modern desk calculator mechanism is due to Odhner (1891), and its electric drive dates from 1920.

1-2 DIFFERENCE ENGINES

Mathematical tables usually display associated pairs of values. The first member of each pair is a value of an independent variable, or *argument;* the second is that of a *function* dependent upon the argument. Thus x might be the argument and $\sin x$ the function shown in a table of sines. The differences between successive values of a function, for equally spaced arguments, are known as *first differences*. The differences between successive first differences are known as *second differences*, etc. It is easy to show that the nth differences of

3

a polynomial of degree* n are constant, and that higher-order differences are zero. This is illustrated in Table 1–1, where the function is the second-degree polynomial $f(x) = x^2 - 5x + 6$. Each of the rightmost columns contains the differences of the entries in the previous column. Any smooth function can be closely approximated over a small range by a polynomial. A table of such a function can be checked for (nonsystematic) errors by verifying that differences of an appropriately high order are nearly constant.

<table>
<tr><td align="center">**Table 1–1**</td><td align="center">**Table 1–2**</td></tr>
<tr><td align="center">DIFFERENCE TABLE FOR</td><td align="center">CONSTRUCTION OF $f(x) = (x + 1)^2$</td></tr>
<tr><td align="center">$f(x) = x^2 - 5x + 6$</td><td align="center">FROM DIFFERENCES</td></tr>
</table>

x	$f(x)$			
0	6			
		−4		
1	2		2	
		−2		0
2	0		2	
		0		0
3	0		2	
		2		0
4	2		2	
		4		
5	6			

x	$f(x)$		
0	1		
		3	
1	4		2
		5	
2	9		2
		7	
3	16		2
		9	
4	25		
5			

Difference tables have long been used in the preparation and verification of mathematical tables. By using difference tables, the values of a polynomial (and hence of a function approximated by a polynomial) can be tabulated without multiplication. This requires only the prior computation of the first n differences at the starting point, for which techniques are available. Since the nth differences are constant, the nth column is known and can be used to compute the $(n - 1)$th column. Each column is computed in turn until the column of function values is obtained. An alternative organization of the work involves computing in turn one value in each of the difference columns. Table 1–2 shows a stage in the calculation of the second-degree polynomial with $f(0) = 1$ and initial first and second differences of 3 and 2, respectively.

In the eighteenth century it was customary to employ hordes of clerks, skilled only in addition, to compute astronomical and navigational tables, under the

---

* See p. 156 for a formal definition.

supervision of mathematicians who could also multiply. Clerical errors*
abounded, of course, and the desire to eliminate them led the English inventor
Charles Babbage to propose in 1811 the construction of a *difference engine* for
calculations involving differences. By 1822 he had a working model with eight
decimal positions that could handle second differences. He then proposed a
20-place machine for sixth differences, but ceased work on that project in 1833,
when his mind turned to a much more powerful type of engine. His plans were
eventually proved practical by the construction in 1855, by the Swedish printer
George Scheutz and his son Edward, of a 14-place fourth-difference machine
based on Babbage's design. The modern accounting machine, although designed for different purposes, can generally be used as a difference engine.

1–3 ANALYTICAL ENGINES

The project for which Babbage abandoned the difference engine in 1833 was
the design of a machine which would not be limited to a single task, but which
would perform a variable sequence of operations to be specified in advance for
each problem. Such a machine had been mentioned by Müller in 1786, but
was first seriously proposed by Babbage. His requirements were far in excess
of what early nineteenth-century technology could produce, and the machine
proved impossible either to build or to finance.

The *analytical engine*, as Babbage called it, was to be organized into five
main units. The *mill* was to perform addition, subtraction, multiplication, and
division, and was to embody an elementary decision operation. The latter
would permit the machine to choose among alternative sequences of computations on the basis of the result of a prior sequence. Intermediate results
were to be held in a *store* with capacity for a thousand 50-digit numbers. The
control unit would direct the operation of all parts of the machine through
holes in punched cards, similar to those introduced by Jacquard at the turn of
the century for controlling automatic looms. *Input* of data to the machine would
also utilize these cards. *Output* would assume either of two forms. Cards would
be punched for later use as input, thus augmenting the internal store with
indefinitely large external storage. For final output, such as mathematical
tables, an automatic typesetting machine was to be included. This would re-
move another major source of errors in printed tables. The organization of
Babbage's analytical engine is recognizable to a remarkable degree in that of
many modern automatic computers.

The gross organization of a typical computer is shown in Fig. 1–1. The more
modern term, *arithmetic and logical unit (ALU)*, has replaced Babbage's *mill*.
Shown with the five major units is an information transfer *bus* used to transmit

---

* It was generally observed that the fewest errors were made by those clerks least
schooled in the intricacies of arithmetic.

data and instructions from one unit to another. The solid arrows represent paths for information flow; the dashed arrows represent the exercise of control.

Babbage's paramount contribution was the concept of automatic sequential control. Any sequence of the elementary arithmetical operations could be specified in advance and the mechanism would execute all steps of the sequence fully automatically. The user had to foresee all eventualities, such as attempts to extract the square root of a negative number; but, once having foreseen them, he could then instruct the engine to follow different courses of action for different data, or even for different intermediate results. The resulting flexibility would enable the analytical engine to carry out not only the simple operations of a difference engine, but also much more elaborate computations.

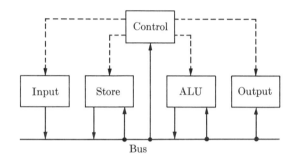

Figure 1–1

Another century passed before Howard Aiken of Harvard University proposed in 1937 the construction of an analytical engine, similar to Babbage's in concept and in power, but more modest in size. This time the technology was adequate, and in 1939 Aiken persuaded IBM to build the machine. Mark I, as it is generally known, was placed in service in 1943 and given by IBM to Harvard in 1944. Its store held 72 signed numbers of 23 decimal digits in counters that also served as part of the mill. A multiply unit and a function generation unit were also included. Punched cards were used for input and output, and electric typewriters (whose copy could be printed by photo offset) served the same purpose as Babbage's automatic typesetter. Operations were controlled by holes in punched paper tape, which was actually uncut card stock. Mark I was the first general-purpose automatic computer ever built.

Meanwhile, George Stibitz and Samuel Williams had started work in 1937 on various special-purpose machines. Their complex number computer (1940) and interpolator (1942) preceded their first general-purpose machine, the Bell Relay Computer, completed in 1944. Electronic components were introduced by J. Presper Eckert and John Mauchly, whose Eniac (1946) employed no fewer than 18,000 vacuum tubes. About this time John von Neumann suggested that a computer's operating instructions be stored, not externally as on punched tape, but within the store of the computer. He showed how the resulting ability of the computer to modify its own instructions could greatly enhance its scope, and embodied his suggestions in a machine built at Princeton in 1948.

Across the Atlantic, Maurice Wilkes built the Edsac in Cambridge in 1949. The first automatic computers offered for sale were the Ferranti Mark I* (England, 1951) and Eckert and Mauchly's Univac (United States, 1951). The subsequent history of automatic computers has been characterized by rapid technological development, by increasing sophistication in the use of computing devices, and by their application to almost every field of human endeavor.

---

* Unrelated to Aiken's machine.

Chapter 2

Digital Computer Use

2-1 PROBLEM PREPARATION

The preparation of problems for solution by means of an automatic digital computer may be described as consisting of three phases: analysis, programming, and coding.

Analysis involves casting the problem as originally stated into a form suitable for manipulation by means of the elementary operations provided in computers. If the original statement is mathematical, the process utilizes *numerical analysis*, the subject of Part IV of this book. More often than not, however, the problem is formulated in the language of a specific discipline and must first be represented as a presumably equivalent mathematical problem by the use of techniques relevant to that discipline. An understanding of the particular field to which the computer is to be applied is therefore of importance equal to that of knowing in general how a computer is used.

Programming is the task of specifying the sequence of events that are to occur during the solution of a problem by an automatic computer. Programming is not wholly distinct from analysis, of course, but it may be viewed as that part of problem preparation most closely concerned with the properties of computers in general. The primary considerations are the organization, completeness, and logical consistency of the specified process.

Coding is the specification of the actual instructions to a given computer. It may be viewed as the translation of the process specified by the programmer into the language used by the specific machine under consideration. This process is not entirely distinct from programming. Indeed, it is included by some writers in their definition of programming.

Although the analysis of a problem necessarily precedes the programming and coding, it is affected by the requirements of computer programming. Accordingly, discussion of analysis will follow that of programming.

(a) Programming

Notation and Elementary Concepts. It is instructive to start with an example almost trivial in its simplicity. Let it be required to program a difference engine to prepare a table of squares of positive integers. Table 2–1 gives the first few integers with their squares and first and second differences. Note that each difference is shown, not as in Table 1–2, but on the same line as the lower-order difference (or function value) to which it is added. The first line of the desired table of squares includes the entries 1, 1. The second line can be calculated by the following additions. The initial value 3 of y is added to the initial value 1 of x to yield the new value 4 of x. The new value 2 of i is obtained by adding 1 to the initial value 1. Finally a new value 5 of y must be produced before further progress is possible. This is the sum of the initial value 3 of y and that of z, which is 2. The process may be repeated indefinitely to produce successive pairs i, x of integers and their squares.

A description of this process in the difference engine can be made very concise by use of statements whose form is particularly simple. The fact that the initial value of x is 1 will be specified by the use of the statement

$$x \leftarrow 1$$

as the first statement involving x. The arrow in the statement may be thought of as pointing to a variable (x in the example) *defined* by the statement. Here, the definition states that the value

Table 2–1

i	x	y	z
1	1	3	2
2	4	5	2
3	9	7	2
4	16	9	2
5	25	11	2

of the variable x is the constant 1. Alternatively, the arrow may be considered to point at the result of an operation (here setting x equal to 1) described by the statement. The right-hand side of a statement need not be limited to constants. The first addition of the process is described by the statement

$$x \leftarrow x + y.$$

Here x is defined as the sum of the previously defined variables x and y. The value of x on the right-hand side is the value before the occurrence of the addition operation corresponding to the definition; the value on the left-hand side is that after the operation.

A computer *program* consists of a series of such statements that describe the process effected by the computer. The first stage in the computation of table values might be specified by Program 2–1. Each statement is to be thought of as being executed after the one immediately above it, and the process starts with the topmost.

Program 2–2 incorporates the printing of the first line of the table. Here a statement without an arrow is used for convenience. Printing of the second and third lines, as well as calculation of the third, is included in Program 2–3. In Program 2–4 the statement "print 1, 1" has been replaced by the statement "print i, x" placed after rather than before the initial definition of i and x. This shows that a single type of print statement suffices to specify the printing of both the initial line of given values and the subsequent lines of computed values. Further lines may be computed and printed as in Program 2–5, where the ellipsis indicates as many repetitions of the basic four-statement pattern (shown by the brace) as are required. Clearly, the program so written becomes longer as the length of the desired table increases. Not only does the program become unwieldy to write, but the corresponding computer instructions occupy more and more of the space in the store. If the same operations are to be repeated, albeit with different numbers, they may as well be repeated in time alone, rather than in both space and time. The written sequence of execution of statements can be broken by a resumption of execution from a place other than that following the last statement executed. This break in sequence or *jump* is shown in Program 2–6 by means of an arrow from one statement to its successor. Program 2–6 describes the repeated calculation and printing of lines of the table of squares. Each statement has been numbered at the left for ease

Program 2–1

$i \leftarrow 1$
$x \leftarrow 1$
$y \leftarrow 3$
$z \leftarrow 2$
$x \leftarrow x + y$
$i \leftarrow i + 1$
$y \leftarrow y + z$

Program 2–3

Print 1, 1
$i \leftarrow 1$
$x \leftarrow 1$
$y \leftarrow 3$
$z \leftarrow 2$
$x \leftarrow x + y$
$i \leftarrow i + 1$
$y \leftarrow y + z$
Print i, x
$x \leftarrow x + y$
$i \leftarrow i + 1$
$y \leftarrow y + z$
Print i, x

Program 2–2

Print 1, 1
$i \leftarrow 1$
$x \leftarrow 1$
$y \leftarrow 3$
$z \leftarrow 2$
$x \leftarrow x + y$
$i \leftarrow i + 1$
$y \leftarrow y + z$

Program 2–4

$i \leftarrow 1$
$x \leftarrow 1$
$y \leftarrow 3$
$z \leftarrow 2$
Print i, x
$x \leftarrow x + y$
$i \leftarrow i + 1$
$y \leftarrow y + z$
Print i, x
$x \leftarrow x + y$
$i \leftarrow i + 1$
$y \leftarrow y + z$
Print i, x

Program 2–5

$i \leftarrow 1$
$x \leftarrow 1$
$y \leftarrow 3$
$z \leftarrow 2$
Print i, x
$x \leftarrow x + y$
$i \leftarrow i + 1$
$y \leftarrow y + z$
Print i, x
$\left. \begin{array}{l} x \leftarrow x + y \\ i \leftarrow i + 1 \\ y \leftarrow y + z \\ \text{Print } i, x \end{array} \right\}$
$\vdots$
$x \leftarrow x + y$
$i \leftarrow i + 1$
$y \leftarrow y + z$
Print i, x

of reference. Here, statement 8 is followed by statement 5. Statements 5 through 8 thus constitute a *loop*, which will be executed repeatedly to generate successive lines of the table.

If a difference engine were actually programmed in the manner of Program 2–6, it would continue to generate table entries indefinitely. The loop of this program is therefore classified as an *endless loop*. The process might fail eventually for lack of paper, or from inability of the machine to hold numbers of ever-increasing size. The user might watch the printed output and stop the computation manually when enough of the table had been prepared. With automatic machinery it is customary, as well as more convenient, to provide means for terminating automatically the repetitions of the loop. Indeed, the endless loop is generally regarded as a programming error.

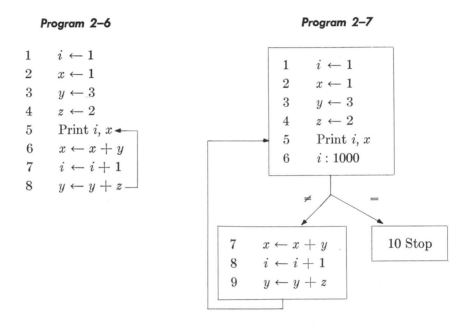

Program 2–6

1    $i \leftarrow 1$
2    $x \leftarrow 1$
3    $y \leftarrow 3$
4    $z \leftarrow 2$
5   Print i, x
6    $x \leftarrow x + y$
7    $i \leftarrow i + 1$
8    $y \leftarrow y + z$

Program 2–7

1    $i \leftarrow 1$
2    $x \leftarrow 1$
3    $y \leftarrow 3$
4    $z \leftarrow 2$
5   Print i, x
6    $i : 1000$

$\neq$ $=$

7    $x \leftarrow x + y$
8    $i \leftarrow i + 1$
9    $y \leftarrow y + z$

10 Stop

A common device for deciding when to terminate a loop is the comparison, usually of a variable with a constant limiting value, but frequently of one variable with another. The statement whose execution follows the comparison is selected from among two or more, according to the result of the comparison. Program 2–7 illustrates the use of a comparison to terminate generation of the table after 1000 entries have been printed. Statement 6 symbolizes the comparison by means of a colon placed between the names of the quantities compared. Here the variable i is compared with the constant 1000. Each arrow emanating from statement 6 is labeled with a symbol. Substitution of this symbol for the colon of statement 6 yields the comparison result for which the direction corresponding to the symbol is followed. Thus if $i \neq 1000$, statement

7 follows statement 6, whereas if $i = 1000$, statement 10 follows instead. The bifurcation of the arrow is termed a *branch point*, or often simply *branch*. Note that the first 999 times statement 6 is reached, the process will follow the loop, whose length has now been increased to five statements by the incorporation of the test. Statement 10 is shown as a reminder that automatic computers must generally be specifically instructed to stop.

An alternative organization of the computation is presented as Program 2–8. Here statement numbers have not been supplied, and the branch has been indicated by two separate arrows. The reader should verify that Programs 2–7 and 2–8 result in the preparation of identical tables. If, instead of a difference engine, an automatic computer capable of performing multiplication were available, Program 2–8 could be replaced by Program 2–9.

The foregoing programs illustrate an important principle. If the functions generated by two processes are equivalent, the processes may nevertheless differ. The processes themselves are the major concern here.

Addressing and Iteration Control. Consider next the use of an automatic computer in a simple data conversion application. Eighty numbers, x_0 through x_{79}, have been obtained from metering devices calibrated in arbitrary units, and are held in the store of the computer. Each number x_i is first to be checked to ensure that it lies between the limits a_i and b_i and is then to be converted into engineering units by use of the formula $y_i = c_i x_i + d_i$. If for any x_i the condition $a_i < x_i < b_i$ is not satisfied, the conversion program is to branch to another program to take care of the error situation. Program 2–10 is one solution. Here only one arrow is shown for each branch. If the condition that labels the arrow is not met, the next statement in sequence is executed rather than the one at the end of the arrow. The stop statement will henceforth be omitted as an indication that the program shown may be only part of a larger program.

When a given computer is coded to execute the preceding program, the instruction used must refer to the specific place in the store where each operand is to be found and each result stored. This is generally achieved in automatic computers by subdividing the store into small compartments, each of which holds a unit of data (e.g., a number). To each compartment, or store *location*, is assigned a number known as the *address* of that location. This address may be used in the program to identify the *content* of the corresponding location, i.e., the data stored there. A convenient notation is to denote by $\{s\}$ the data stored in the location whose address is s. Thus, if storage location 107 contains the number 3, one may write $\{107\} = 3$. It is common, too, to speak of s as being the address of the data as well as that of the storage location.

In the conversion program previously introduced, suppose that each of the quantities x_i, a_i, b_i, c_i, d_i, or y_i constitutes one unit of data, and that its storage address is $X + i$, $A + i$, $B + i$, $C + i$, $D + i$, or $Y + i$, respectively. Here x_i is the ith of the input numbers x_0 through x_{79}; $X + i$ is the number, or address, assigned to the storage location that contains x_i. The other addresses

Program 2–8

$$i \leftarrow 0$$
$$x \leftarrow 0$$
$$y \leftarrow 1$$
$$\rightarrow x \leftarrow x + y$$
$$y \leftarrow y + 2$$
$$i \leftarrow i + 1$$
$$\text{Print } i, x$$
$$\xleftarrow{\neq} i : 1000 \xrightarrow{=} \text{Stop}$$

Program 2–9

$$i \leftarrow 0$$
$$\rightarrow i \leftarrow i + 1$$
$$x \leftarrow i \times i$$
$$\text{Print } i, x$$
$$\xleftarrow{\neq} i : 1000 \xrightarrow{=} \text{Stop}$$

Program 2–10

$$i \leftarrow 0$$
$$\rightarrow x_i : a_i \xrightarrow{\leq} \text{Error program}$$
$$x_i : b_i \xrightarrow{\geq} \text{Error program}$$
$$y_i \leftarrow c_i \times x_i$$
$$y_i \leftarrow y_i + d_i$$
$$i \leftarrow i + 1$$
$$\xleftarrow{\leq} i : 79$$
$$\text{Stop}$$

Program 2–11

1          $i \leftarrow 0$
2     $\rightarrow \{X + i\} : \{A + i\} \xrightarrow{\leq} \text{Error program}$
3     $\{X + i\} : \{B + i\} \xrightarrow{\geq} \text{Error program}$
4     $\{Y + i\} \leftarrow \{C + i\} \times \{X + i\}$
5     $\{Y + i\} \leftarrow \{Y + i\} + \{D + i\}$
6          $i \leftarrow i + 1$
7     $\xleftarrow{\leq} i : 79$

are defined similarly. The previous program may be rewritten as Program 2–11. The execution of statement 6 implies the incrementation of i in each of its occurrences in statements 2 through 5, where it is used as part of an address. Since each such address must be incorporated in the instructions that correspond to statements 2 through 5, the computer has effectively been programmed to modify its own instructions. This is the means whereby eighty sets of tests and conversions can be specified by merely seven statements, which will generally correspond to only a handful of computer instructions.

In Program 2–11, one execution of the loop results in ten numbers being brought from the store to the mill as operands or returned from the mill to the store as results. Each of these references to the store corresponds to one of the ten occurrences of $X + i$, $A + i$, or a similar address, in the program. In most computers such access to the store is relatively costly in time. As a result, computers are often provided with a small amount of storage space in the mill

Program 2–12	**Program 2–13**

$$i \leftarrow 0$$

$$r \leftarrow \{X + i\}$$

$$r : \{A + i\} \xrightarrow{\leq} \text{Error program}$$

$$r : \{B + i\} \xrightarrow{\geq} \text{Error program}$$

$$r \leftarrow r \times \{C + i\}$$

$$r \leftarrow r + \{D + i\}$$

$$\{Y + i\} \leftarrow r$$

$$i \leftarrow i + 1$$

$$\xrightarrow{<} i : 80$$

$$i \leftarrow 0$$

$$r \leftarrow \{X\}$$

$$r \leftarrow \{A\} \xrightarrow{\leq}$$

$$r \leftarrow \{B\} \xrightarrow{\geq}$$

$$r \leftarrow r \times \{C\}$$

$$r \leftarrow r + \{D\}$$

$$\{Y\} \leftarrow r$$

$$X \leftarrow X + 1$$

$$A \leftarrow A + 1$$

$$B \leftarrow B + 1$$

$$C \leftarrow C + 1$$

$$D \leftarrow D + 1$$

$$Y \leftarrow Y + 1$$

$$i \leftarrow i + 1$$

$$\xrightarrow{\leq} i : 79$$

itself, in the form of one, two, or perhaps several *registers*. Each register, like a storage location, might hold one unit of data. Note how, in Program 2–12, a single register (whose content is r) permits the reduction from ten to six in the number of references to the store, at the cost of only two more statements.

Some computers have instructions, corresponding for example to statements of the type $r \leftarrow \{X + i\}$, that compute a storage address by addition before fetching or storing the data. The addition of the *index i* to the basic address or *origin X* is known as *indexing*. If indexing is available in the computer used to implement Program 2–11, the single incrementation of i by unity realizes the incrementation by unity of each of the six *effective addresses* $X + i$, $A + i$, etc. If indexing is not available, each of these six addresses must be incremented explicitly, as in Program 2–13. This program looks as though it will properly test and convert the eighty values. A line-by-line analysis of the program shows this to be indeed the case, yet Program 2–13 is wholly unacceptable. Why is this so?

The glaring defect of Program 2–13 is that it will work only once. Consider, for example, the second statement: $r \leftarrow \{X\}$. After the program has been executed once, the address X will have been augmented by 80, and this is true of every other storage address as well. The second time the program is used, the first number will be not x_0 but whatever the content of location $X + 80$ might be. Unless one of the limit tests fails, the results of computing with these unknown numbers will lead to the loss of the data originally in storage locations $Y + 80$ through $Y + 159$. These might be valuable data, perhaps even part of the computer program itself. Such a state of affairs is clearly intolerable.

Program 2–14   **Program 2–15**

$i \leftarrow 0$

$X' \leftarrow X$ $X' \leftarrow X$

$A' \leftarrow A$ $A' \leftarrow A$

$B' \leftarrow B$ $B' \leftarrow B$

$C' \leftarrow C$ $C' \leftarrow C$

$D' \leftarrow D$ $D' \leftarrow D$

$Y' \leftarrow Y$ $Y' \leftarrow Y$

$r \quad \leftarrow \{X'\}$ $r \leftarrow \{X'\}$

$r \quad : \{A'\} \xrightarrow{\leq}$ $\xleftarrow{\leq} r \quad : \{A'\}$

$r \quad : \{B'\} \xrightarrow{\geq}$ $\xleftarrow{\geq} r \quad : \{B'\}$

$r \quad \leftarrow r \times \{C'\}$ $r \quad \leftarrow r \times \{C'\}$

$r \quad \leftarrow r + \{D'\}$ $r \quad \leftarrow r + \{D'\}$

$\{Y'\} \leftarrow r$ $\{Y'\} \leftarrow r$

$X' \leftarrow X' + 1$ $X' \leftarrow X' + 1$

$A' \leftarrow A' + 1$ $A' \leftarrow A' + 1$

$B' \leftarrow B' + 1$ $B' \leftarrow B' + 1$

$C' \leftarrow C' + 1$ $C' \leftarrow C' + 1$

$D' \leftarrow D' + 1$ $D' \leftarrow D' + 1$

$Y' \leftarrow Y' + 1$ $Y' \leftarrow Y' + 1$

$i \quad \leftarrow i + 1$ $Y' : Y + 79 \xrightarrow{\leq}$

$\xleftarrow{\leq} i : 79$

The cure, fortunately, is simple. One need merely ensure that whenever
any loop is entered for the first time, values modified by the loop have been
preset to the proper initial state. This process of *initialization* of the loop is
of the utmost importance. The initialization of the loop of Program 2–14 is
provided by the first seven statements, all of which lie, of course, outside the
loop. The program is now satisfactory, although a minor improvement is
possible. The quantity i, used here only as a counter, is unnecessary, because
one of the addresses can be used for counting. This modification is shown in
Program 2–15.

It may be desirable to reflect in a program more or less of the structure of a
given computer. Program 2–10, for example, stresses the definition of the
conversion problem, whereas Program 2–15 emphasizes the address modification that may be required for its solution. Program 2–12 differs from the other
conversion programs in the comparison used to control the number of iterations.
The referent is 80 rather than 79, and the branch back to the start of the loop
occurs if the first operand is strictly less than the second, instead of less than or
equal to the second. One type of *conditional branch*, as such statements are

called, may be available in one computer but not in another. Accordingly, the programmer should design his program for ease of implementation on the particular computer he plans to use.

Many other variations exist for the control of iteration. The decision whether to repeat the loop may occur at the head of the loop as well as at its foot. The decision can precede or follow the modification of the count. The count can be decremented instead of incremented. In view of the greater ease in many computers of comparing a variable with zero rather than with an arbitrary number, Program 2–16 is conveniently organized. The computer to be used may be considered to offer indexing or, alternatively, addressing techniques may be felt to be unemphasized. Statement 1 alone constitutes the initialization. Statement 2 is a conditional branch incorporating a test prior to both index modification and computation. Statement 3 counts not up, but down through the original data, limits, coefficients, and results. The branch from statement 7 occurs in all cases and is therefore termed *unconditional*. Whereas Program 2–16 enjoys the conceptual advantage of setting i equal initially to the number of iterations, Program 2–17 uses one less branch.

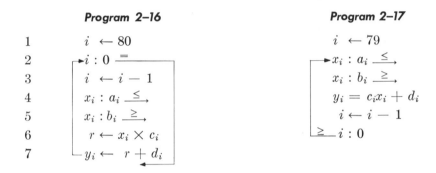

	Program 2–16	*Program 2–17*
1	$i \leftarrow 80$	$i \leftarrow 79$
2	$i : 0 \xrightarrow{=}$	$x_i : a_i \xrightarrow{\leq}$
3	$i \leftarrow i - 1$	$x_i : b_i \xrightarrow{\geq}$
4	$x_i : a_i \xrightarrow{\leq}$	$y_i = c_i x_i + d_i$
5	$x_i : b_i \xrightarrow{\geq}$	$i \leftarrow i - 1$
6	$r \leftarrow x_i \times c_i$	$\xrightarrow{\geq} i : 0$
7	$y_i \leftarrow r + d_i$	

In the latter program, the formation of y_i is shown in less detail than in the former. For different purposes, different levels of detail may be advantageous. A complex process is often best described by one program showing with little detail the over-all organization, in conjunction with a series of more detailed programs for each of its subprocesses.

Flow Charts, Efficiency, and Multiple Loops. A process frequently encountered in automatic computation is that of sorting. A public utility company may have account information for several tens or hundreds of thousands of customers in a master file, recorded very possibly on magnetic tape for computer use. If the company issues bills monthly, it can expect to receive, on the average, account payments from 4 or 5 percent of its customers every business day. Suppose that 1000 daily payments arrive at random and must be credited to the correct customers among 21,000 accounts. If for each payment record the master file must be searched to locate the corresponding account, and if the average length of search is one-third the length of the file (as is the case for accounts in random sequence), the computer will have to examine 7,000,000 accounts in order to make 1000 postings. In order to avoid such inefficient use of equipment, it is customary to assign to each customer an identifying account number, and maintain the master file in sequence according to the account numbers. Each day the company can sort the 1000 payment records into sequence according to account number and then compare this list against the master file, making all postings with only one pass through the file. A mere 21,000 master file accounts are examined, rather than 7,000,000. The price of this saving is the prior sorting of 1000 payment records. Clearly this requires not more than 1,000,000 examinations: 1000 to find the lowest account number, 1000 to find the next higher, etc. Moreover, the payment records are much shorter than the complete account records. Furthermore, many sorting techniques have been developed for reducing the number of examinations to well below a million, to even as few as 10,000 for randomly ordered account numbers.

Thus sorting is a topic worthy of attention; it occurs in such diverse applications as maintaining warehouse inventories and updating the engineering records of a manufacturer. A comprehensive treatment of sorting will not be attempted here, however. Instead, the problem of sorting three numbers into ascending sequence will be used to illustrate some further topics in programming. Let three numbers x, y, z be stored in locations A, B, C, respectively. The re-

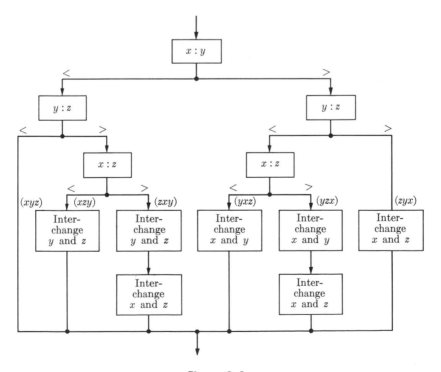

Figure 2–1

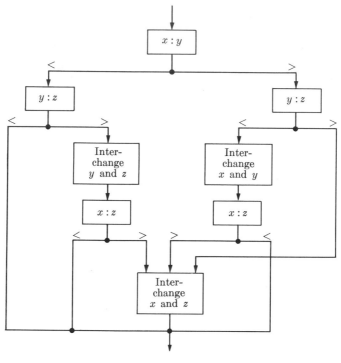

Figure 2–2

quired task is to rearrange the three numbers, no two of which are equal, so that the least is in A, the greatest in C, and the third in B.

One approach is to program a sequence of comparisons to determine the relative magnitudes of the three numbers. Each of the six possible outcomes is then followed by the appropriate rearrangement. Figure 2–1 shows the resulting process in the pictorial form of a *flow chart*. Here the emphasis is less on individual statements, as in a program, than on the interrelationships of different parts of the process. Each of the six paths through the chart is labeled with the corresponding ascending sequence of the numbers x, y, z. Figure 2–2 is the result of a simple rearrangement of comparisons and interchanges. The operands x and z that enter the third comparison will be drawn from different store locations in the two programs.

The basic strategy in Fig. 2–1 or 2–2 is first to determine which rearrangement is required, and then to effect it. For 3 numbers there are $3! = 6$ possible rearrangements,* and the appropriate one is selected by the program. For n numbers, there are $n!$ rearrangements. Unless n is rather small, however, $n!$

---

* The factorial function $n!$ (read "n factorial") is defined for the positive integer n as the product of the first n positive integers, $n! = 1 \times 2 \times \cdots \times n$. Thus $3! = 1 \times 2 \times 3 = 6$ and $10! = 3,628,800$. The factorial can also be defined recursively as $n! = n \cdot (n - 1)!$; the convention $0! = 1$ makes the two definitions consistent.

is exceedingly large, and more efficient procedures are mandatory. When one has an automatic computer available which is capable of performing thousands or millions of elementary operations each second, it is tempting to program the machine to examine all possible cases of a complex situation. The user must realize, however, that such a brute force attack is often completely impractical and should be eschewed in favor of more subtle techniques. The number of microseconds in a year is only 3×10^{13}, and 17! already exceeds that figure, not to mention the utility company's 1000! rearrangements.

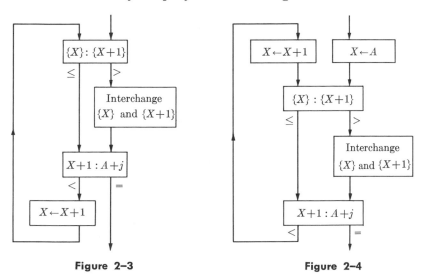

Figure 2–3   Figure 2–4

An alternative approach to the sorting problem is to perform an interchange whenever, and as soon as, two numbers are discovered to be in the wrong relative order in the store. The key is to plan the comparisons wisely. One frequently used method is the following. The first two items are compared and, if the first is larger, interchanged. The (possibly new) second item is compared with the third, and the process is continued to the end of the list of numbers. After one such pass through the list, the greatest number will have been placed in the last location. A second pass will ensure that the second greatest number is delivered to the second last location. The $(n - 1)$th pass will deliver the second smallest number to the second location, and the smallest will then necessarily occupy the first. In this method each pass is shorter than its predecessor. Whereas the first pass must examine all $n - 1$ pairs of adjacent numbers, the second need not compare the last pair, because the greatest number will be known to be in the last location. The third pass need not examine the last two pairs, and so forth, until the last or $(n - 1)$th pass, which need make but a single comparison. The total number of comparisons, and the maximum possible number of interchanges, is therefore

$$(n - 1) + (n - 2) + \cdots + 2 + 1 = n(n - 1)/2.$$

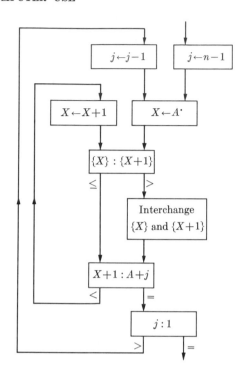

Figure 2–5

A program to effect the foregoing sorting process will now be developed. The easiest method is to start, not with initialization, but with the core of the process. Let the n numbers, no longer assumed to be distinct from each other, be stored in locations A through $A + n - 1$. The last number examined on the first pass is $\{A + n - 1\}$. The last number examined on the second is $\{A + n - 2\}$, and $\{A + j\}$ is the last number examined on the $(n - j)$th pass. Consider the comparison, on this $(n - j)$th pass, of some pair of consecutive numbers, whose addresses may be called X and $X + 1$. The central process is described by Fig. 2–3. Since the first numbers to be compared are the pair $\{A\}$ and $\{A + 1\}$, the correct initial value of X for all $n - 1$ passes is A. The loop of Fig. 2–3, with the initialization of X added, is repeated as Fig. 2–4, which describes one complete sorting pass. It is necessary now to determine whether the pass just described is the last, or whether another is to follow. On the last pass, $n - j = n - 1$, and $j = 1$. Thus a comparison of j with 1 will determine whether the process is to be repeated. If so, j must be decremented by 1, so that the subsequent pass will be of the correct length. The incorporation of the decrementation of j and of its initialization to the value $n - 1$ results in the finished flow chart of Fig. 2–5. The program incorporates two loops, one within the other. Note that the initialization of the inner loop lies outside the inner loop but within the outer. The initialization of the outer loop lies necessarily without both. Such use of multiple loops is one of the most powerful tools available to the programmer.

(b) Analysis

The first step in using a digital computer to perform a numerical computation is to analyze the problem whose solution is required. It is necessary to specify a method of solution in terms of the operations of which the computer is capable, usually the four basic arithmetical operations. Moreover, it is highly desirable to cast the computation into a form that combines repetitive operations into both simple and multiple loops. A tedious computation can thus be carried out with only a short list of instructions to the computer. Indeed, if the list were excessively long, it might be easier to perform the operations by hand than to prepare the instructions.

A common goal in analysis is a procedure to refine an approximation to the answer of a problem. Given a suitable initial approximation, the procedure can be applied repetitively until an approximation is obtained which is sufficiently accurate to be taken as the answer. Consider, for example, the problem of extracting the square root of the positive number N, not necessarily an integer. The formula

$$x_i = \frac{1}{2}\left(x_{i-1} + \frac{N}{x_{i-1}}\right) \tag{2-1}$$

can be used to improve an approximation x_{i-1} to $\sqrt{N}$. Equation (2–1) will not be derived until Part IV, but its validity can be illustrated by computing the sequence of numbers x_i generated by $N = 4$ and $x_0 = 1$:

$$x_1 = \tfrac{1}{2}(1 + \tfrac{4}{1}) \qquad = 2.5,$$

$$x_2 = \frac{1}{2}\left(2.5 + \frac{4}{2.5}\right) = 2.05,$$

$$x_3 \qquad\qquad\qquad = 2.006,$$

$$x_4 \qquad\qquad\qquad = 2.000000009.$$

Calculate $\sqrt{N}$

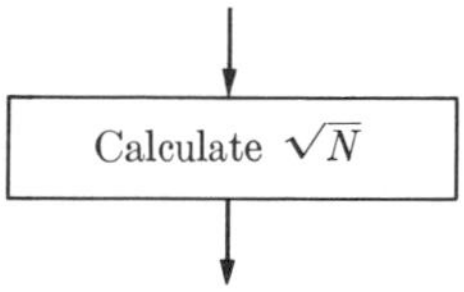

Figure 2–6

The sequence converges very rapidly to a square root of 4. It can be shown in general that Eq. (2–1) will generate a sequence of numbers converging for any positive initial approximation x_0 to the positive square root of N. A convenient choice of x_0 independent of N is unity.

A major question in the use of an iterative process is the determination of the number of iterations to be performed. For some problems, mathematical analysis may permit the determination of the number needed to achieve specified accuracy for input data in a certain range. Alternatively, the process itself may be used to give information about the rate of convergence and to determine the number of iterations required for the particular data being used. For a rapidly convergent process, the difference between two successive approximations is a good estimate of the error in the earlier approximation. A common technique is to repeat the process until the absolute value $|x_i - x_{i-1}|$ is less than some preassigned tolerance T.

In organizing a calculation for computer solution, care must be taken to provide for all possible contingencies. The tolerance T may be so small that two successive approximations will never differ by less than T. This is because once the process has converged to a neighborhood of the solution, successive x_i may alternate between two values on account of approximations due to rounding. It is also conceivable that T be erroneously preassigned a negative value. It is possible, too, that an attempt be made to extract the square root of a negative number. In all the foregoing cases, the process will never terminate. For $N < 0$ the process will diverge, and for T negative or too small convergence will occur but remain unrecognized. The careful computer user will test for the existence of such conditions or ensure that they cannot arise.

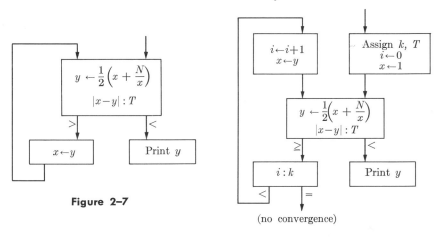

Figure 2–7

(no convergence)

Figure 2–8

The result of the computer user's analysis is commonly a flow chart, from which a program can then be developed. The level of detail specified should be so chosen as to be most helpful in the context. The flow chart of Fig. 2–6 for the square root extraction gives no information about the details of the process. It could be useful, however, in the context of a larger process, such as solving a quadratic equation. In Fig. 2–7 is shown a more detailed chart for the central part of the square-root extraction process just developed. Note that x_i of the problem explanation does not appear as an indexed variable in the program, because $x_0, x_1, \ldots$ is a sequence in time rather than in space. This flow chart still lacks provision for avoiding an endless loop, or for the case in which $|x - y|$ exactly equals the tolerance. The possible equality with the tolerance is taken care of by arbitrarily assigning that condition to either of the two branches. The endless loop can be avoided by maintaining a count of the number of iterations. If the approximation is refined more than k times without convergence, an error program is entered. These features, along with initialization, are incorporated in the flow chart of Fig. 2–8. This is only one of many possible flow charts for the given process. Different workers and different organizations use different conventions with regard to symbols, box shapes, and other matters. The amount of detail can vary, as it does between Figs. 2–6 and 2–8. Further detail than is illustrated in Fig. 2–8 might include the steps in the computation of y, in the comparison, and in editing the output data for printing. Each computer user must find a compromise useful to himself and to others, while avoiding the extremes of over- and under-specification of detail.

(c) Coding

It is necessary ultimately to translate the general specifications of the flow chart into explicit instructions for the computer. Typical of the operations initiated by a single instruction are the following:

(1) add the number in storage location 71 to the number in the accumulator,* leaving the sum in the accumulator;

(2) take the next instruction from storage location 275 only if the number in the accumulator is negative;

(3) record the contents of storage locations 100 through 199 on an output magnetic tape;

(4) copy the number from the accumulator into storage location 100.

The choice of instructions available and their most effective use to implement various processes vary widely from one computer to another. A thorough introduction to coding must therefore be couched in terms of a specific computing machine. The detailed description, for this purpose, of any one existing machine would not be of much service to a reader without access to a copy of that machine. On the other hand, the use of a hypothetical machine suffers from certain disadvantages. One is the difficulty of mirroring the idiosyncrasies encountered in almost any real machine. Another is the fact that, after having learned how to code for the hypothetical machine, the reader would have no place to test his skill. Accordingly, the details of machine coding will not be further treated here. Instead, the reader is advised to supplement this book by consulting sources relating to the computing machine available to him.

The task of preparing instructions for a computing machine is a very tedious one. This is due in part to the large amount of bookkeeping involved, especially in the assignment of storage locations for both data and instructions. Another cause is the fact that the instructions usually bear no resemblance to statements in natural language, such as English. Instead, the rules for the formation of instructions are essentially those of an artificial language, the *machine language*. This language is

Program 2–18

100	C 320 C 320
101	B 200 C 102
102	B 320 A- 440
103	C 320 B 102
104	A- 201 H 102
105	L 202 Q3 107
106	00 000 U 102
200	B 320 A- 440
201	000000 000001
202	B 320 A- 540

* The name accumulator is often given to a register in the mill. It is normally connected to addition circuitry in a manner which permits it to accumulate sums.

usually designed with engineering considerations of primary importance and it is generally neither easily used by the programmer nor convenient for the statement of problems. A portion of the machine-language coding for one automatic computer is presented as Program 2–18.

Fortunately, it is possible to use the computer to perform the most tedious parts of the machine-language coding. Artificial languages, which are more convenient than machine languages but use the symbols normally read by the computer, have been developed for many computers. With each such language a machine-language program is also prepared to translate from the synthetic language to the machine language. Such programs generally incorporate provisions for performing much of the bookkeeping associated with coding.

Among the advantages of using a language different from the machine language are the following: (1) usually fewer instructions need be written; (2) the language* can be designed for the programmer's convenience; (3) the bookkeeping is reduced; and (4) the chances of error are lessened by the other three advantages cited. The principal disadvantage in the use of a synthetic language is the necessity of translating from it to machine language.

Two principal types of translating programs are in common use. The *interpretive* program, or *interpreter*, translates the synethetic-language program into machine language and executes it as it translates. Only one computer run is required. The *compiling* program, or *compiler*, performs only the translation, in one computer run, and a second run is required with the newly compiled program. Symbolic diagrams of the two different types of translation are shown in Figs. 2–9 and 2–10. The rectangular box represents the computer, as well as the machine-language program controlling its operation. The circular boxes, similar in shape to magnetic tape reels, depict the input and output.

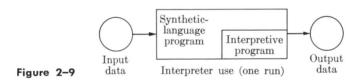

Figure 2–9   Input data   Interpreter use (one run)   Output data

Although the compiler requires two runs, as opposed to only one for the interpreter, it offers compensating advantages. In the translation, or *compiling* phase, deviations from the rules of the synthetic language can be signaled to the user by the compiler. This occurs prior to the run on which final results are expected. If a process is to be performed repeatedly, use of a compiler permits the translation to be performed only once, rather than each time it is desired to run the program. Moreover, even if the program is to be run only once, individual instructions may be executed many times, but need be translated only once.

---

* Such a language is often called a *user-oriented* or *problem-oriented* language.

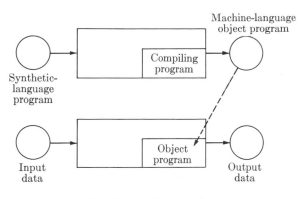

Compiler use (two runs)

Figure 2–10

A special class of compilers are known as *assemblers*. These are distinguished primarily by the feature that one synthetic-language instruction corresponds to one machine-language instruction, whereas for the compiler the correspondence is generally one-to-many. Assemblers are used chiefly to reduce bookkeeping work, and the structure of the assembly language is usually rather similar to that of machine language.

The language to be used by the reader will be dictated primarily by the nature of the computer and installation available to him. No attempt has been made here, therefore, to explain any particular programming language in detail. Instead, the reader is urged to learn at least one such language thoroughly from other sources.

2–2 CONTROL OF ERROR

Neither computing machines nor the people who use them function perfectly at all times. That people make mistakes is of course well known. Many people believe, however, that computers never do. This is not true and it is, on the contrary, remarkable that automatic computers performing even millions of electronic operations per second fail as rarely as they do.

It is convenient to classify errors in machine computation into three types: machine, numerical, and programming. A machine error is one caused by the steady or intermittent failure of some component of the machine. A numerical error is essentially due to inaccuracy in mathematical analysis. A programming error is any other error in problem preparation, especially one in coding.

The effect of an error may be anything from nil to catastrophic. A temporary component failure may not affect any information used in a particular computation. Some errors can lead to the calculation of obviously incorrect results, or even of no results at all. A particularly insidious outcome is the calculation of slightly incorrect results that may be difficult to recognize as being in error. A permanent electronic failure may be so centrally situated as to incapacitate the computer completely.

(a) Detection and Correction

The detection of error serves two purposes. One is to ensure the correctness of a final result; the other is to locate the point at which an error may have occurred. Over-all checking of a final result can be performed only by program. The best technique is the computation of final results by two distinct independent processes from data known to be correct. This is often embodied in the use of a mathematical identity. The tabulation of $\sin x$ may be checked, for example, by the independent computation of $\cos x$ and verification of the identity $\sin^2 x + \cos^2 x = 1$, but there are pitfalls in blind reliance on mathematical identities (see Exercise II–22).

Diagnostic, as opposed to final, checking may be performed either by programming checks on part of a computation or by incorporating error-detecting features in the machine itself. In some computers the arithmetic circuitry is duplicated and the results constantly compared. Instructions and data can be checked for validity according to almost any desired criterion. A technique widely used with both external and internal storage is the incorporation of redundant information. Alphabetic characters are often represented by seven symbols, each zero or one, of which only six are independent and the seventh is chosen according to the parity* of the sum of the other six. For example, the seventh may be zero if the sum is odd, or one if the sum is even. A single error in any one of the seven symbols is then easily detected, as the reader can verify.

Extra checking circuitry or extra program sections for checking are no more immune from error than the parts they are meant to check. A delicate balance must be sought by the builder and user of the machine between incorporating too much and too little checking. It is easily assumed that machine detection catches only machine errors and programmed detection catches only program errors, but this is not the case. A computer may be able to detect the programmer's use of an invalid instruction; the programmer should be able to detect the incorrect execution of a multiplication.

The correction of error is usually less difficult than its detection. If an error is found in the program, the appropriate portion of the program is changed. Great care must be taken in doing this, lest the "correction" introduce yet further errors. In one computer installation it was found that two-thirds of the program errors were introduced in the correction of other errors. If a permanent machine error is discovered, the machine must be repaired. If a machine error is intermittent, it may be possible to run the program by means of a *rerun*. If the error is detected by the program, provision may be made in the program

---

* The parity of a number is its evenness or oddness; the parity is even or odd accordingly as the number is even or odd.

to repeat part of the computation in the hope that the error will not repeat. In some computers, the occurrence of a machine error can be used to transfer control from the problem program to a monitor program that can try the same operation. A technique often acceptable is to program the machine to stop in case of error and to restart manually at an appropriate point; this is efficient only if the computer is not so fast that the loss of time is intolerable.

Prevention of error is fully as important as its detection. The most common means for the prevention of machine error is known as *marginal checking*. Test programs are run with the power supplies set to abnormally low levels, and components that fail under these conditions are replaced on the grounds that they would be the first to fail in normal operation.

When a compiler is employed, the first pass can be used to hunt program errors that would occur on the second pass. The output of the first pass will then usually consist not of an object program, but rather of a list of errors in the source program. An execution pass is not even attempted until no further errors are detected in the compilation pass.

(b) Checkout and Debugging

Most computer programs are so complex that the programmer should assume that he has made one or more programming errors. Rather than just run his program and accept the results, if any, he will go through a process of checking out his program, and of pin-pointing errors or *bugs* in it.

There are as many checkout procedures as there are programmers, but some general suggestions can be made. A long program should be checked out in parts, and only when the parts appear to operate correctly should the entire program be tested. Sometimes a checkout program can be written to monitor this phase of the checkout. It is often helpful to prepare test values for which intermediate and final results are computed by hand and compared with those generated by the program.

Once a discrepancy is noted, the debugging process commences. There are two general types of debugging, *on-machine* and *off-machine*, both of which can tax the programmer's ingenuity. In on-machine debugging, the older of the two methods, the programmer uses the control console to examine the contents of various storage locations, makes changes manually in data and/or instructions, and tries by experiment to determine what has gone wrong. During this time the computer is not productive, in the narrowest sense of the word, and the advent of faster and more expensive computers led to the use of off-machine debugging. When trouble is encountered, in this technique a *dump* is taken. This is a printed record of the contents of all or part of the store, including input data, instructions, and intermediate results. The programmer then looks at this static record and tries to deduce what happened. A dump of the complete store is often wasteful and confusing; a more useful tool is the programmed partial dump. Advance preparation is required, and may be incorporated in the checkout features of the program. With the advent of *multiprogramming* systems, whereby several programs can share a computer, on-machine debugging is once more finding favor for fast computers because the machine need no longer be idle while a programmer cogitates. Instead, the computer executes one program while another is being debugged.

References for Part I

ALT, F. L., *Electronic Digital Computers*. New York: Academic Press, 1958.

BOOTH, A. D., and K. H. V. BOOTH, *Automatic Digital Calculators*. London: Butterworth, 1953. Chapter 2.

BOWDEN, B. V., ed., *Faster Than Thought*. London: Pitman, 1953.

BROOKS, F. P., JR., and K. E. IVERSON, *Automatic Data Processing*. New York: Wiley, 1963.

IVERSON, K. E., *A Programming Language*. New York: Wiley, 1962.

LEEDS, H. D., and G. M. WEINBERG, *Computer Programming Fundamentals*. New York: McGraw-Hill, 1961.

McCORMICK, E. M., *Digital Computer Primer*. New York: McGraw-Hill, 1959.

McCRACKEN, D. D., *Digital Computer Programming*. New York: Wiley, 1957.

MORRISON, P., and E. MORRISON, eds., *Charles Babbage and His Calculating Engines*. New York: Dover, 1961.

SHERMAN, P. M., *Programming and Coding Digital Computers*. New York: Wiley, 1963.

WILKES, M. V., *Automatic Digital Computers*. London: Methuen, 1956.

WRUBEL, M. H., *A Primer of Programming for Digital Computers*. New York: McGraw-Hill, 1959.

Exercise Set for Part I

1. A function is tabulated below for nine values of the argument. Introduce an error (say, the transposition of adjacent digits) in one of the middle values. Prepare a difference table for the modified function values and observe how the behavior of the differences indicates the presence of error. Explain the phenomenon.

x	$f(x)$
6.06	0.15481 76536 49793
6.07	0.15456 66882 16177
6.08	0.15430 03654 53749
6.09	0.15401 87178 38843
6.10	0.15372 17793 63046
6.11	0.15340 95855 29243
6.12	0.15308 21733 47503
6.13	0.15273 95813 30827
6.14	0.15238 18494 90744

2. Write a computer program for the flow chart of Fig. 2–2.

3. Recast Fig. 2–5 for $n = 3$, then simplify the result, and finally write a corresponding program.

4. Write a program for the flow chart of Fig. 2–8.

5. Program a computer to extract the square roots of five numbers that lie in the range $0 \leq N \leq 10^6$ and that are specified with as many as four places after the decimal point. The square roots are to be rounded to six places after the decimal point. The five input values may be presented in any convenient format.

6. Program a computer to generate prime numbers.

7. Consider the numbers described in Section 2–2(a) for the representation of alphabetic characters. The *distance* between any pair of these numbers is defined as the number of places in which they differ. Thus, if $x = 0011010$ and $y = 1011101$, then $d(x, y) = 4$. Show that the parity rule imposed requires that $d \geq 2$ for every pair of distinct admissible numbers. Show that this suffices for the detection, but not the correction, of any single error. What minimum distance d is required for single-error correction? For the detection of n simultaneous errors? For their correction?

Part II

Numbers

Digital computers process numbers. Despite the wealth of nonnumerical applications of computers, such as language translation and pattern recognition, numerical problems are fundamental. Knowledge of the ways in which numbers are represented and of the elementary arithmetical operations, so often taken for granted, is therefore invaluable. Of great importance, too, is an understanding of sources and effects of errors in numerical data. The foregoing subjects form the content of Part II.

Chapter 3

Representation of Numbers

Man's first need for numbers was almost certainly in counting. It is believed that what we now know as the natural numbers $(1, 2, \ldots)$ were represented in prehistoric times by piles of small objects, such as pebbles. Sequences of marks or tallies were probably also used, one mark for each item in the collection being counted. Such means are unwieldy for large numbers, and different symbols were introduced as abbreviations for tally sequences of various lengths. The Romans retained simple vertical strokes for numbers under five, but used the familiar abbreviations V for five marks, X for ten marks, etc. The juxtaposition of symbols indicated combination by simple addition or subtraction, as in VI and IV, but not all sequences of symbols were meaningful. The number which we would call eighteen hundred forty-seven had to be represented as MDCCCXLVII, and the sequence CCMVXLCIID was usually not permitted, although it contains the same symbols.

3-1 POSITIONAL NOTATION

The type of representation in common use today was developed in the middle ages. It is a *positional notation*, in which the value of a symbol depends only on its identity and its position, and is independent of the values of neighboring symbols. Furthermore, all sequences of symbols are meaningful.

A set of b symbols is used, each of which represents a distinct nonnegative integer less than b, which is termed the *base* or *radix* of the system. An arbitrary nonnegative integer N can be expressed as a weighted sum of powers of the base b as follows.

$$N = a_{n-1}b^{n-1} + a_{n-2}b^{n-2} + \cdots + a_1b^1 + a_0b^0. \tag{3-1}$$

If the coefficients a_i are restricted by the constraint $0 \leq a_i < b$ for all i, then the specification of the coefficients is unique, as is demonstrated by Exercise II-1. Clearly, the coefficients of all powers of b higher than some given power, which depends upon N, will be zero. This fact was used in writing the expression (3–1) with only n coefficients displayed. It is to be understood that a_i may be considered to exist for $i \geq n$, but with $a_i = 0$ for such cases. The conventional representation of the integer N is simply the symbols for the coefficients $a_{n-1}, \ldots, a_0$ juxtaposed in the order in which they appear in the form (3–1).

(a) Choice of Radix

It is clear that the choice $b = 1$ is unsatisfactory, because the coefficients a_i would all be zero as a result of the constraint $0 \leq a_i < b$, and only $N = 0$ could be expressed in the form (3–1). Any integer greater than 1 can serve as the base of a positional number system.

The fact that man has ten fingers is almost certainly responsible for the widespread use of the *decimal* system with base ten. The ten symbols used in our society to represent the first ten nonnegative integers are

$$0, 1, 2, 3, 4, 5, 6, 7, 8, 9.$$

The symbols are here displayed in natural order, and it should be understood that 0 precedes 1, instead of following 9, as on the telephone dial. The decimal expansion

$$361 = 3 \cdot 10^2 + 6 \cdot 10^1 + 1 \cdot 10^0$$

should not surprise the reader.

Desk calculators generally employ the decimal system. The store of a desk calculator usually holds very few numbers, and intermediate results must be copied for later reintroduction. This process is most convenient for the user if the numbers are represented in a familiar form. Moreover, ten-position number wheels are fast enough to keep pace with a human operator.

The widespread availability of fast, cheap, and reliable two-state devices for use in automatic computing machinery has created great interest in the use of the *binary* system, with base two. The two symbols used are commonly 0 and 1. Corresponding to each symbol is one of the two states of the device employed. This may be, for example, a pair of relay contacts either open or closed, or a transistor either saturated with current or cut off from carrying current.

The relative paucity of symbols in the binary system, as contrasted with the decimal system, has the advantage that the rules of arithmetic are simpler, and the circuitry required to effect them less complex. The binary system suffers from the corresponding disadvantage that more symbols must be displayed to represent a given number.

This disadvantage is alleviated by use of the *octal* system, whose base, eight, is a power of two. Binary and octal representations are so closely related that either can be transformed into the other upon inspection.* The octal system

* See Exercise II–4.

profits from the simplicity of the binary, but it uses most of the digits of the decimal in yielding shorter representations. Octal desk calculators have been built to facilitate the checking of intermediate results on binary automatic computers.

Another power of two that is often employed as a base is sixteen. The resulting *hexadecimal* system combines the easy translation to and from the binary system with the ability to represent any decimal digit by a single hexadecimal digit.

Certain groups have recommended the general adoption of the *duodecimal* system, with base twelve. The duodecimalists argue that the fact that twelve has many integer divisors makes it especially appropriate as a base, particularly in the representation of fractions. A later section will make clear why such an advantage would obtain. Twelve symbols would be required, presumably those of the decimal system plus two more to be specified.

Remnants of the *sexagesimal* system have come down to us in the use of sixty divisions in reckoning latitude and longitude, and the closely related subdivision of the hour. Man has used other systems, too, and it is possible to consider the merits and drawbacks of almost every integer as a radix. Space does not permit such a digression, however, and the subsequent discussion will be illustrated primarily with reference to the most widespread bases in computation, two and ten.

(b) Determination of Coefficients 1316112

A computational method, or *algorithm*, for finding the coefficients of the base b representation of an arbitrary integer N can easily be derived from the expansion (3–1), repeated here for convenience:

$$N = a_{n-1}b^{n-1} + \cdots + a_0 b^0. \tag{3–1}$$

Dividing the equation by b, one obtains

$$\frac{N}{b} = a_{n-1}b^{n-2} + \cdots + a_2 b^1 + a_1 b^0 + \frac{a_0}{b}. \tag{3–2}$$

The sum on the right-hand side, exclusive of the last term, can be recognized as the expansion of some new integer N', and Eq. (3–2) may be rewritten as

$$\frac{N}{b} = N' + \frac{a_0}{b}, \tag{3–3}$$

where

$$N' = a_{n-1}b^{n-2} + \cdots + a_2 b^1 + a_1 b^0. \tag{3–4}$$

The coefficient a_0 is seen to be the remainder after the division of N by b. The same process may be repeated on N', and the coefficient a_1 will be obtained as the remainder after the division of N' by b, as shown in the following equation:

$$\frac{N'}{b} = N'' + \frac{a_1}{b}. \tag{3–5}$$

This process may be applied repetitively to find all the coefficients. Although all the successive quotients and remainders are defined, the process may be stopped once a zero quotient is obtained.

It may be objected that the division process cannot be performed without a prior knowledge of the coefficients with respect to at least one radix system in which rules of arithmetic have been established. This is not the case, however, because the division can be performed with a nonpositional representation of N. Consider, for example, a pile of N coins. Let it be required to determine the base ten representation of N. The coins can be dealt into ten stacks of equal numbers of coins, with fewer than ten coins left over. The number of coins in any stack is the quotient and the number not assigned to a stack is the remainder, after the division of N by ten. Suppose that this process yields ten stacks of coins and a remainder of four coins. The coefficient a_0 in the base ten representation of N must therefore be 4. If the division process is repeated with the coins in any one stack alone, the remainder might be 7, which would then be the coefficient a_1. If each stack produced by this second division process contained two coins, the division of the coins in any one such stack by ten would yield a quotient of zero and a remainder of two. The base ten representation of the number N of coins would in this case be 274.

Normally, an integer will already be represented in some number system rather than as a pile of coins. The successive divisions can be performed in the system in which the number is represented, and the coefficients of its representation in a second system will be obtained directly. Consider, for example, the conversion of 361 from base ten to base two. This can be performed under the assumption, to be justified later, that the common procedures for arithmetical operations in base ten are valid. Table 3–1 shows the successive quotients and remainders obtained by dividing by

Table 3–1

361		
180	1	a_0
90	0	a_1
45	0	a_2
22	1	a_3
11	0	a_4
5	1	a_5
2	1	a_6
1	0	a_7
0	1	a_8

the new base, two. The base two number obtained is 101101001. One may refer to 361 and 101101001 as different *numerals* for the same number. A convenient way to express the fact that 361 and 101101001 represent the same integer in two different systems is to write $(361)_{10} = (101101001)_2$. The subscript indicates the base used in representing the associated number. In order to avoid confusion, it is necessary to agree on the notation to be used for this subscript. The integer b expressed in the system of base b is always represented by 10. It is clearly inadequate for the subscript to be written in its own base. The standard convention, adopted here, is to write the subscript b in base ten notation.

The number $(101101001)_2$ can be converted back to the decimal system as a check on the conversion just performed. Division by ten in the binary system must await the development of rules for binary arithmetic. An alternative method, easily applied in this case, is to evaluate in base ten the expansion (3–1) for the coefficients given. The only intermediate step is to calculate the needed powers of 2, which can be saved in a table for repeated use:

$$N = 1 \cdot 2^8 + 0 \cdot 2^7 + 1 \cdot 2^6 + 1 \cdot 2^5 + 0 \cdot 2^4 + 1 \cdot 2^3 + 0 \cdot 2^2 + 0 \cdot 2^1 + 1 \cdot 2^0$$
$$= 256 + 0 + 64 + 32 + 0 + 8 + 0 + 0 + 1 = (361)_{10}.$$

The division process requires the ability to perform arithmetic in the original base; the evaluation process just illustrated depends upon arithmetic in the new base. In order to be able to perform conversions between arbitrary bases, it is necessary to develop rules of arithmetic for an arbitrary base. This will be the subject of Section 4–2.

(c) Negative Powers

The expression (3–1) can be extended to include negative powers of the base, yielding

$$M = a_{n-1}b^{n-1} + \cdots + a_1b^1 + a_0b^0 + a_{-1}b^{-1} + a_{-2}b^{-2} + \cdots + a_{-m}b^{-m} \tag{3–6}$$

as the expansion of the *mixed* number M. The first n terms on the right-hand side constitute the expansion of an integer $\lfloor M \rfloor$, known as the *integral part* of M. The m remaining terms constitute the *fractional part* $M - \lfloor M \rfloor$ of M. The fractional part is always less than unity. The conventional representation of the mixed number M is simply the symbols for the coefficients $a_{n-1}, \ldots, a_{-m}$, juxtaposed in that order, with a period, or *radix point*, between the symbols for a_0 and a_{-1} to separate the integral and fractional parts. If the base is 10, the radix point is called the *decimal point;* however, this name should properly be reserved for use with the decimal system. Calculation of the coefficients of the expansion (3–6) is best performed by considering the sum $M = N + F$, where N is the integral part of M, and F is its fractional part. The coefficients $a_0, \ldots, a_{n-1}$ can be calculated from N by the method previously introduced; they are clearly independent of F. The coefficients of F, which are similarly independent of N, can be calculated by the following process. Since

$$F = a_{-1}b^{-1} + a_{-2}b^{-2} + \cdots + a_{-m}b^{-m}, \tag{3–7}$$

on multiplying Eq. (3–7) by b, one obtains

$$bF = a_{-1}b^0 + a_{-2}b^{-1} + \cdots + a_{-m}b^{-m+1}. \tag{3–8}$$

The sum on the right-hand side, exclusive of the first term, can be recognized as the expansion of some new fraction F' and, since $b^0 = 1$, Eq. (3–8) may be rewritten as

$$bF = a_{-1} + F', \tag{3–9}$$

where

$$F' = a_{-2}b^{-1} + a_{-3}b^{-2} + \cdots + a_{-m}b^{-m+1}. \tag{3–10}$$

The coefficient a_{-1} is seen to be the integral part $\lfloor bF \rfloor$ of the product of b and F. The same process may be repeated on F', and the coefficient $a_{-2} = \lfloor bF' \rfloor$ is obtained from

$$bF' = a_{-2} + F''. \tag{3–11}$$

This process may be applied repetitively to find all the coefficients.

Consider the conversion of $(0.6875)_{10}$ to the binary system. Each line of Table 3–2 is a number equal to twice the fractional part of the preceding number. The coefficients a_{-1} through a_{-4} are seen to be 1, 0, 1, 1, and the fraction is $(0.1011)_2$. It has been assumed throughout the foregoing discussion that the number of coefficients needed to represent F is finite. That this restriction is unnecessary is shown by the conversion, outlined in Table 3–3, of $(0.2)_{10}$ to the binary system. After four coefficients have been calculated, the new fractional part is the same as the original F. A fractional part 0 is never obtained, and the base-two representation of F consists of an infinitely repeated sequence of four digits. One may write $(0.2)_{10} = (0.00110011\ldots)_2 = (0.\overline{0011})_2$. The overbar in the last expression covers the repeating digits. The conversion may be checked by direct decimal evaluation. Equation (3–7) must first be rewritten as an infinite* sum:

$$F = a_{-1}b^{-1} + a_{-2}b^{-2} + \cdots + a_{-m}b^{-m} + \cdots,$$

$$(0.\overline{0011})_2 = (2^{-3} + 2^{-4} + 2^{-7} + 2^{-8} + 2^{-11} + 2^{-12} + \cdots)$$

$$= (2^{-3} + 2^{-4})(1 + 2^{-4} + 2^{-8} \cdots)$$

$$= (3 \cdot 2^{-4})\left(\frac{1}{1 - 2^{-4}}\right) = \frac{3 \cdot 2^{-4}}{15 \cdot 2^{-4}} = \frac{3}{15}$$

$$= (0.2)_{10}. \tag{3–12}$$

Table 3–2

0.6875
1.3750
0.7500
1.5000
1.0000

Table 3–3

0.2
0.4
0.8
1.6
1.2
0.4
0.8
1.6
1.2

---

* It will be recalled that if $|r| < 1$, the sum of the infinite geometric series $a + ar + ar^2 + ar^3 + \cdots$ equals $a/(1 - r)$. Further results on nonterminating representations are developed in Exercise II–7.

To convert a mixed number from one base to another requires the use of two different algorithms, one for the integral part and one for the fractional part. If the given representation is terminating, the need for two algorithms can be obviated at the expense of performing an extra division in the new system. This result is achieved by multiplying the mixed number M by b^m, where b is the base before conversion, yielding the integer Mb^m. Division by b^m is then performed explicitly in the new base after conversion of the two integers Mb^m and b^m. The base b multiplication by b^m is trivial, inasmuch as it requires only that the radix point be *shifted* to the right m places. The following conversion illustrates the method:

$$(111.01)_2 = \frac{(11101.)_2}{(100)_2} = \frac{(29)_{10}}{(4)_{10}} = (7.25)_{10}.$$

3–2 RATIONAL NUMBERS

When man began to make measurements and to refine them by subdividing standard units, he found the integers inadequate to express these measurements. Moreover, he was troubled by the fact that the exact quotient of two integers is not necessarily an integer. In other words, the class of integers is not *closed* with respect to division. Both of these situations were remedied by the introduction of *rational* numbers, usually defined as the quotient, or *ratio*, of two integers.

It is precisely these rational numbers that yield representations in terms of negative powers of the base. Let an arbitrary rational number be given as the quotient of two integers. If the two integers are then represented with respect to base b and the indicated division performed in base b arithmetic, a representation of the rational number is obtained in terms of positive and negative powers of the base. It can be shown, moreover, that if the fractional part is nonterminating, it must be periodic. Furthermore, every terminating or periodic sequence of coefficients in any base represents a rational number.

3–3 REAL NUMBERS

It is customary for the mathematician at this point to introduce irrational numbers, in order to express such quantities as the square root of 2 or the ratio of the circumference of a circle to its diameter. He can prove, of course, that there exist no integers p and q such that the rational number p/q is equal to $\sqrt{2}$, or to π. Nevertheless, although one makes frequent use of the concept of such *real* numbers, in actual computation they are invariably approximated by rational numbers. In computers, moreover, only those rational numbers that have terminating representations in the base used are employed, because machines of limitless size are not available nor, if they were, would they be practical. Although periodic representations of rational numbers can be manipulated with paper and pencil, the effort involved is not always adequately repaid. Such approximations, although necessary to permit computation, introduce errors. Estimation of the corresponding errors in the computed results will be studed in Section 5–2.

It is often convenient to place the real numbers in correspondence with the points of a straight line, the distance of an arbitrary point from a fixed reference location, or *origin*, being proportional to the magnitude of the number. This correspondence serves as the basis of analytic geometry, in which the line is taken as an axis of a system of coordinates. Although considerable use will be made of real numbers in the remainder of the book, it is to be understood that terminating rational approximations will be made for them in all computations.

3–4 COMPLEX NUMBERS

No real number z satisfies the equation $z^2 + 4 = 0$. In order to be able to express solutions of this and similar equations, mathematicians have invented the *imaginary* unit i with the property $i^2 = -1$. The sum of x real units and y imaginary units is said to be the *complex* number $z = x + iy$, where the real numbers x and y are known as the real and imaginary parts of z, respectively. The terms "real" and "imaginary" are, of course, misnomers. The imaginary part of z has neither less nor more reality than its real part, but the terms have become entrenched in common usage. It can be verified that the complex number $z = 2i$ satisfies the given equation $z^2 + 4 = 0$, because $z^2 = (2i)^2 = 2^2 i^2 = 4(-1) = -4$. Such a complex number, whose real part is zero, is often called an imaginary number. A complex number whose imaginary part is zero is equal to a real number, and as a result the complex numbers are ordinarily considered to include the real numbers, just as the reals can be thought of as including the rationals.

A useful correspondence can be established between complex numbers and points of a plane by setting the real and imaginary parts of the number equal

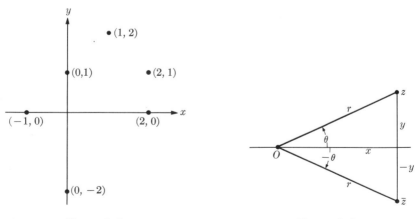

Figure 3–1   **Figure 3–2**

to the cartesian coordinates of the point. The horizontal, or real, axis corresponds to the real numbers and the vertical, or imaginary, axis corresponds to the imaginary numbers. Each complex number $z = x + iy$ can be represented by its real and imaginary parts in the ordered pair (x, y) of real numbers. Figure 3–1 shows the cartesian representation of several points in the *complex plane*. The imaginary number i is represented by the point whose coordinates are $(0, 1)$; the real number -1 by the point $(-1, 0)$.

Just as real numbers may be considered to represent distances, so can complex numbers be thought of as representing both distance and direction with respect to the origin. Any complex number may be represented by the real numbers that specify the distance and direction. In the usual polar coordinate representation, the distance is measured out from the origin and the direction is measured counterclockwise from the axis of reals, as shown in Fig. 3–2. The distance r is known as the *modulus* of z, and is often written as $r = |z|$. This notation is consistent with that for the absolute value of a real number, and serves as a reminder that $r \geq 0$. The angle θ is known as the *argument* of z and is commonly, although not invariably, restricted to the range $0 \leq \theta < 2\pi$. Zero is an exception in that it has no argument.

Conversion between cartesian and polar representations is easily performed by considering the upper triangle of Fig. 3–2. One immediately deduces the following equations:

$$x = r \cos \theta, \qquad r^2 = x^2 + y^2,$$
$$y = r \sin \theta, \qquad \theta = \text{arc tan } \frac{y}{x}. \qquad (3\text{--}13)$$

The *conjugate* $\bar{z}$ of the complex number z is obtained by reflecting z in the real axis. Figure 3–2 shows that the conjugate of (x, y) is $(x, -y)$ and that the conjugate of (r, θ) is $(r, -\theta)$. A real number is clearly its own conjugate; the conjugate of an imaginary number is its negative.

3–5 REPRESENTATION IN COMPUTERS

Information in automatic digital computers is ultimately represented by binary digits. A string of such digits, having a fixed length equal to the capacity of one addressable location in the store, is generally called a *word*. Typical word lengths might be a few dozen bits.* The programmer might use a word as the binary representation of an integer, fraction, or mixed number, or he might consider the binary digits to be grouped together in *characters*. Four-bit groups are often used as *numeric* characters, in which 10 of the 16 four-digit numbers represent decimal digits. A word of $4n$ binary digits can thus be used to represent an n-digit decimal number. Such a *binary-coded decimal* representation

---

* The expression "binary digit" is frequently contracted to "bit." This usage is at variance with the more correct definition of a bit as a unit of information, but has become entrenched in computer jargon.

is normally understood when reference is made to a "decimal" computer, for truly decimal representation is usually encountered only in desk calculators. Three binary-coded decimal representations that have been used in automatic computers are shown in Table 3–4.

Table 3–4

0	0 0 0 0	0 0 1 1	1 1 0 0
1	0 0 0 1	0 1 0 0	0 0 0 1
2	0 0 1 0	0 1 0 1	0 0 1 0
3	0 0 1 1	0 1 1 0	0 0 1 1
4	0 1 0 0	0 1 1 1	0 1 0 0
5	0 1 0 1	1 0 0 0	0 1 0 1
6	0 1 1 0	1 0 0 1	0 1 1 0
7	0 1 1 1	1 0 1 0	1 0 0 0
8	1 0 0 0	1 0 1 1	1 0 0 1
9	1 0 0 1	1 1 0 0	1 0 1 0

Five binary digits suffice to encode the letters of the alphabet, but six or more are commonly used, to permit inclusion of the decimal digits as well. The resulting *alphanumeric* characters normally include not only the alphabet and the decimal digits, but also many special characters, such as punctuation marks. The *American Standard Code for Information Interchange* uses seven bits and includes the alphabet in both lower and upper cases. The use of redundant binary digits for error detection has already been described. Such redundancy may be incorporated in each character, or only in each word.

Provision is often made for storing explicitly with each number its sign. The most common methods are the use of the leftmost or rightmost binary digit to indicate the sign. Sometimes the magnitude of the number will be represented differently for positive and negative numbers. It will be assumed in the following discussion that some provision exists for indicating the sign, although its nature is not germane, and its absence would not be an essential limitation on the schemes to be described. Attention will henceforth be limited to numeric words.

It is easiest to build arithmetic units to process purely numeric words in which the radix point does not appear explicitly. Each character then represents a successive coefficient in the radix expansion of a number, and all characters are handled in the same manner. Only the location of the radix point remains to be specified. This can be done by either of two essentially different types of representations, *fixed (radix) point* and *floating (radix) point* numbers.

In fixed-point numbers, the location of the radix point of all numeric words is fixed once and for all by the machine builder. The two most common conventions are placement of the radix point at the extreme left, in which case all numbers are fractions less than unity, or at the extreme right, in which case all numbers are integers. The radix point does not appear explicitly, of course, but the arithmetic unit is designed to deliver results whose radix point can be considered to lie in the place corresponding to that of the operands. Although the radix-point location does not affect addition and subtraction, it is of vital importance for multiplication and division. At least one computer has been built in which the radix-point location, although fixed during the execution of any one program, can be set manually at any position between the left- and right-hand ends of the word.

A major problem in the use of fixed-point representation is that of *scaling*. There is no reason to expect the numbers in the problem being solved to be restricted to the range of numbers representable by the computer. The programmer will usually multiply a number outside that range by a power of the base suitable to bring it within the range, and he must then keep track of all such changes of scale. An alternative interpretation of the adjustment is that the programmer adopts for each number a radix-point location which is not necessarily that inherent in the computer. He must then make adjustments appropriate to the arithmetical operations by shifting words right or left. Consider, for example, the representation of 3600 pounds in a 10-place decimal computer with radix point leftmost. The number 3600000000 may be used. Either it represents 0.36 of a new unit, 10^4 pounds, or the decimal point is understood by the user to have been shifted four places to the right. The principal disadvantage of scaling is that approximate magnitudes of all intermediate and final results must be determined in the course of programming a problem.

For a given base b, any nonzero number x can be expressed uniquely in the form $x = a \times b^n$, where n is integral and $b^{-1} \le a < b$. The floating-point representation of x specifies the *mantissa* or *fraction* a and the *characteristic* or *exponent* n. If $x = 0$, it may be represented either by $a = 0$ with n arbitrary or by sufficiently large negative n with a arbitrary. Some base ten examples are the following:

$$\pi = 0.314159 \times 10^1$$
$$1000 = 0.1 \quad \times 10^4$$
$$0.0073 = 0.73 \quad \times 10^{-2}.$$

Separate words may be used to store a and n, each of which is a signed number. The radix points of a and n are understood to be at the left- and right-hand ends, respectively. The main advantage of such floating-point representation is the tremendous range of numbers that can be represented. The range of nonzero magnitudes that can be represented by two-word floating-point numbers in a 10-digit decimal computer is from $0.1 \times 10^{-9999999999}$ to nearly $10^{+9999999999}$. The price paid for this advantage is twofold. First, twice as much storage is required per number; second, either programs must be written, or special equipment built, to perform arithmetic upon the floating-point representations. Many modern computers have arithmetic units that will operate either on fixed-point or on one-word floating-point numbers. In the one-word floating-point representation, a and n share the space available in one word. No more storage is needed than for a fixed-point number, but fewer digits are available for the precise specification of the magnitude. A typical method of storage in a binary computer with words of 47 digits and sign might be to use the sign position for the sign of a, 35 digits for the magnitude of a, and 12 digits for the positive integer $n + 2^{11}$. Here n is constrained to the range $-2^{11} \leq n < 2^{11}$.

With floating-point numbers, the need for scaling is obviated, except in extreme cases, and the labor of problem analysis is correspondingly reduced. However, either the speed of computation is diminished by the need to program floating-point operations in terms of the fixed-point ones commonly available in computers, or more expensive floating-point arithmetic units are required. Moreover, some precision is lost by the provision of storage space for the exponent.

When great precision is required, a number may be spread over two or even more words, in either fixed- or floating-point form. Special programs, or *subroutines*, are usually required to handle such representations. The two-word storage of complex numbers is similar to double-precision representations, in which one word contains the high-order and the other word the low-order digits. Either cartesian or polar forms may be used, with one word each for the real and imaginary parts or for the modulus and argument.

Chapter 4

Transformation of Numbers

4-1 COMPLEX ARITHMETIC

The performance of arithmetical operations on complex numbers will be developed in terms of arithmetical operations on the real number pairs used to represent them. It will be assumed for the present, and justified later, that methods are known for doing arithmetic with the real numbers x, y, r, θ.

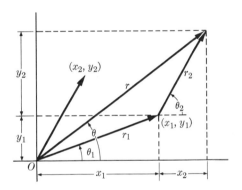

Figure 4-1

The addition of two complex numbers is represented vectorially in Fig. 4-1. In the cartesian representation the addition becomes simply

$$(x_1 + iy_1) + (x_2 + iy_2) = (x_1 + x_2) + i(y_1 + y_2). \qquad (4\text{-}1)$$

Two real additions are therefore necessary to perform one complex addition. For multiplication, one obtains

$$(x_1 + iy_1)(x_2 + iy_2) = x_1x_2 + ix_1y_2 + iy_1x_2 + i^2y_1y_2,$$

$$(x_1 + iy_1)(x_2 + iy_2) = (x_1x_2 - y_1y_2) + i(x_1y_2 + x_2y_1). \qquad (4\text{-}2)$$

This requires six arithmetical operations on real numbers, four multiplications and two additions.

The labor of multiplication can be reduced by using polar representations. Let the product in Eq. (4–2) be the complex number $x + iy$:

$$x = x_1 x_2 - y_1 y_2,$$

$$r \cos \theta = r_1 \cos \theta_1 r_2 \cos \theta_2 - r_1 \sin \theta_1 r_2 \sin \theta_2$$

$$= r_1 r_2 \cos (\theta_1 + \theta_2),$$

$$y = x_1 y_2 + x_2 y_1,$$

$$r \sin \theta = r_1 \cos \theta_1 r_2 \sin \theta_2 + r_2 \cos \theta_2 r_1 \sin \theta_1$$

$$= r_1 r_2 \sin (\theta_1 + \theta_2),$$

$$r^2 (\cos^2 \theta + \sin^2 \theta) = (r_1 r_2)^2 [\cos^2 (\theta_1 + \theta_2) + \sin^2 (\theta_1 + \theta_2)],$$

$$r = r_1 r_2 \text{ and } \theta = \theta_1 + \theta_2. \tag{4–3}$$

In the polar representation, a single multiplication and a single addition suffice. It might be asked whether a similar advantage accrues to the polar representation in complex addition. Let the sum in Eq. (4–1) be the number $x + iy$:

$$x = x_1 + x_2,$$

$$y = y_1 + y_2,$$

$$r \cos \theta = r_1 \cos \theta_1 + r_2 \cos \theta_2,$$

$$r \sin \theta = r_1 \sin \theta_1 + r_2 \sin \theta_2,$$

$$r^2 \cos^2 \theta = r_1^2 \cos^2 \theta_1 + r_2^2 \cos^2 \theta_2 + 2 r_1 r_2 \cos \theta_1 \cos \theta_2,$$

$$r^2 \sin^2 \theta = r_1^2 \sin^2 \theta_1 + r_2^2 \sin^2 \theta_2 + 2 r_1 r_2 \sin \theta_1 \sin \theta_2,$$

$$r^2 = r_1^2 + r_2^2 + 2 r_1 r_2 (\cos \theta_1 \cos \theta_2 + \sin \theta_1 \sin \theta_2),$$

$$\left. \begin{array}{l} r = \sqrt{r_1^2 + r_2^2 + 2 r_1 r_2 \cos (\theta_1 - \theta_2)}, \\[2mm] \theta = \text{arc cos } \dfrac{r_1 \cos \theta_1 + r_2 \cos \theta_2}{r}. \end{array} \right\} \tag{4–4}$$

The resulting equations (4–4) are seen to be hopelessly intricate. To perform addition with polar representations, one might as well convert them to cartesian form, add, and then convert back. The cartesian representation is the more convenient of the two for addition (and for subtraction), and the polar representation is more convenient for multiplication (and, as is demonstrated in Exercise II–9, for division).

4–2 INTEGER ARITHMETIC

The foregoing discussion is predicated on having means of performing arithmetic with real numbers. Such means will be explored in the present section. The only real numbers on which arithmetic is performed in practice are rational numbers with terminating representations. The treatment of such rational numbers is a very simple extension of that of natural numbers, which will now be examined in detail.

(a) Addition

Consider the addition of two n-digit numbers N and N', where

$$N = a_{n-1}b^{n-1} + \cdots + a_1b^1 + a_0b^0,$$

$$N' = a'_{n-1}b^{n-1} + \cdots + a'_1b^1 + a'_0b^0.$$

Their sum $N + N'$ is given by

$$N + N' = (a_{n-1} + a'_{n-1})b^{n-1} + \cdots + (a_1 + a'_1)b^1 + (a_0 + a'_0)b^0,$$

where $0 \le a_i + a'_i \le 2(b - 1)$. The term $(a_0 + a'_0)$ may be rewritten as $\lambda_0 b^1 + \alpha_0 b^0$, where λ_0 is zero or unity, and $0 \le \alpha_0 < b$. The sum $N + N'$ then becomes

$$N + N' = (a_{n-1} + a'_{n-1})b^{n-1} + \cdots + (a_1 + a'_1 + \lambda_0)b^1 + \alpha_0 b^0.$$

The rightmost coefficient in the base b representation of $N + N'$ is therefore α_0, and the next coefficient is obtained from the integral part of the quotient:

$$(N + N')/b = (a_{n-1} + a'_{n-1})b^{n-2} + \cdots + (a_1 + a'_1 + \lambda_0)b^0 + \alpha_0/b.$$

The term $(a_1 + a'_1 + \lambda_0)$ may be rewritten as $\lambda_1 b^1 + \alpha_1 b^0$, where λ_1 is zero or unity, and $0 \le \alpha_1 < b$. The same process is carried out repeatedly, yielding the digits that represent $N + N'$, until the term $(\lambda_{n-1}b^1 + \alpha_{n-1}b^0)$ is obtained. If $\lambda_{n-1} = 0$, then α_{n-1} is the leftmost digit of an n-digit representation of the sum. If $\lambda_{n-1} = 1$, then $\alpha_n = \lambda_{n-1} = 1$ is the leftmost digit of an $(n + 1)$-digit representation.

Table 4–1

	0	1	2	3	4	5	6	7	8	9
0	0	1	2	3	4	5	6	7	8	9
1	1	2	3	4	5	6	7	8	9	10
2	2	3	4	5	6	7	8	9	10	11
3	3	4	5	6	7	8	9	10	11	12
4	4	5	6	7	8	9	10	11	12	13
5	5	6	7	8	9	10	11	12	13	14
6	6	7	8	9	10	11	12	13	14	15
7	7	8	9	10	11	12	13	14	15	16
8	8	9	10	11	12	13	14	15	16	17
9	9	10	11	12	13	14	15	16	17	18

$$b = 10$$

	0	1
0	0	1
1	1	10

$$b = 2$$

In order to perform the computation above, it is clearly sufficient to be able to determine the *sum* digit α_i and the *carry* digit λ_i for all possible pairs of summand digits a_i, a'_i. This information is readily listed in an *addition table*, which lists for each pair a_i, a'_i the corresponding number $\lambda_i\alpha_i$. It is customary not to display zero values of λ_i. Decimal and binary addition tables are presented in Table 4–1. Note that, because of the commutativity (see Exercise II–10) of addition, the tables are symmetric about the main diagonal. Either the entries above the diagonal or those below it may be considered redundant. The addition table gives the sum $a_i + a'_i + \lambda_{i-1}$ only if the carry λ_{i-1} from the previous stage is zero. If $\lambda_{i-1} = 1$, it must be added to the sum obtained from the table. If that sum is $b - 1$, then addition of unity raises it to b, which is represented by $\lambda_i = 1$, $\alpha_i = 0$. If that sum is any other number, then λ_i remains unchanged, and the new α_i can be obtained from the table by addition of unity to the original α_i.

Examples are provided by the following additions of $N = 217$ to $N' = 168$ in both decimal and binary arithmetic. Each nonzero carry λ_i is written above the summands.

$$
\begin{array}{ll}
\quad 1 & \quad 1\ 1\ 1\ 1\ 1 \\
\quad 217 & \quad 1\ 1\ 0\ 1\ 1\ 0\ 0\ 1 \\
\quad 168 & \quad 1\ 0\ 1\ 0\ 1\ 0\ 0\ 0 \\
\hline
\quad 385 & \quad 1\ 1\ 0\ 0\ 0\ 0\ 0\ 1
\end{array}
$$

(b) Subtraction

If $N > N'$, the difference $N' - N$ will be negative, but equal in magnitude to $N - N'$. It suffices, therefore, to consider the positive difference $N - N'$, which may be written as

$$N - N' = (a_{n-1} - a'_{n-1})b^{n-1} + \cdots + (a_1 - a'_1)b^1 + (a_0 - a'_0)b^0$$

$$= (a_{n-1} - a'_{n-1})b^{n-1} + \cdots + (a_1 - a'_1 - \lambda_0)b^1 + (\lambda_0 b + a_0 - a'_0)b^0,$$

where $\lambda_0 = 0$ or 1 and $0 \le \lambda_0 b + a_0 - a'_0 < b$. If $a_0 \ge a'_0$, then $\lambda_0 = 0$; if $a_0 < a'_0$, then $\lambda_0 = 1$. The rightmost coefficient in the base b representation of the difference is $(\lambda_0 b + a_0 - a'_0)$. The next coefficient is $(\lambda_1 b + a_1 - a'_1 - \lambda_0)$, where $\lambda_1 = 1$ only if $a_1 - a'_1 - \lambda_0 < 0$. Succeeding coefficients are obtained in the same manner. Just as it is necessary in addition to propagate carry, in subtraction it is required to propagate *borrow*, represented by the λ_i. The construction of a *subtraction table*, giving the difference and borrow digits as a function of the operand digits a_i and a'_i, will be left as an exercise.

In organizing the propagation of borrow, two alternatives are available, each based on one of the following equations:

$$a_i - a'_i - \lambda_{i-1} = (a_i - \lambda_{i-1}) - a'_i \tag{4–5}$$

$$a_i - a'_i - \lambda_{i-1} = a_i - (a'_i + \lambda_{i-1}). \tag{4–6}$$

The method of subtracting the borrow from the appropriate digit of the *minuend* N corresponds to Eq. (4–5); the method of adding the borrow to the *subtrahend* N' corresponds to Eq. (4–6). The two methods are illustrated below on successive lines for $N = 217$ and $N' = 168$.

217	207	107	107
168	168	168	168
9	49	049	049

217	217	217	217
168	178	278	278
9	49	049	049

(c) Multiplication

The product of the two numbers N and N' may be expanded as

$$NN' = (a_{n-1}b^{n-1} + \cdots + a_1b^1 + a_0b^0)(a'_{n-1}b^{n-1} + \cdots + a'_1b^1 + a'_0b^0)$$
$$= (a_{n-1}b^{n-1} + \cdots + a_1b^1 + a_0b^0)a'_0 + (a_{n-1}b^n + \cdots + a_0b^1)a'_1$$
$$+ \cdots + (a_{n-1}b^{2n-2} + \cdots + a_1b^n + a_0b^{n-1})a'_{n-1}.$$

Each digit a'_i of the *multiplier* N' multiplies the entire *multiplicand* N, and the n subproducts thus formed can be added by means already discussed. It is sufficient, therefore, to provide for the multiplication of N by a single multiplier digit. Consider, for example, the subproduct

$$Na'_0 = a_{n-1}a'_0b^{n-1} + \cdots + a_1a'_0b^1 + a_0a'_0b^0.$$

Since $a_0a'_0 \le (b-1)^2$, we can write $a_0a'_0 = \mu_0b + \pi_0$, where $0 \le \mu_0, \pi_0 < b$, obtaining

$$Na'_0 = a_{n-1}a'_0b^{n-1} + \cdots + (a_1a'_0 + \mu_0)b^1 + \pi_0b^0.$$

The rightmost coefficient of the subproduct Na'_0 is clearly π_0. The term $a_1a'_0 + \mu_0$ cannot exceed $(b-1)^2 + (b-1) < b^2$, and can therefore also be written in the form $\mu_1b + \pi_1$, where $0 \le \mu_1, \pi_1 < b$. The process is repeated until all the π_i are generated. If $\mu_{n-1} \ne 0$, then $\pi_n = \mu_{n-1}$ and the subproduct has $n+1$ digits; otherwise it has n digits. The product NN' may require as many as $2n$ digits for its representation, either because the subproduct Na'_{n-1} requires n digits or because of carry generated in the addition of the subproducts. In general, the product of an m-digit by an n-digit number, where leading zeros are not counted, will be $m + n$ or $m + n - 1$ digits in length (see Exercise II–14).

A *multiplication table*, giving the product $\mu\pi$ of the digits a and a' for all pairs a, a' is a great convenience. Like the addition table, it is symmetric about its main diagonal. It is customary not to display zero values of μ. Multiplication tables for $b = 10$ and $b = 2$ are presented in Table 4–2. Nearly every child has memorized the decimal multiplication table; the properties of the binary multiplication table are less widely known. The carry digit μ is always zero, and the product digit π is zero in every case but one. This great simplicity of binary multiplication is one of the reasons for the widespread use of the base two system in high-speed computing machinery.

Examples of the decimal and binary multiplication of $N = 217$ by $N' = 168$ are given below. In the binary multiplication, the zero subproducts may be omitted, as in the example on the right.

	114	115	
217	217	217	217
1	6	8	168
217	1302	1736	1736
			1302
			217
			36456

```
                    1 1 0 1 1 0 0 1              1 1 0 1 1 0 0 1
                    1 0 1 0 1 0 0 0              1 0 1 0 1 0 0 0
                    0 0 0 0 0 0 0 0          1 1 0 1 1 0 0 1
                    0 0 0 0 0 0 0 0          1 1 0 1 1 0 0 1
                    0 0 0 0 0 0 0 0      1 1 0 1 1 0 0 1
                    1 1 0 1 1 0 0 1      1 0 0 0 1 1 1 0 0 1 1 0 1 0 0 0
                    0 0 0 0 0 0 0 0
                1 1 0 1 1 0 0 1
                0 0 0 0 0 0 0 0
            1 1 0 1 1 0 0 1
    1 0 0 0 1 1 1 0 0 1 1 0 1 0 0 0
```

(d) Division

The following is an elementary theorem of number theory.

> **Theorem 4–1.** Every integer a is uniquely representable in terms of a given positive integer b in the form $a = bq + r$, where q and r are integers and $0 \le r < b$.

Proof. The existence of such a representation is guaranteed by taking bq as the greatest multiple of b not exceeding a. Its uniqueness is shown by assuming $a = bq' + r'$, where $0 \le r' < b$. It then follows that $a - a = b(q - q') + (r - r')$, whence $r - r' = b(q' - q)$ is seen to be a multiple of b. But the

Table 4–2

	0	1	2	3	4	5	6	7	8	9			0	1
0	0	0	0	0	0	0	0	0	0	0		0	0	0
1	0	1	2	3	4	5	6	7	8	9		1	0	1
2	0	2	4	6	8	10	12	14	16	18				
3	0	3	6	9	12	15	18	21	24	27				
4	0	4	8	12	16	20	24	28	32	36				
5	0	5	10	15	20	25	30	35	40	45				
6	0	6	12	18	24	30	36	42	48	54				
7	0	7	14	21	28	35	42	49	56	63				
8	0	8	16	24	32	40	48	56	64	72				
9	0	9	18	27	36	45	54	63	72	81				

conditions on r and r' yield $|r - r'| < b$, and the only multiple $r - r'$ of b satisfying this constraint is zero. Therefore $r = r'$ and $q = q'$.

The number q is called the *quotient* and the number r is the *remainder*. If $r = 0$, then the quotient $q = a/b$ is *exact*.

Given a number or *dividend* N and another number or *divisor* D, the object of division is to determine the unique quotient Q and remainder R such that $N = DQ + R$, with $0 \leq R < D$. Assume that the dividend N has n digits and can be written as

$$N = a_{n-1}b^{n-1} + \cdots + a_1b^1 + a_0b^0,$$

and that the divisor D has $m \leq n$ digits and can be written as

$$D = d_{m-1}b^{m-1} + \cdots + d_1b^1 + d_0b^0.$$

It follows from repeated application of Theorem 4–1 that

$$N = N' + q_{n-m}(b^{n-m}D), \qquad 0 \leq N' < b^{n-m}D,$$
$$N' = N'' + q_{n-m-1}(b^{n-m-1}D), \qquad 0 \leq N'' < b^{n-m-1}D,$$
$$\vdots \qquad\qquad\qquad \vdots$$
$$N^{(n-m-1)} = N^{(n-m)} + q_1(b^1D), \qquad 0 \leq N^{(n-m)} < b^1D,$$
$$N^{(n-m)} = R + q_0(b^0D), \qquad 0 \leq R < b^0D.$$

Adding equations, one obtains

$$N = q_{n-m}b^{n-m}D + q_{n-m-1}b^{n-m-1}D + \cdots + q_1b^1D + q_0b^0D + R$$
$$= D(q_{n-m}b^{n-m} + \cdots + q_1b^1 + q_0b^0) + R$$
$$= DQ + R.$$

It remains to be shown that the q_i are indeed the coefficients of the base b expansion of Q. Because D and the $N^{(i)}$ are all nonnegative, every q_i must be nonnegative. Assume now that some $q_i \geq b$. Since

$$N^{(n-m-i)} = N^{(n-m-1+i)} + q_i b^i D, \qquad 0 \leq N^{(n-m-i)} < b^{i+1} D,$$

it follows that

$$
\begin{aligned}
N^{(n-m-i+1)} &= N^{(n-m-i)} - q_i b^i D \\
&\leq N^{(n-m-i)} - b^{i+1} D \\
&< b^{i+1} D - b^{i+1} D = 0,
\end{aligned}
$$

which contradicts the condition $0 \leq N^{(n-m-i+1)} < b^i D$.   Therefore $0 \leq q_i < b$, and the successive quotients q_i constitute the $n - m$ digits of the base b representation of Q.   It is possible for q_{n-m} to be zero, but in this case $q_{n-m-1} \neq 0$.   In other words, the quotient Q will have either $n - m$ or $n - m + 1$ digits.

There are several ways to perform the division of N by $b^{n-m}D$ and the divisions of the succeeding remainders by $b^i D$. It should be observed first of all that $b^i D$ is obtained by shifting D left through i places. An equivalent result can be obtained by shifting N right through i places. One method of determining the largest multiple $q_i b^i D$ that can be subtracted from $N^{(n-m-i)}$ is to list the b multiples of D by the integers 0 through $b - 1$. A comparison of this list with the leftmost digits of the current dividend indicates which multiple is to be subtracted. This method is particularly suitable for hand computation with long numbers, as in the example below. The digits in parentheses are customarily omitted.

0	0 0 0 0	(0)4 9 1 1 6
1	2 7 4 1	2 7 4 1) 1 3 4 6 2 9 0 4 7
2	5 4 8 2	1 0 9 6 4 (0 0 0 0)
3	8 2 2 3	2 4 9 8 9 (0 4 7)
4	1 0 9 6 4	2 4 6 6 9 (0 0 0)
5	1 3 7 0 5	3 2 0 0 (4 7)
6	1 6 4 4 6	2 7 4 1 (0 0)
7	1 9 1 8 7	4 5 9 4 (7)
8	2 1 9 2 8	2 7 4 1 (0)
9	2 4 6 6 9	1 8 5 3 7
		1 6 4 4 6
		2 0 9 1

A method frequently used in desk calculators is to subtract $b^i D$ repeatedly until the dividend has become negative. The divisor is then added back once, *restoring* the dividend to obtain a remainder less than the divisor. The net number of subtractions is taken as the corresponding digit of the quotient. The reason for subtracting the divisor once too often is that it is extremely easy to provide in a desk calculator for the recognition of sign change, much easier than it is to compare the magnitudes of dividend and divisor. The first few steps of this process are shown in the following division of 34726 by 11. In the left column, the subtractions and additions are shown explicitly; in the right column, the resulting values of the quotient and remainder are shown.

$$
\begin{array}{rr}
\quad\ 31 & \quad 0000 \\
11\overline{)34726} & 11\overline{)34726} \\
-11 & \\
\overline{\ 23726} & 1000 \\
-11 & 11\overline{)23726} \\
\overline{\ 12726} & \\
-11 & 2000 \\
\overline{\ \ 1726} & 11\overline{)12726} \\
-11 & 3000 \\
\overline{-9274} & 11\overline{)01726} \\
+11 & \\
\overline{\ \ 1726} & 4000 \\
-11 & 11\overline{)-9274} \\
\overline{\ \ \ 626} & 3000 \\
-11 & 11\overline{)01726} \\
\overline{\ -474} & \\
+11 & 3100 \\
\overline{\ \ \ 626} & 11\overline{)00626} \\
 & 3200 \\
 & 11\overline{)-0474} \\
 & 3100 \\
 & 11\overline{)00626}
\end{array}
$$

A third method, known as *nonrestoring* division, is often employed in automatic computers. Once the dividend has been driven negative, the same divisor is not added back once as in restoring division. Instead, the divisor is shifted right one place and added until the dividend is driven positive. For each time the divisor is added, unity is subtracted from the corresponding quotient digit. Once the dividend has become positive again, the further shifted divisor is subtracted while one is added to the quotient, and the process continues until the remaining dividend is smaller than the divisor. The example below shows the first stages of this process with the same numbers as in the previous example.

$$
\begin{array}{rr}
+- & \\
\underline{49} & \underline{0000} \\
11)34726 & 11)34726 \\
-11 & \\
\overline{23726} & \underline{1000} \\
-11 & 11)23726 \\
\overline{12726} & \\
-11 & \underline{2000} \\
\overline{1726} & 11)12726 \\
-11 & \\
\overline{-9274} & \underline{3000} \\
+11 & 11)01726 \\
\overline{-8174} & \\
+11 & \underline{4000} \\
\overline{-7074} & 11)-9274 \\
+11 & \\
\overline{-5974} & \underline{3900} \\
+11 & 11)-8174 \\
\overline{-4874} & \\
+11 & \underline{3800} \\
\overline{-3774} & 11)-7074 \\
+11 & \\
\overline{-2674} & \underline{3700} \\
+11 & 11)-5974 \\
\overline{-1574} & \\
+11 & \underline{3600} \\
\overline{-474} & 11)-4874 \\
+11 & \\
\overline{+626} & \underline{3500} \\
 & 11)-3774 \\
\end{array}
$$

(e) Extension to Nonintegral Operands

The processes described above apply with only trivial modification to operations on nonintegral numbers. The coefficients being manipulated are coefficients of negative as well as positive powers of the base. The various rules previously derived made use only of the fact that successive coefficients multiplied successive powers of b, not that these powers were positive. Accordingly, it is sufficient to mark the radix points in the operands in the usual manner. For addition and subtraction, the radix points should be aligned, and the radix point of the result will have the corresponding position. For multiplication, the radix point in the product should leave as many digits to the right as the sum of the numbers of digits to the right of the operand radix points. In division, both the dividend and divisor radix points can be shifted so that the divisor becomes an integer, and the quotient radix point will then lie above that of the dividend. A few examples are given below.

$$
\begin{array}{rrr}
 & 1\,0\,0.1\,0\,0 & 1101.1001 \\
1\,0.1\,0\,)\,1\,0\,1\,1.0\,1\,0\,0\,1 & 1010.1000 \\
\hline
1\,0\,1\,0 & 11000.0001 \\
1\,0\,1\,0 & \\
1\,0\,1\,0 & \\
\hline
0\,1 &
\end{array}
$$

$$
\begin{array}{r}
2\,1.7 \\
1.6\,8 \\
\hline
1\,7\,3\,6 \\
1\,3\,0\,2 \\
2\,1\,7 \\
\hline
3\,6.4\,5\,6
\end{array}
$$

Chapter 5

Error in Numbers

Errors occur in numbers for a variety of reasons. The sources of uncertainty are many, and will be described in Section 5–1. The way in which calculation projects uncertainty from the data into the results will be described in Section 5–2. Uncertainty in acquired numbers will be considered in Section 5–4. This latter study will require the prior development of some elementary probability theory (Section 5–3) and will lead to some simple results of statistics (Sections 5–4 and 5–5).

5–1 TYPES OF UNCERTAINTY

(a) Precision, Accuracy, and Error

Before undertaking a study of errors, it will be helpful to establish precise meanings for some of the descriptive phrases commonly employed. The statement that $\pi = 3.1416$ is not normally understood to mean that π is equal to the rational number given. It means instead that π is more nearly equal to the rational 3.1416 than to any other rational expressible with the same number of digits. In other words, $3.14155 \leq \pi \leq 3.14165$. If some convention is adopted to govern rounding, at least one of the weak inequality signs $\leq$ can be replaced by the strong one $<$.

The term *precision* is used to refer to the narrowness of the range of specification of the number. The term *accuracy* is used to refer to the correctness of the specification. Consider the following examples:

$$\text{(a) } \pi = 3.1416;$$
$$\text{(b) } \pi = 3.14160;$$
$$\text{(c) } \pi = 3;$$
$$\text{(d) } \pi = 2.984327654;$$
$$\text{(e) } \pi = 3.1415927.$$

Of the five statements, (d) is at once the most precise and the least accurate;

(c) is not very precise, but it is accurate; (b) is more precise than (a), but its last digit is not accurate; (e) is accurate in all eight digits given.

The term *significant digit* has at least two common meanings. With respect to numbers in general, it refers to any digit other than a leading zero. In this sense, the numbers 256, 2.56, 2.06, 0.00256 all have three significant digits. With respect to numbers derived by calculation, the term is often used to refer only to digits (other than leading zeros) known to be correct. Suppose, for example, that the length and height of a rectangle are measured to within one percent as 5.1 and 4.3 inches, respectively. The area is calculated as 21.93 square inches, to within two percent. According to the first meaning, the number 21.93 has four significant digits; according to the second it has but two. It may be that the actual area of the rectangle is 21.87, in which case the number 21.93 has three digits of accuracy. A common phrase in this connection is that the number is "accurate to three places" or "good to three places."

A further confusion is occasionally introduced by the fact that "places" is often, but not invariably, used to refer only to digits to the right of the radix point. It is generally understood, for example, that four-place decimal logarithm tables are accurate to 10^{-4}. It is permissible, however, to refer to 3.1416 as a five-place representation of π, provided that the context is clear.

It is important to distinguish between *absolute* error and *relative* error. If the number x^* is represented for any reason by the number x, the absolute error is defined as $\epsilon = x - x^*$, the difference between the value x actually employed and the (possibly unknown) "true" value x^*. The relative error is defined as ϵ/x^*. Either the absolute or the relative error may be large or small, independently of the other. In the use of 3.14 to represent π, the absolute error ϵ is approximately -0.0016 and the relative error ϵ/π approximately -0.0005. When bounds on a number are known, a common notation is $x^* = x \pm \delta x$, which is to be interpreted as meaning $x - \delta x \leq x^* \leq x + \delta x$. An example is $\pi = 3.14 \pm 0.002$.

(b) Sources of Uncertainty

Manipulations with numbers can be classified, though somewhat arbitrarily, as acquisition of numbers and computation with the numbers acquired. Among the errors introduced by computation are truncation, blunders, and propagation of acquired errors.

Truncation is essentially the use of fewer terms of a series than are required to define a number without error. Truncation may take many forms. Among these are the use of rationals to approximate irrationals and the use of rationals with terminating representations to approximate those with nonterminating representations. Another is *rounding*, the use of fewer digits than are already available in some representation of a number. Rounding is often dictated by the desire for efficient use of the storage space in a computer. The resulting *roundoff error* is distinguished by some authors from truncation, which in its narrowest sense is the use of only a finite number of terms of an infinite defining series. Thus, for example, the sine of a real number can be defined by the infinite series

$$\sin x = \sum_{i=0}^{\infty} (-1)^i \frac{x^{2i+1}}{(2i+1)!} = x - \frac{x^3}{3!} + \frac{x^5}{5!} - \frac{x^7}{7!} + \cdots \qquad (5\text{–}1)$$

If only the first four terms on the right-hand side of Eq. (5–1) are used, the approximation

$$y = x - \frac{x^3}{3!} + \frac{x^5}{5!} - \frac{x^7}{7!}$$

will differ from $\sin x$ by an amount whose estimation is one of the important problems of analysis.

Arithmetical and clerical blunders contribute their share of error; one of the most common among the latter is the transposition of adjacent digits. The manner in which *inherited* errors, those already present in arithmetic operands, are propagated to the results is the subject of Section 5–2.

Numbers other than the results of previous computations are generally acquired either by measurement or by sampling. Measurement errors occur among the most careful workers; the reader may wish to invite several friends to measure the dimensions of this book to the best precision they can attain. Some variation in the answers is likely, and theoretical tools are available for deciding both which value to use and what error bounds to assign to it. Sampling errors are related to the size of the sample, the size of the population sampled, the nature of the population, and to many other factors, not the least of which is chance. Some of these factors are amenable to quantitative treatment.

5–2 PROPAGATION OF UNCERTAINTY

Errors in operands are transmitted to the results of arithmetical operations, and it is important to be able to determine the extent to which error is thus *propagated*. It is as grossly pessimistic to assume that the maximum error will be generated at each step as it is naive to hope that all errors will compensate. On the other hand, it is an extremely difficult statistical task to compute an average or reasonable value of the propagated error. It is dangerous to ignore this accumulation of error, and instructive to compute approximately the errors in results of the elementary arithmetical operations. It will be assumed that further errors are not introduced in the calculation process.

Consider two numbers $A + a$ and $B + b$. For each, the upper-case letter represents the true value, and the lower-case letter represents the absolute error. These values may be positive or negative. The relative errors are a/A and b/B. In general, of course, it is not known how much of each number is the true value and how much is the error, but it will be assumed that the relative errors are small, that is, that $|a| \ll |A|$ and $|b| \ll |B|$.

(a) Addition and Subtraction

These two operations can both be represented by the algebraic addition of signed numbers

$$(A + a) + (B + b) = (A + B) + (a + b).$$

It is seen that the absolute error of the sum is the sum of the absolute errors of the summands. The relative error of the sum can be very large if $A + B$ is nearly zero. Such an error is usually termed *difference* error, because it arises in taking the difference of two nearly equal quantities. Consider the tabulation for several small values of x of the function

$$f(x) = \left(\frac{15}{x^3} - \frac{6}{x}\right) \sin x - \left(\frac{15}{x^2} - 1\right) \cos x. \tag{5-2}$$

If eight-place tables are used for the sine and cosine, the function is evaluated directly for $x = 0.1$ as

$$f(x) = 1491.51129480 - 1491.51125083 = 0.00004397.$$

For small x, however, substitution of series expansions for the sine and cosine yields

$$f(x) = \frac{x^4}{105} - \frac{x^6}{1890} + \cdots \tag{5-3}$$

By using the series (5–3), $f(0.1)$ is evaluated to eight places as 0.00000095. Direct use of the defining formula (5–2) leads to an answer with a relative error of 45.

(b) Multiplication and Division

For multiplication,

$$(A + a)(B + b) = AB + aB + bA + ab.$$

The term ab can be neglected in comparison with aB and bA because of the relations $|ab| \ll |aB|$ and $|ab| \ll |Ab|$. The absolute error in the product is then approximately $aB + bA$ and the relative error is $(aB + bA)/AB = a/A + b/B$. It is seen that, whereas addition adds absolute errors, multiplication adds relative errors. For division,

$$\frac{A + a}{B + b} = \frac{A + a}{B(1 + b/B)} = \frac{A + a}{B}\left(1 - \frac{b}{B} + \cdots\right).$$

The first term omitted from the series* is $(b/B)^2$, which can be neglected, yielding

$$\frac{A + a}{B + b} = \frac{A + a}{B}\left(1 - \frac{b}{B}\right) = \frac{A}{B} + \frac{a}{B}\left(1 - \frac{b}{B}\right) - \frac{Ab}{B^2}.$$

---

* The expansion
$$1/(1 + b/B) = 1 - b/B + b^2/B^2 - b^3/B^3 + \cdots = \sum_{i=0}^{n} (-b/B)^i$$
is easily verified, in light of the footnote on p. 38.

The absolute error in division is thus found to be approximately

$$\frac{a}{B} - \frac{Ab}{B^2} = \frac{a - (A/B)b}{B} .$$

This shows that a small divisor B leads to a large error. The relative error is

$$\frac{a - (A/B)b}{B} \div \frac{A}{B} = \frac{a}{A} - \frac{b}{B},$$

and it is seen that relative errors are subtracted by the division operation. This should not be construed to mean that division is guaranteed to reduce relative error. After all, the signs and magnitudes of the operand errors must be considered. If maximum values, or *bounds*, can be placed on the magnitudes of the relative errors, the only safe conclusion is that multiplication or division adds these bounds.

Let it be required to estimate the maximum error in

$$t = \frac{(u + v)(w - x)}{y + z} ,$$

where

$$
\begin{aligned}
u &= 1 \pm .03, & x &= 2 \pm .04, \\
v &= 2 \pm .04, & y &= 3 \pm .01, \\
w &= 6 \pm .02, & z &= 3 \pm .03.
\end{aligned}
$$

Since the signs of the errors in the six variables are not known, the errors are added. The bounds on absolute errors in $u + v$, $w - x$, and $y + z$ are 0.07, 0.06, and 0.04, respectively. The relative errors can be estimated by using the sums $u + v$, etc., good approximations to the unknown true sums, yielding $\frac{7}{3}$ percent for the bound on relative error in $u + v$, $\frac{3}{2}$ percent for $w - x$, and $\frac{2}{3}$ percent for $y + z$. For the multiplication and division, the relative-error magnitudes are added, yielding a possible 4.5 percent relative error in the computed value 2 of t. The result of this analysis is that $t = 2 \pm 0.09$.

(c) Powers

If n is a positive integer, then the nth power $(A + a)^n$ may be approximated from the binomial expansion*

$$(A + a)^n = A^n + nA^{n-1}a + \binom{n}{2} A^{n-2}a^2 + \cdots$$

as $(A + a)^n = A^n + naA^{n-1}$, by neglecting powers of a which are higher than the first. The absolute error is naA^{n-1} and the relative error is

---

* $\binom{m}{n}$ is the binomial coefficient $m!/n!(m - n)!$.

$naA^{n-1}/A^n = n(a/A)$, representing an n-fold increase in the relative error of the operand.

If $n = \frac{1}{2}$, the operation in question is the very common one of square-root extraction. The binomial expansion may be used to obtain

$$(A + a)^{1/2} = \left[A \left(1 + \frac{a}{A} \right) \right]^{1/2} = A^{1/2} \left(1 + \frac{a}{A} \right)^{1/2}$$

$$= A^{1/2} \left[1 + \frac{1}{2} \frac{a}{A} - \frac{1}{8} \left(\frac{a}{A} \right)^2 + \cdots \right].$$

By neglecting powers of a/A which are higher than the first, one finds that the absolute error is approximately $a/2\sqrt{A}$, and that the relative error is $a/2A$.

For large A, both types of error are diminished. For small A, however, the foregoing analysis is inapplicable because $a \ll A$ does not hold, and serious problems can arise. A common source of annoyance is that the number zero, when computed, is often represented, because of roundoff and truncation errors, as a very small but nonzero number. Suppose that zero is represented in a ten decimal digit calculator by a roundoff of unity in the last place, that is, $N = 10^{-10}$. Then $\sqrt{N} = 10^{-5}$ and the absolute error in the square root will be 10^5 times that in the number.

(d) Exponentials and Logarithms*

The absolute error in $e^{(A+a)} = e^A e^a$ is $e^A (e^a - 1)$ and the relative error is $e^A (e^a - 1)/e^A$ or $e^a - 1$. For small a, $e^a = 1 + a + a^2/2 + \cdots$, and by neglecting powers of a higher than the first, one finds that the relative error $e^a - 1$ is approximately equal to a, the absolute error of the exponent.

The natural logarithm of $A + a$ may be expanded as follows:

$$\ln (A + a) = \ln \left[A \left(1 + \frac{a}{A} \right) \right] = \ln A + \ln \left(1 + \frac{a}{A} \right)$$

$$= \ln A + \left[\frac{a}{A} - \frac{1}{2} \left(\frac{a}{A} \right)^2 + \cdots \right],$$

from which one obtains, by neglecting higher powers of a, the absolute error a/A, which is equal to the relative error of the operand.

The inverse operations of exponentiation and logarithm extraction are thus seen to have complementary properties with respect to error. Exponentiation transforms an absolute error into a relative one; the opposite transformation occurs when the logarithm is taken.

---

* This section may be omitted without loss of continuity by the reader unfamiliar with the Taylor or Maclaurin series expansions of exponential and logarithmic functions.

5–3 FREQUENCY DISTRIBUTIONS OF ONE VARIABLE

Many of the data on which computation is performed are obtained by sampling or measurement. Some familiarity with the methods of statistics is essential to an understanding of the significance of such data. Moreover, the propagation of errors, whose magnitudes of course are not known exactly, is often best treated statistically. Statistics is itself based on the concepts of frequency distributions and probability theory, which are both introduced in this section.

Almost any collection of qualitatively similar data can be viewed as constituting a *frequency distribution*, so called because of the emphasis on the frequency of occurrence of the different possible results. The data need not be numerical, but they must represent results of the same type. A collection of the heights and weights, mixed together, of a group of school children would not be considered a frequency distribution. Even the set of heights alone would not qualify if all were not expressed in terms of the same unit.

(a) Discrete Distributions

Table 5–1(a) records whether a coin landed heads (H) or tails (T) on each of ten successive tosses. Table 5–1(b) presents the same data as a frequency distribution. The presentation as a distribution shows only the numbers of occurrences of each result, but not the sequence in which the results were obtained. Although such sequence information is important in some studies, its removal often leads to no harm and usually permits a simplification of the subsequent analysis. From the numbers of occurrences of heads (6) and of tails (4), their frequencies of occurrence can readily be calculated as 60 and 40 percent, respectively, or as 0.6 and 0.4.

Table 5–1

Toss	1	2	3	4	5	6	7	8	9	10
Result	T	H	H	T	H	H	H	T	T	H

(a)

Heads	6
Tails	4
Total	10

(b)

The scores (out of a possible 55 points) on an examination taken by 21 students are presented in Table 5–2. Their organization as a frequency distribution is also shown in the table, with scores below 20 omitted. One can easily compute from the table that the frequency of the score 43, for example, is $\frac{2}{21}$.

Table 5–2

Scores		Frequency distribution							
33	51	20	0	29	2	38	1	47	0
36	43	21	0	30	0	39	0	48	0
35	32	22	1	31	1	40	1	49	1
49	43	23	0	32	3	41	0	50	0
44	53	24	0	33	1	42	0	51	2
46	40	25	0	34	0	43	2	52	0
38	29	26	1	35	1	44	1	53	1
26	51	27	0	36	1	45	0	54	0
32	29	28	0	37	0	46	1	55	0
31	32								
22									

It is often more convenient to express the characteristics of a frequency distribution by means of a small number of parameters than by a large table of frequencies. Such statistical parameters can be computed from the data that define the distribution, provided that these data are numerical. Nonnumerical data can sometimes be converted for this purpose to numerical by the arbitrary assignment of numbers to the different results. Thus for coin tossing one might assign 1 to heads and 0 to tails.

One parameter that is often required is a measure of the location of the distribution. There are many ways of specifying such an *average* of n values x_i, where $1 \leq i \leq n$. Foremost among them is the *(arithmetic) mean* $\bar{x}$ defined as

$$\bar{x} = \frac{1}{n} \sum_{i=1}^{n} x_i. \tag{5–4}$$

The summation index will be the same in subsequent formulas, and will not be shown explicitly.* The *geometric* mean is a multiplicative rather than additive average and is given by $(\Pi x_i)^{1/n}$. The *harmonic mean* is the reciprocal of the arithmetic mean of the reciprocals of the values and is equal to $n/\sum x_i^{-1}$. The *mode*, if it exists, is that value of x_i which appears most frequently in the distribution. The *median* is the middle value of the x_i in the list of all x_i in numerical sequence. If n is even, and the two middle values of x_i are different, the median is taken to be their arithmetic mean. The test score distribution has arithmetic mean 37.9, median 36, and mode 32. Calculation of its geometric and harmonic means is left to the industrious reader.

---

* Although $\bar{x}$ was used in Chapter 3 to represent the complex conjugate of x, its present use for the arithmetic mean also follows custom. The reader may as well recognize the fact that the proper understanding of mathematical notation is not always independent of the context in which it is used.

Of the various parameters of location the mean and the median are the most commonly encountered. The mean is often preferred because it is easily computed, as in Program 5–1. The sum $\sum x_i$ can be calculated by adding each x_i to the previous partial sum, without storing any of the x_i. The median cannot be computed without storing all n values of x_i and sorting them into numerical sequence. For many purposes, however, the median is a better measure of location than the mean. Suppose that a village has 110 families of whom 100 have annual incomes of $5000 and the remaining 10 have incomes of $50,000. The mean income is $9091, which is far removed from that of any of the families. The median, however, is $5000.

A second parameter of importance is a measure of the variation or spread in the data. The *deviation* of the ith value is defined as $x_i - \bar{x}$. The sum of the deviations is given by

$$\sum(x_i - \bar{x}) = \sum x_i - \sum \bar{x} = n\bar{x} - n\bar{x} = 0,$$

and hardly serves as a useful measure. The sum of the magnitudes $|x_i - \bar{x}|$ of the deviations could be used, but absolute values, although convenient for numerical work, are inconvenient for mathematical analysis, and it is usual to employ the squares of the deviations instead. This has the further advantage of accentuating measurements that differ widely from the mean. Thus the *variance* s^2 is defined as

$$s^2 = \frac{1}{n}\sum(x_i - \bar{x})^2, \tag{5–5}$$

and its positive square root s, which is seen to have the same units as x, is termed the *standard deviation*.

It is highly inconvenient to use the formula (5–5) to calculate s^2, because $\bar{x}$ is not known until all the x_i have been examined once. They must be stored for the subsequent computation of each deviation. An equivalent formulation which allows a more efficient organization of the computation will now be derived.

$$
\begin{aligned}
ns^2 &= \sum(x_i - \bar{x})^2 \\
&= \sum x_i^2 - 2\sum x_i \bar{x} + \sum \bar{x}^2 \\
&= \sum x_i^2 - 2\bar{x}\sum x_i + n\bar{x}^2 \\
&= \sum x_i^2 - 2n\bar{x}^2 + n\bar{x}^2 \\
&= \sum x_i^2 - n\bar{x}^2, \\
s^2 &= \frac{1}{n}\sum x_i^2 - \bar{x}^2, \\
s^2 &= \overline{x^2} - \bar{x}^2. \tag{5–6}
\end{aligned}
$$

Program 5–1

$$
\begin{aligned}
&i \leftarrow 0 \\
&y \leftarrow 0 \\
&\rightarrow i \leftarrow i+1 \\
&\left\lfloor \neq \begin{array}{l} y \leftarrow y + x_i \\ i : n \end{array} \right. \\
&\bar{x} \leftarrow y/n
\end{aligned}
$$

Program 5–2

$$
\begin{aligned}
&i \leftarrow 0 \\
&y \leftarrow 0 \\
&z \leftarrow 0 \\
&\rightarrow \begin{array}{l} y \leftarrow y + x_i \\ w \leftarrow x_i \times x_i \\ z \leftarrow z + w \\ i : n \end{array} \\
&\neq \\
&\bar{x} \leftarrow y/n \\
&y \leftarrow \bar{x} \times \bar{x} \\
&z \leftarrow z/n \\
&s^2 \leftarrow z - y
\end{aligned}
$$

A single pass through the data suffices to implement Eq. (5–6). Each x_i is squared, and both the squared and unsquared values are accumulated. The sum $\sum x_i^2$ is divided by n to yield $\overline{x^2}$ and the sum $\sum x_i$ is divided by n and then squared to yield $\overline{x}^2$. Program 5–2 illustrates the process. Despite the simplicity of Eq. (5–6), its use may result in substantial difference error if the deviations are small compared to the mean.

Other measures of variation occasionally encountered are the *mean (absolute) deviation*, already discussed, and the *range*. The latter is defined simply as the difference of the greatest and smallest values of x_i and of course yields no information about the distribution of the nonextreme values.

Both the mean and the variance are special cases of *moments* of the distribution of measurements. The kth moment about c is defined in general as

$$\frac{1}{n} \sum (x_i - c)^k.$$

The mean is thus seen to be the first moment about zero, and the variance is the second moment about the mean. Higher-order moments are of great theoretical importance in the study of frequency distributions, but will not be used here.

Table 5–3

Deaths x_i	Frequency $f(x_i)$
0	109
1	65
2	22
3	3
4	1

Although the data in discrete frequency distributions are constrained to assume discrete values, the admissible values need not be finite in number, as in the examples cited. The number of consecutive times a coin may fall the same way as the first time has no limit, although very large values are exceedingly unlikely. A celebrated frequency distribution is that of Table 5–3. The variable x_i is the number of deaths from the kick of a horse per year per corps for 10 Prussian Army Corps during 20 years. The distribution can be represented graphically either as the conventional *histogram* of Fig. 5–1(a) or the cartesian plot of Fig. 5–1(b).

The distribution of Table 5–3 agrees closely with the theoretical *Poisson* distribution. This distribution is defined by the *discrete frequency function*

$$f(x) = \frac{a^x e^{-a}}{x!}, \tag{5–7}$$

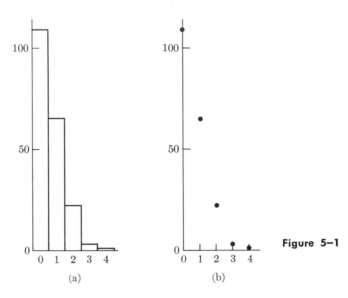

(a)   (b)   **Figure 5–1**

where $f(x)$ is the frequency of occurrence of the value x, which, in this case, can be any nonnegative integer. By use of the relation

$$e^a = 1 + a + \frac{a^2}{2!} + \cdots = \sum_{i=0}^{\infty} \frac{a^i}{i!} \tag{5-8}$$

the reader can verify that the Poisson frequency function obeys the general law

$$\sum_j f(x_j) = 1. \tag{5-9}$$

The Poisson distribution is obeyed fairly closely by many rare events, such as the occurrence of raisins in a small volume of dough or of particle emissions per unit time by a radioactive source.

The mean and standard deviation of a distribution are easily calculated from its frequency function. The n values x_i that enter into Eq. (5–4) are really $nf(x_j)$ occurrences of each of the values x_j. Equation (5–4) can therefore be rewritten to identify the mean as

$$\bar{x} = \frac{1}{n} \sum_{i=1}^{n} x_i$$

$$= \frac{1}{n} \sum_j nf(x_j)x_j$$

$$= \sum_j x_j f(x_j). \tag{5-10}$$

The variance s^2 can similarly be shown to be

$$s^2 = \sum_j (x_j - \bar{x})^2 f(x_j) \tag{5-11}$$

and to be computable by Eq. (5–6), where $\overline{x^2}$ is now determined as $\sum_j x_j^2 f(x_j)$.

From Eq. (5–10) and the fact that x_j is just the integer j, one obtains the mean of the Poisson distribution as follows:

$$\bar{x} = \sum_{j=0}^{\infty} j \frac{a^j e^{-a}}{j!}$$

$$= \sum_{j=1}^{\infty} j \frac{a^j e^{-a}}{j!}$$

$$= e^{-a} \sum_{j=1}^{\infty} \frac{ja^j}{j!}$$

$$= e^{-a} \sum_{j=1}^{\infty} \frac{a \cdot a^{j-1}}{(j-1)!}$$

$$= ae^{-a} \sum_{j=1}^{\infty} \frac{a^{j-1}}{(j-1)!}$$

$$= ae^{-a} \sum_{i=0}^{\infty} \frac{a^i}{i!} \qquad (\text{where } i = j - 1)$$

$$= ae^{-a}e^{a}$$

$$= a.$$

(b) Continuous Distributions

The distributions of the preceding section were all discrete, in that the variable could assume discrete values only. Continuous frequency distributions arise when the variable is not so constrained. This may occur as the result of a limiting process of some sort, or because the variable in question can assume any real value, perhaps within certain limits.

Whereas a discrete frequency function expresses the frequency of occurrence of a particular value of the variable, a continuous frequency function expresses the frequency of occurrences of values of the variable within an interval. Thus $f(x_i)\,dx$ is the frequency of occurrence of values of x in the infinitesimal range $x_i \le x \le x_i + dx$. The value $f(x_i)$ is seen to be the limit at x_i, as dx approaches zero, of the number of occurrences of x within a unit interval. The function $f(x)$ is therefore often called the *density* function of the distribution.

Since the frequency of occurrence of values of x within the range (a, b) for which the distribution is defined is unity, it follows that

$$\int_a^b f(x)\,dx = 1. \tag{5-12}$$

Equation (5–12) is the continuous counterpart of the law (5–9), in which the discrete sum has been replaced by an integral. The limits of integration will be omitted when no ambiguity is possible. The kth moment of the continuous distribution about c is defined as

$$\int (x - c)^k f(x) \, dx,$$

from which the following expressions for the mean and variance are easily derived.

$$\bar{x} = \int x f(x) \, dx, \tag{5–13}$$

$$s^2 = \int (x - \bar{x})^2 f(x) \, dx. \tag{5–14}$$

A simple example of a continuous distribution is the *uniform* distribution. Here, all values of the variable within a finite interval occur with equal density $f(x) = C$; values outside the interval do not occur. If that interval is $(-1, 1)$, C can be evaluated from Eq. (5–12):

$$\int_{-1}^{1} C \, dx = 1,$$

$$2C = 1,$$

$$C = \tfrac{1}{2}.$$

A plot of this distribution is given in Fig. 5–2. Since the distribution is symmetric about the origin, the mean is clearly zero, as can be verified by using Eq. (5–13). The variance is calculated from Eq. (5–14) as $s^2 = \tfrac{1}{3}$ and the standard deviation is therefore $s = \sqrt{\tfrac{1}{3}} = 0.58$. The values $\bar{x} \pm s$ are indicated in the figure by dashed lines. The uniform distribution describes the random selection of a point on a line segment or of a real number within a finite interval.

A continuous distribution over the half-open infinite interval is defined by $f(x) = Ce^{-x}$ for nonnegative x. The constant C is easily determined by substitution in Eq. (5–12):

$$1 = \int_0^{\infty} Ce^{-x} = C.$$

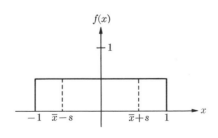

Figure 5–2

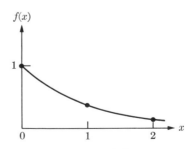

Figure 5–3

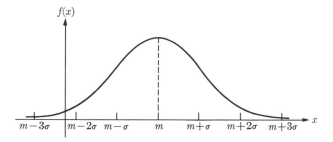

Figure 5–4

The frequency function is therefore $f(x) = e^{-x}$, which characterizes the *exponential* distribution, shown in Fig. 5–3. The reader can verify by use of Eqs. (5–13) and (5–14) that $\bar{x} = s = 1$.

Of great practical and theoretical importance is the gaussian or *normal* distribution, illustrated in Fig. 5–4. The normal distribution is a good approximation to the frequency distributions exhibited by many physical measurements on manufactured articles and on living organisms. It will be seen later to be useful in much statistical analysis.

The normal distribution is defined for all x by the frequency function

$$f(x) = \frac{1}{\sigma\sqrt{2\pi}} e^{-(x-m)^2/2\sigma^2}. \tag{5–15}$$

This function satisfies the general law (5–12) for any value of m and any positive value of σ. The verification is difficult and will be omitted. Since the density function (5–15) is symmetric about $x = m$, one would expect the mean $\bar{x}$ to equal m. This is readily shown by making the change of variable $z = x - m$ in applying the definition (5–13).

$$\bar{x} = \int_{-\infty}^{\infty} x \frac{1}{\sigma\sqrt{2\pi}} e^{-(x-m)^2/2\sigma^2} \, dx$$

$$= \int_{-\infty}^{\infty} (z + m) \frac{1}{\sigma\sqrt{2\pi}} e^{-z^2/2\sigma^2} \, dz$$

$$= \frac{1}{\sigma\sqrt{2\pi}} \int_{-\infty}^{\infty} z e^{-z^2/2\sigma^2} \, dz + m \int_{-\infty}^{\infty} \frac{1}{\sigma\sqrt{2\pi}} e^{-z^2/2\sigma^2} \, dz. \tag{5–16}$$

The first integral in Eq. (5–16) is evaluated as

$$-\sigma^2 e^{-z^2/2\sigma^2} \Big]_{-\infty}^{\infty} = 0,$$

and the second integral, being a special case of that of Eq. (5–12), is unity. It follows that $\bar{x} = m$. The reader skilled in integration by parts is invited to verify that the variance is σ^2, and the standard deviation is therefore σ. Geometrically, the standard deviation of this distribution is the distance from the mean at which the curve that represents the frequency function has inflection points.

The frequency of occurrence of values in the range $x = m \pm k\sigma$ is often of interest. It is given by the integral of the frequency function (5–15) from $m - k\sigma$ to $m + k\sigma$. Introduction of the variable $y = (x - m)/\sigma$ reduces the integral as follows.

$$\int_{m-k\sigma}^{m+k\sigma} \frac{1}{\sigma\sqrt{2\pi}} e^{-(x-m)^2/2\sigma^2} \, dx = \int_{-k}^{k} \frac{1}{\sqrt{2\pi}} e^{-y^2/2} \, dy$$

$$= 2\int_{0}^{k} \frac{1}{\sqrt{2\pi}} e^{-y^2/2} \, dy. \qquad (5\text{–}17)$$

The integral in (5–17) cannot be evaluated analytically, but it can be evaluated numerically by techniques similar to those described in Part IV. The integrand in (5–17) is the frequency function $f(y) = (1/\sqrt{2\pi})e^{-y^2/2}$ of the normal distribution in *standard units* $y = (x - m)/\sigma$, and has mean zero and standard deviation unity. Extensive tabulations of this standardized normal distribution function, its integral, and its derivatives are available. Table 5–4 gives a few values of its integral from 0 to k. It is seen from the table that about 68 percent of the variable values lie within plus or minus one standard deviation of the mean, and about 95 percent within two standard deviations.

Table 5–4

k	0.0	0.5	1.0	1.5	2.0	2.5	3.0	∞
I	0.000	0.191	0.341	0.433	0.477	0.494	0.499	0.500

(c) Probability Theory

If a coin were tossed repeatedly, one would normally observe that the frequency of heads approached $\frac{1}{2}$ as the number of tosses increased without limit. A physical theory might predict a certain distribution of velocities for the molecules of a gas. Each possible outcome of a real or hypothetical experiment (tossing a coin or measuring the velocity of a gas molecule) is called in probability theory an *event*. The statistician would view the limiting frequency of heads in the first case, or the theoretical frequency of velocities within a certain range in the second, as the *probability* of occurrence of the corresponding events. The attempt to give precise meaning to the notion of probability leads to advanced philosophical arguments that have no place here. For present purposes it will be sufficient to define the probability of an event as the theoretical or limiting frequency of its occurrence.

The variables used to describe the results of the real or conceptual experiments that are performed are called *random variables*. The variable may be an observed quantity, such as the number of deaths plotted in Fig. 5–1, or an arbitrarily defined one, such as a variable equal to 1 for heads and 0 for tails. The random variable and the frequency function, which can now be given its proper name of *probability density function*, are together assumed to obey certain rules. For every value x of the random variable under consideration, the probability density function $f(x)$ is defined; it obeys the restriction $f(x) \geq 0$ and either the law (5–9) (if the random variable assumes discrete values only) or the law (5–12) (if the random variable has a continuous range). Moreover, for every event with nonzero probability density $f(x)$, the random variable is assigned a unique value x. Probabilities are so defined that they always fall in the interval $(0, 1)$.

An important concept in probability and statistics is that of the independence of events or of random variables. A formal definition of independence can be based upon the definition of joint probability distributions for two or more random variables. The intuitive notion that two random variables are independent if the probability distribution function of each is independent of the values assumed by the other is adequate for present purposes. Thus two successive tosses of a coin or rolls of a die are usually considered to be independent. The scores made by a given student on two examinations in the same course would not generally be considered independent.

Two events that cannot occur simultaneously are called *mutually exclusive*. They are clearly not independent, for the occurrence of one precludes that of the other. Two such events in the roll of a die are rolling an ace and rolling an even number. The probability of obtaining either one or the other of two mutually exclusive events is the sum of their individual probabilities. Thus if the probability of an ace is $\frac{1}{6}$ and that of an even number is $\frac{1}{2}$, the probability of rolling 1, 2, 4, or 6 is $\frac{2}{3}$.

If two events are independent, the probability that both will occur is the product of the probabilities of each occurring. Thus the probability of tossing a coin heads and rolling an ace is $\frac{1}{12}$.

An important application of the foregoing principles is in repeated experiments. Suppose that for a given experiment a certain result has probability p. The probability q that the result will not occur is determined from Eq. (5–9) and the addition principle for mutually exclusive events as $q = 1 - p$. The probability that the result will occur exactly x times in n independent trials is determined as follows. There are $\binom{n}{x}$ ways, each mutually exclusive, in which the compound event of x *successes* and $n - x$ *failures* of the single event or result can occur. The probability of each of these is the product $p^x q^{n-x}$ of the individual probabilities for the x successes and $n - x$ failures. The sum of these $\binom{n}{x}$ equal probabilities is

$$f(x) = \binom{n}{x} p^x q^{n-x}. \tag{5-18}$$

The distribution (5–18) is called the Bernoulli or *binomial* distribution in view of the binomial expansion

$$(p + q)^n = \sum_{x=0}^{n} \binom{n}{x} p^x q^{n-x} = 1. \tag{5–19}$$

The probability of rolling exactly three times out of four neither an ace nor a six is obtained from Eq. (5–18) by substituting $p = \frac{2}{3}$, $q = \frac{1}{3}$, $x = 3$, and $n = 4$. The result is

$$f(3) = \binom{4}{3}\left(\frac{2}{3}\right)^3\left(\frac{1}{3}\right) = 4\left(\frac{2}{3}\right)^3\left(\frac{1}{3}\right) = \frac{32}{81}.$$

The probability of tossing heads 6 times in a sequence of 10 tosses, as in the experiment of Table 5–1, is calculated from $p = q = \frac{1}{2}$, $x = 6$, and $n = 10$ as

$$f(6) = \binom{10}{6}\left(\frac{1}{2}\right)^6\left(\frac{1}{2}\right)^4 = 210\left(\frac{1}{2}\right)^{10} = \frac{105}{512}, \qquad \text{or about 20.5 percent.}$$

The probability of tossing heads 12 times in 20 trials might appear to the uninitiated to be the same as that of heads 6 times out of 10, because both sequences have 60 percent heads. Actually Eq. (5–18) yields for 20 trials

$$f(12) = \binom{20}{12}\left(\frac{1}{2}\right)^{12}\left(\frac{1}{2}\right)^8 = \frac{62985}{524288}, \qquad \text{or only about 12.0 percent.}$$

The reader might ponder why these results are different.

The mean of the binomial distribution is readily calculated from Eqs. (5–10) and (5–18):

$$\bar{x} = \sum_{x=0}^{n} x \binom{n}{x} p^x q^{n-x}$$

$$= \sum_{x=1}^{n} x \frac{n!}{x!(n-x)!} p^x q^{n-x}$$

$$= \sum_{x=1}^{n} n \binom{n-1}{x-1} p^x q^{n-x}$$

$$= np \sum_{x=1}^{n} \binom{n-1}{x-1} p^{x-1} q^{n-x}$$

$$= np \sum_{y=0}^{n-1} \binom{n-1}{y} p^y q^{(n-1)-y}$$

$$= np,$$

because the last sum is unity in virtue of the expansion (5–19). The average number of successes is merely the number of trials times the probability of success on each. The reader can apply Eq. (5–6) to show that the standard deviation of the binomial distribution is $\sqrt{npq}$.

5–4 SAMPLING AND MEASUREMENT

A manufacturer of electrical resistors may measure the resistance of every unit produced in order to segregate (for sale at a higher price) those whose resistance lies within 5 percent of the nominal value. For many purposes, however, it is sufficient to select a *sample* of the production of an article and use measurements made on items in the sample to yield information concerning the nature of the *population* from which the sample is drawn. Moreover, use of the entire population is often impractical because of its size (pre-election preferences of voters) or cost (destructive testing of television sets). Physical measurement may itself be viewed as a form of sampling among the possible values of a physical quantity.

If a population is finite, it is convenient to return to the population each item sampled before a further item is drawn. This is known as sampling with replacement, and serves to keep the population size constant. The population possesses a frequency distribution with respect to some variable of interest. In order to permit use of the calculus, it is generally assumed that the population is infinite in size, and that the distribution is continuous. Departures in practice from these assumptions are often of minor consequence.

A sample will yield reliable information about a population only to the extent that it is representative of the population. The ideal is a *random* sample. An intuitive definition of random sampling is representative sampling, but a formal definition can be given in terms of repeated drawings of samples of the same size. Let x_i be a variable representing the ith value of the variable x in each sample, where $i = 1, \ldots, n$. The sampling is random if the x_i are all independent and each possesses the population distribution. The results of this section depend upon each sample being random. In practical situations, the attainment of randomness in sampling is often the most difficult task facing the statistician.

The size of the sample is important for two reasons. The simplest statistical tools apply only to fairly large samples, say $n = 30$ or 50 or more. Moreover, the precision with which estimates of population parameters can be deduced from sample parameters increases with n, as will be seen. The remainder of this section presents a few items from so-called *large-sample* statistics. Small-sample theory will be left to more specialized texts.

(a) Distribution of Sample Parameters

Consider the drawing of repeated samples of size n from a population. For each sample the mean is calculated as $\bar{x} = (1/n)\sum x_i$. Just as the x_i of the various samples are random variables, so $\bar{x}$ is a random variable. The distribution of the sample means provides a measure of the precision in using the sample mean as an estimate of the population mean. The following theorem is stated without proof.

Theorem 5–1. Let repeated samples of size n be drawn from a normal population with mean m and standard deviation σ. Then the sample mean is also normally distributed, with mean m but with standard deviation $\sigma/\sqrt{n}$.

Suppose that a manufacturer of tires has found over a long period that the endurance of tires of a particular grade on a test stand is normally distributed with mean 32,200 miles and standard deviation 3700 miles. After modifying the processing of the rubber at a certain stage he tests 100 tires and finds a mean endurance of 33,500 miles. Is it reasonable to conclude from this result that the modification has reduced tire wear?

The standard method for approaching problems of this type is to set up a *statistical hypothesis*, which is then tested on the basis of the assumptions made. In this case, the hypothesis will be that the modification has not affected the endurance of the tires. The sample may be treated as a random sample of size 100 from a normal population with mean 32,200 and standard deviation 3700. Consequently $\bar{x}$ will be normally distributed with $m = 32,200$ and $\sigma = 3700/\sqrt{100} = 370$. Corresponding to the value 33,500 of $\bar{x}$ is the number

$$y = \frac{\bar{x} - m}{\sigma} = \frac{33,500 - 32,200}{370} = \frac{1300}{370} = 3.51$$

of standard units. Since 3.51 lies well outside the interval $(-2, 2)$, which includes, according to Table 5–4, about 95 percent of the variable values, the hypothesis is rejected at the 95-percent *confidence level*. The new process indeed appears to improve the tires.

If 12-month-old male mice delivered by a certain breeder have a mean weight in the neighborhood of 30 grams, with a standard deviation of 3.5 grams, how many mice should be sampled to determine the mean weight to within 1 gram? To make the determination with certainty would entail weighing all mice delivered. To make the determination with 95-percent confidence requires a sample large enough to yield a standard deviation of 0.5 gram for the sample mean. Since the population standard deviation is assumed known to be 3.5, or 7 times as great, a sample of 49 mice is required.

Suppose that the mean weight of such a sample were found to be 31.6 grams. The interval 31.6 ± 1.0 would then be considered a 95-percent *confidence interval* for the population mean m, because the probability that m lies within 2σ of the sample mean is just 0.95. It is important to observe that the foregoing analyses are valid only if the standard deviation σ of the population is known. If σ is not known, a confidence interval for the population mean must be determined on the basis of the standard deviation of the sample. This process, which is rather complex, will not be developed here.

A common method of determining whether a significant difference exists between two sets of similar data is based upon a second theorem, the proof of which will also be omitted.

Theorem 5–2. Let the random variables x_1 and x_2 each be normally distributed with means m_1 and m_2 and standard deviations σ_1 and σ_2, respectively. Then their sum (difference) $x_1 \pm x_2$ is a random variable, normally distributed with mean $m_1 \pm m_2$ and standard deviation $\sqrt{\sigma_1^2 + \sigma_2^2}$.

Let $\bar{x}$ and $\bar{y}$ be the means of random samples of sizes n_x and n_y from normal populations with means m_x and m_y and standard deviations σ_x and σ_y, respectively. Then $x_1 = \bar{x}$ is normally distributed with mean $m_1 = m_x$ and standard deviation $\sigma_1 = \sigma_x/\sqrt{n_x}$. Similarly $y_1 = \bar{y}$ is normally distributed with $m_2 = m_y$ and $\sigma_2 = \sigma_y/\sqrt{n_y}$. Application of Theorem 5–2 yields the result that $\bar{x} - \bar{y}$, the difference of the sample means, is normally distributed with mean $m = m_x - m_y$ and standard deviation $\sigma = \sqrt{\sigma_x^2/n_x + \sigma_y^2/n_y}$.

Suppose that mice of the strain sampled previously are raised on a diet differing from the previous one. A sample of sixty 12-month-old male mice has mean weight $\bar{y} = 30.9$ and standard deviation $s_y = 3.0$ grams. Is the decrease in mean weight from that of the previous sample ($\bar{x} = 31.6$, $\sigma_x = 3.5$, $n = 49$) significant? Although the standard deviation of the first population is assumed known to be 3.5, that of the second population is unknown. The error in using the sample standard deviation $s_y = 3.0$ in place of the unknown σ_y can be shown to be fairly small for samples of the size under consideration.

The statistical hypothesis to test here is that the two samples came from populations (assumed normal) with the same means. Under this hypothesis, $\bar{x} - \bar{y}$ would be normally distributed with mean $m_x - m_y = 0$ and standard deviation

$$\sigma = \sqrt{\frac{(3.5)^2}{49} + \frac{(3.0)^2}{60}} = \sqrt{\frac{12.25}{49} + \frac{9}{60}} = \sqrt{0.4} = 0.63.$$

The observed difference $\bar{x} - \bar{y} = 0.7$ lies well within the interval $0 \pm 2(0.63)$. The hypothesis is accordingly accepted at the 95-percent confidence level, or 0.05 *significance level*. It appears that the change in diet has no effect on the weight of the mice.

(b) Limits of Distributions

Some of the frequency distributions studied thus far are of interest not merely for their intrinsic properties, but also for the fact that they are limiting forms of other distributions. Frequently the limiting form provides a basis for simpler computations than the original with remarkably little loss of accuracy. A few of these limiting cases are considered in this section, with proofs omitted.

The binomial distribution has already been defined in Eq. (5–18) by

$$f(x) = \binom{n}{x} p^x q^{n-x}.$$

It gives the probability of x successes in n independent trials each with probability p of success. This distribution tends to a different limit under each of two different sets of circumstances.

If the number n of trials increases without limit while the probability p of success decreases toward zero in such a manner that the product $np = a$ remains constant, the binomial distribution approaches as a limit the Poisson distribution

$$f(x) = \frac{a^x e^{-a}}{x!}. \tag{5–7}$$

If n increases without limit while p remains constant, then the distribution of the normalized binomial variable $y = (x - np)/\sqrt{npq}$ approaches the standard normal distribution with $m = 0$ and $\sigma = 1$. Put otherwise, the binomial distribution for fixed n and p is approximated by the normal distribution with $m = np$ and $\sigma = \sqrt{npq}$.

The utility of the approximation to the binomial provided by the Poisson and normal distributions is apparent even for such a nonlimiting case as $n = 20$ and $p = 0.2$. The probabilities of x successes in 20 trials are shown in Table 5–5 for $x = 0, \ldots, 12$, calculated according to each of the three distributions. For $x > 12$, the probabilities are all zero to the precision used.

The methods of computing the numbers in each of the three columns of Table 5–5 illustrate the judicious use of shortcuts. For the binomial distribution, substitution of $p = \frac{1}{5}$ and $q = \frac{4}{5}$ in Eq. (5–18) yields

$$f(0) = \binom{20}{0} \left(\frac{1}{5}\right)^0 \left(\frac{4}{5}\right)^{20} = \frac{4^{20}}{5^{20}},$$

$$f(1) = \binom{20}{1} \left(\frac{1}{5}\right)^1 \left(\frac{4}{5}\right)^{19} = \frac{20 \cdot 4^{19}}{5^{20}} = \frac{20}{4} f(0),$$

$$f(2) = \binom{20}{2} \left(\frac{1}{5}\right)^2 \left(\frac{4}{5}\right)^{18} = \frac{20 \cdot 19 \cdot 4^{18}}{2 \cdot 5^{20}} = \frac{19}{8} f(1).$$

It is much simpler to compute $f(x)$ from $f(x - 1)$ than directly from the definition. The successive multipliers are readily computed in advance as $20/(1 \cdot 4)$, $19/(2 \cdot 4)$, $18/(3 \cdot 4)$, $17/(4 \cdot 4)$, and so forth. Several guard digits should be carried to absorb loss of significance due to rounding. Two good final checks are available. The first is to compute the last term from the definition and compare it with the value obtained by the process outlined. The other is to verify that the sum of the probabilities is unity.

The normal distribution desired is that with mean $m = np = 4$ and standard deviation $\sigma = \sqrt{npq} = \sqrt{3.2} = 1.789$. The use of a table is especially convenient here, and the statistical worker will usually have access to a considerably expanded version of Table 5–4. The chief problem is fitting a continuous distribution to discrete points. The standard method is to associate with x the interval $(x - \frac{1}{2}, x + \frac{1}{2})$. Thus $f(5)$ is determined as the difference

Table 5–5

x	Binomial	Normal	Poisson
0	0.012	0.019	0.018
1	0.058	0.056	0.073
2	0.137	0.120	0.147
3	0.205	0.189	0.195
4	0.218	0.220	0.195
5	0.175	0.189	0.156
6	0.109	0.120	0.104
7	0.055	0.056	0.060
8	0.022	0.019	0.030
9	0.007	0.005	0.013
10	0.002	0.001	0.005
11	0.000	0.000	0.002
12	0.000	0.000	0.001
	1.000	0.994	0.999

of the tabular values for 4.5 and 5.5. The data must first be converted to standard units. Repeated division by σ can be avoided by the one-time calculation of $1/\sigma = 0.559$. Repeated additions of $1/\sigma$ to $y = (x - m)/\sigma = 0.2795$ for $x = 4.5$ yield values of the standard variable y for $x = 5.5, 6.5$, etc. Corresponding to $x = 4.5$ and 5.5 are $y = 0.2795$ and 0.8385, whose tabular values are 0.1101 and 0.2991, yielding $f(5) = 0.2991 - 0.1101 = 0.189$.

A secondary problem is the treatment of the minimum and maximum values of the finite variable. The problem arises here in determining $f(0)$. There appears to be a choice between using $x = -\frac{1}{2}$ and $x = -\infty$ as a lower limit of the interval used. The former choice results in $f(0) - f(8)$, preserving the symmetry of the normal distribution, but the latter choice results in the sum of all the probabilities equaling unity. The symmetric choice usually gives a better approximation, but requires the computation of a dummy value for the unused interval, here $(-\infty, -\frac{1}{2})$, to avoid loss of the $\Sigma f(x) = 1$ check.

For the Poisson distribution $a = 4$, and the first few values are obtained as

$$f(0) = \frac{4^0 e^{-4}}{0!} = e^{-4}, \qquad f(1) = \frac{4^1 e^{-4}}{1!} = 4f(0), \qquad f(2) = \frac{4^2 e^{-4}}{2!} = \frac{4}{2}f(1).$$

The method used is similar to that described for the binomial distribution, but with multipliers $\frac{4}{1}, \frac{4}{2}, \frac{4}{3}$, etc. This method of computation can be summarized by the pair of equations

$$f(0) = e^{-4} \qquad \text{and} \qquad f(x) = \frac{4}{x}f(x - 1).$$

The initial value e^{-4} can be computed directly from $e = 2.71828$ in this case, because a is integral. Normally, a table of logarithms or of natural exponentials would be required. For limited precision a log-log slide rule would suffice.

The theorem was stated in the previous section that the sample mean is normally distributed if the population is normal. For a great many different population distributions the distribution of the sample mean approaches the normal as the sample size increases. This is a consequence of the central limit theorem, which holds under very liberal conditions. One condition that is sufficient is that all moments about zero of the population distribution be finite. If the population distribution has mean m and standard deviation σ, the central limit theorem states that the distribution of $y = (\bar{x} - m)/(\sigma/\sqrt{n})$ approaches the standard normal distribution as n increases without limit.

One consequence of this important result is that if the sample size is large enough, the sample mean for almost any population likely to be encountered in practice will be approximately normally distributed with mean m and standard deviation $\sigma/\sqrt{n}$. Therefore the various tests of Section 5–4(a) are applicable even in the absence of population normality.

Another consequence appears in the study of errors which occur in repeating a given physical measurement. Such errors are presumably caused by many factors unknown to the measurer. If the error is viewed as the mean of a large number of elements from an unknown, but reasonably well-behaved, distribution, then the central limit theorem applies. As a result, measurement errors should tend to be normally distributed. It has often been observed in practice that physical measurements are normally distributed. These two distributions are consistent only if the mean value of the measurements is normally distributed about their correct value. For this reason it is customary to use the mean of a set of measurements as the best estimate of the correct value.

Another view of measurements is that they constitute random sampling from an infinite population, whose mean is the correct value. The mean measurement value should be normally distributed with mean equal to the correct value.

5–5 FREQUENCY DISTRIBUTIONS OF TWO VARIABLES

Only two of the many subjects concerning bivariate frequency distributions will be explored here. The first is to determine the extent to which two variables are related. The second is to find the "best" straight line expressing this relationship if it can be assumed to be linear. These two subjects are known respectively as *correlation* and *linear regression*.

(a) Correlation

One intuitively considers variables which increase together to be correlated, as are, for example, the ages and weights of a group of children. The statistician would call this an example of *positive* correlation, and would term *negative* correlation the relation that would normally be found between outside temperature in a given city and amount of fuel oil delivered there. In both of these examples, a cause and effect may be postulated, but this is not necessarily the case for correlated variables. An example of variables that are uncorrelated might be the number of marriage license applications and the number of automobile collisions.

Suppose that n pairs x_i, y_i of measurements are made of two variables x, y. The *correlation coefficient* of x and y is defined as

$$r = \frac{\sum (x_i - \bar{x})(y_i - \bar{y})}{n s_x s_y}, \tag{5–20}$$

where $\bar{x}$, $\bar{y}$, s_x, and s_y are the means and standard deviations of x and y. The use of the deviations $x_i - \bar{x}$, $y_i - \bar{y}$, rather than the variables x_i, y_i, makes r independent of the origins for measuring the variables. Division by s_x and s_y makes r independent of the sizes of units, or scales, for x and y. These are elementary consequences of the result of Exercise II–30. It is clear that r is dimensionless, and that the appearance of n in the denominator makes r an average for the n pairs of measurements. It can be proved that $|r| \leq 1$. Positive (negative) values of r correspond to positive (negative) correlation; the greater the magnitude of r, the greater the extent of the correlation.

A cartesian plot of the points x_i, y_i, often called a *scatter diagram*, gives some qualitative information about the correlation of x and y. Figure 5–5 presents such a diagram for the data of Table 5–6, which are the test scores (out of a possible 55 points) of 21 students on two different hour examinations in the same course. If the axes of the coordinate system are taken to be the lines $x = \bar{x}$ and $y = \bar{y}$, which have been drawn in the figure, points in the first and third quad-

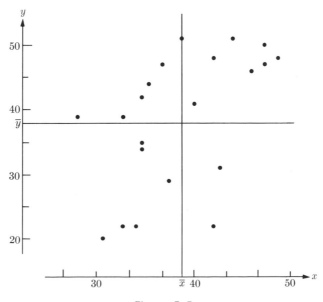

Figure 5–5

Table 5–6

STUDENT TEST SCORES

x	y	x	y	x	y
33	44	26	20	43	22
36	29	32	35	53	48
35	47	31	22	40	41
49	46	22	39	29	39
44	31	51	50	51	47
46	51	43	48	29	22
38	51	32	42	32	34

rants will contribute positively to r and those in the second and fourth quadrants will contribute negatively. Two-thirds of the points in Fig. 5–5 lie in the first or third quadrant, and their distances from the axes are greater than those of the points in the other quadrants. This indicates that the variables x and y are positively correlated, as might have been guessed from knowledge of the source of the data. Actually, $r = 0.52$.

The definition (5–20) is not convenient for computing r, because $\bar{x}$ and $\bar{y}$ are not known until all the data have been processed once. A more convenient form for calculation will now be derived, by using Eq. (5–6) for expressing s_x and s_y.

$$\frac{\sum(x_i - \bar{x})(y_i - \bar{y})}{ns_xs_y} = \frac{n\sum(x_i - \bar{x})(y_i - \bar{y})}{n^2\sqrt{(\overline{x^2} - \bar{x}^2)(\overline{y^2} - \bar{y}^2)}}$$

$$= \frac{n(\sum x_iy_i - \bar{x}\sum y_i - \bar{y}\sum x_i + \sum \overline{xy})}{\sqrt{n^2(\overline{x^2} - \bar{x}^2)n^2(\overline{y^2} - \bar{y}^2)}}$$

$$= \frac{n(\sum x_iy_i - \bar{x}n\bar{y} - \bar{y}n\bar{x} + n\bar{x}\bar{y})}{\sqrt{[n^2\overline{x^2} - (n\bar{x})^2][n^2\overline{y^2} - (n\bar{y})^2]}}$$

$$= \frac{n(\sum x_iy_i - n\bar{x}\bar{y})}{\sqrt{[n(n\overline{x^2}) - (n\bar{x})^2][n(n\overline{y^2}) - (n\bar{y})^2]}}$$

$$= \frac{n\sum x_iy_i - (\sum x_i)(\sum y_i)}{\sqrt{[n\sum x_i^2 - (\sum x_i)^2][n\sum y_i^2 - (\sum y_i)^2]}}. \qquad (5–21)$$

From the data of Table 5–6, one finds $n = 21$, $\sum x_i = 795$, $\sum y_i = 808$, $\sum x_i^2 = 31691$, $\sum x_iy_i = 30695$, and $\sum y_i^2 = 33302$. By substituting these values into Eq. (5–21), the previously stated value $r = 0.52$ of the correlation coefficient is obtained.

(b) Linear Regression

When two variables are linearly or almost linearly related, that is, when the magnitude of r is unity or nearly unity, it is often of interest to determine the equation of a straight line that fits the available measurements as closely as possible. If there are only two points, a unique straight line is determined. If there are more points, a compromise is to be found among many possible lines. Let x be considered an independent and y a dependent variable. Then any particular value y_i will differ in general from the value $y(x_i)$ assigned to the corresponding measurement x_i by a straight line. The task is to find a straight line that renders these differences, or *residuals*, as small as possible. Minimizing the sum of the residuals is clearly inadequate, because large positive residuals can compensate for large negative ones. Minimizing the sum of the magnitudes of the residuals would be more reasonable, but will be avoided because of the difficulty of analyzing absolute values. The criterion generally used is the sum of the squares of the residuals, and minimizing this sum leads to the so-called *least-squares* straight-line approximation to the data.

Let the equation of the desired line be

$$y = m(x - \bar{x}) + b,$$

where m and b are to be chosen so as to minimize the sum of the squares of the residuals. The ith residual is $y_i - m(x_i - \bar{x}) - b$, and the sum of the squares may be written as the function of m and b,

$$F(m, b) = \Sigma[y_i - m(x_i - \bar{x}) - b]^2.$$

Just as a function of one variable can have a minimum only where its derivative with respect to the variable vanishes, so a function of two variables can have a minimum only where its *partial derivatives* with respect to each variable vanish simultaneously. The partial derivative of $f(x, y)$ with respect to x is obtained by treating y as a constant and differentiating the resulting function $f_y(x)$ of the single variable x in the usual manner. The partial derivative with respect to y is obtained similarly and is denoted by $\partial f(x, y)/\partial y$ or just $\partial f/\partial y$.

For $F(m, b)$ the derivatives in question are

$$\frac{\partial F}{\partial m} = \Sigma 2[y_i - m(x_i - \bar{x}) - b][-(x_i - \bar{x})],$$

$$\frac{\partial F}{\partial b} = \Sigma 2[y_i - m(x_i - \bar{x}) - b](-1).$$

Setting both derivatives equal to zero, one obtains

$$\Sigma[y_i - m(x_i - \bar{x}) - b][x_i - \bar{x}] = 0,$$

$$\Sigma[y_i - m(x_i - \bar{x}) - b] = 0.$$

These equations may be rewritten in terms of m and b as

$$[\sum(x_i - \bar{x})^2]m + [\sum(x_i - \bar{x})]b = \sum(x_i - \bar{x})y_i,$$
$$[\sum(x_i - \bar{x})]m + [\sum 1]b = \sum y_i.$$

But $\sum(x_i - \bar{x}) = 0$ and $\sum 1 = n$, and the equations become

$$[(x_i - \bar{x})^2]m = \sum(x_i - \bar{x})y_i,$$
$$nb = \sum y_i,$$

from which follow the solutions

$$b = \bar{y},$$

$$m = \frac{\sum(x_i - \bar{x})y_i}{\sum(x_i - \bar{x})^2}. \tag{5–22}$$

The equation of the least-squares line may be written as

$$y - \bar{y} = m(x - \bar{x}).$$

The computation of m directly from Eq. (5–22) is very inefficient. The determination of a more suitable form for computation will be left as an exercise.

References for Part II

BEERS, Y., *Introduction to the Theory of Error*. Reading: Addison-Wesley, 1957.

BROOKS, F. P. JR., and K. E. IVERSON, *Automatic Data Processing*. New York: Wiley, 1963. Chapter 1.

CHURCHILL, R. V., *Complex Variables and Applications*. 2nd ed. New York: McGraw-Hill, 1960. Chapter 1.

FLORES, I., *The Logic of Computer Arithmetic*. Englewood Cliffs: Prentice-Hall, 1963.

HARDY, G. H., and E. M. WRIGHT, *An Introduction to the Theory of Numbers*. 4th ed. Oxford: Oxford University Press, 1960. Chapter IX.

HOEL, P. G., *Introduction to Mathematical Statistics*. 2nd ed. New York: Wiley, 1954. Chapters 4 and 7.

ORE, O., *Number Theory and its History*. New York: McGraw-Hill, 1948. Chapters 1 and 2.

SMITH, D. E., and J. GINSBURG, "From Numbers to Numerals and from Numerals to Computation," in *The World of Mathematics*. Vol. 1, pp. 442–464. New York: Simon and Schuster, 1956.

USPENSKY, J. V., *Theory of Equations*. New York: McGraw-Hill, 1948. Chapter 1.

WEISNER, L., *Introduction to the Theory of Equations*. New York: Macmillan, 1949. Chapter 1.

Exercise Set for Part II

1. Prove that the coefficients in Eq. (3–1) are uniquely determined by N. Assume that there exist two different representations of some integer N. Subtract one from the other and show that the resulting representation of zero is invalid.

2. (a) Construct addition and multiplication tables for bases three, five, eight, and twelve.

   (b) Perform the following arithmetical operations in the bases indicated. Show all steps clearly. Check each operation by converting the given values and final results to decimal.

   (i) $(110101)_2 + (111)_2$ (ii) $(2011)_3 \times (1022)_3$
   (iii) $(413)_5 \times (203)_5$ (iv) $(13642)_8 - (61471)_8$
   (v) $(21021)_3 \div (121)_3$

   (c) Prove that the square of the greatest digit in the system of any radix is a number whose less significant digit is unity and whose more significant digit is two less than the radix.

3. Use the general algorithm of pp. 35–36 to make the following base conversions. Check each conversion by using the same algorithm to convert the result back to the original base.

   (a) $(2120)_3$ to base ten;   (b) $(16.214)_{10}$ to base two;
   (c) $(105)_8$ to base three;   (d) $(1432)_5$ to base ten;
   (e) $(0.3)_{14}$ to base ten.

4. Show that an octal number can be converted to binary notation by converting each digit independently of the others. Show that a binary number can be converted to octal by first grouping digits in triples, starting at the radix point, and then converting each triple independently of the others.

5. Devise a procedure for using a table of powers of two (in decimal notation) in conversion from decimal to binary without division.

6. Using arithmetic in base two only, find the decimal representation of the integer $(1101011010001)_2$. [*Hint:* The binary representation of ten is 1010.]

7. (a) Convert $(0.10111 \ldots)_2 = (1.10\bar{1})_2$ to base ten.

   (b) Convert your answer for (a) back to base two and compare it with the original number.

   (c) State the conditions under which a number has both a terminating and a nonterminating representation.

   (d) Prove that a nonterminating representation of a rational number must be periodic.

   (e) Prove that every terminating or periodic representation is that of a rational number.

8. Program a computer to implement the base conversion algorithm of Eqs. (3–1) through (3–5).

9. (a) Prove for an arbitrary complex number z that $z\bar{z} = |z|^2$.

   (b) Derive formulas for the division of complex numbers in both cartesian and polar representations. Do they apply invariably?

10. Real numbers obey the following commutative, associative, and distributive laws:

   (a) $x + y = y + x$ (commutativity of addition);
   (b) $xy = yx$ (commutativity of multiplication);
   (c) $(x + y) + z = x + (y + z)$ (associativity of addition);
   (d) $(xy)z = x(yz)$ (associativity of multiplication);
   (e) $x(y + z) = (xy) + (xz)$ (distributivity of multiplication over addition).

   Use these laws for real numbers to prove that they hold for the addition and multiplication of complex numbers.

11. Prove for arbitrary complex numbers z_1 and z_2 that

   (a) $\overline{(z_1 + z_2)} = \bar{z}_1 + \bar{z}_2$ and $\overline{(z_1 z_2)} = \bar{z}_1 \bar{z}_2$;
   (b) $|z_1 z_2| = |z_1|\,|z_2|$.

12. How many unsigned integers can be represented by 48 binary digits in

   (a) pure binary notation,   (b) binary coded decimal notation,
   (c) alphanumeric decimal notation?

   How is your answer modified if one binary digit is reserved for the sign?

13. Construct a decimal subtraction table. Is it symmetric about the main diagonal?

14. Prove for the division of integers that if the dividend has n digits and the divisor has m digits, then the quotient has either $n - m$ or $n - m + 1$ digits. Prove for multiplication that if one factor has m digits and the other n, then the product has either $m + n$ or $m + n - 1$ digits.

15. Complete the examples of restoring and nonrestoring division on pp. 53–54. Do the results agree?

16. Program a computer capable of adding, subtracting, and shifting to carry out restoring division. Repeat for nonrestoring division.

17. (a) The *excess-3* binary encoding of decimal digits derives its name from the property that the decimal digit d is represented by the 4-digit binary number $b = d + 3$. Show that the binary sum of the excess-3 representations of two decimal digits is less than or greater than, by a fixed amount k, the excess-3 representation of the decimal sum of the digits, accordingly as the sum of the digits exceeds 9 or not.
   (b) What is the number k? How can one tell from the binary addition alone whether to add or subtract k in order to obtain the excess-3 representation of the correct sum?

18. Find the absolute and relative errors in

   (a) cube root extraction,   (b) quadratic equation solution.

19. The quotient $x + iy = (a + ib)/(c + id)$ of two complex numbers can be calculated from the formulas

$$x = (ac + bd)/(c^2 + d^2) \quad \text{and} \quad y = (bc - ad)/(c^2 + d^2).$$

   Suppose that a, b, c, d are each known to within ± 0.03, and that their values are approximately 3.2, 6.4, 5.0, 4.7, respectively. Estimate in percent the maximum relative error in the calculated value of x.

20. Round 0.174557 to three places.   Round the result to two places.   Round the original number to two places and compare.

21. Show that if the error e_i in the ith approximation to $\sqrt{N}$ is small, then the error in the next approximation produced by formula (2–1) is approximately $e_{i+1} = e_i^2/2\sqrt{N}$.

22. Explain why the identity $\sin^2 x + \cos^2 x = 1$ is not a sensitive error test for x close to zero.   Suggest an alternative trigonometric identity that is sensitive for small x.   Does it lack sensitivity elsewhere?

23. Write a computer program to determine the geometric mean of a set of numbers. Pay particular attention to exceptional cases.

24. Show that the logarithm of the geometric mean of a set of positive measurements is the arithmetic mean of the logarithms of the measurements.

25. Determine the mean, median, mode, variance, standard deviation, and range of the following test scores.

24	166	152	82	160
109	88	79	117	148
155	129	126	87	82
158	133	95	77	148
167	159	134	123	135
95	156	137	150	56
85	119	121	135	129
162	83	78	139	136
3	105	161	134	142
120	120	156	158	

26. Program a computer to solve Exercise 25 for arbitrary data.

27. Program the calculation of the variance by use of Eq. (5–5) and compare the result with Program 5–2.

28. Calculate the mean and variance of the data of Table 5–3 and compare the data with the Poisson distribution having the same mean.

29. Find the standard deviation of the Poisson distribution.

30. (a) Prove for both discrete and continuous distributions that the addition of the constant a to each member of a collection of data increases the mean by a but does not affect the variance.
    (b) Prove that the multiplication of each item by a multiplies the mean by a and the variance by a^2.

31. Find $\bar{x}$ and s for the exponential distribution.

32. (a) Give an example of an event with probability 1 which is not certain to occur.
    (b) Give an example of an event with probability 0 which is not impossible.

33. What is the probability of tossing heads exactly 5 times in 10 trials?

34. Prove that the variance of the binomial distribution is $s^2 = npq$.

35. Sketch the distribution of the resistance of electrical resistors sold as having a 100-ohm resistance plus or minus 20 percent.

36. Show that the distribution of the difference of two sample means is approximately normal, even though neither population is normal, provided that the samples are sufficiently large.

37. Prove that if $y = ax + b$, where $a \neq 0$, then the correlation of x and y is $r = $ sgn a. The function sgn a (sign of a) is defined as $+1$ for $a > 0$ and -1 for $a < 0$.

38. Program a computer to determine correlation coefficients from arbitrary data.

39. Prove that the correlation coefficient of two points is generally 1 or -1. Discuss the exceptions to this rule.

40. Derive from Eq. (5–22) an expression more suitable for computation.

41. A watchmaker records the deviation of a timepiece at the same hour on different mornings. By what amount is the timepiece losing daily?

Date	Deviation (seconds)	Date	Deviation (seconds)
Oct. 29	+36	Nov. 8	+3
Oct. 30	+34	Nov. 9	−0.5
Oct. 31	+31	Nov. 13	−13
Nov. 1	+27	Nov. 14	−15.5
Nov. 2	+24	Nov. 20	−36
Nov. 5	+11.5		

42. Program a computer to solve Exercise 41 for arbitrary data.

Part III

Analog Computation

The variables in digital computation are represented by rational numbers. The numbers assume discrete values only, and are combined according to the rules of arithmetic. Precision is limited by the number of digit positions available; accuracy is limited by the errors discussed in Part II.

In analog computation each variable is represented by a measurable physical quantity, which serves as an analog of the variable. The physical quantities assume continuous values and are combined by physical devices. Precision is limited by the capacity to measure; accuracy is limited by the construction of the devices.

Among the physical quantities used in analog computation are length, rotational or translational displacement, electrical current, and voltage. Because of the relative ease of constructing devices to manipulate such quantities, analog computers are generally less expensive than digital computers, which must incorporate discrimination among and quantization to the admissible discrete variable values. Analog computers are frequently faster than the digital in solving complex problems, because tasks performed successively by a digital ALU can often be performed simultaneously by interconnected analog devices. Analog computers, although often less versatile than digital computers, are nevertheless easier to use for many problems.

One might wonder, in view of the foregoing advantages of analog computation, why digital computers have achieved such tremendous importance. One reason is their versatility; the sequential nature of digital computation affords a high degree of flexibility. Another reason is the greater precision obtainable. Analog computers of reasonable cost are limited to a precision of 1 part in 10^4 or 10^5. For digital computers there is no limit; time and equipment can both be traded for precision.

Analog computers are widely used, however, when high precision is unnecessary or, as in the case of imprecise input data, illusory. Some graphical techniques to illustrate the analog power of paper and pencil are presented in Chapter 6. Chapter 7 describes some mechanical and electronic analog devices, and Chapter 8 is an introduction to electronic analog computation.

Chapter 6

Graphical Methods

6-1 NOMOGRAMS

Algebraic relationships among various quantities or functions are often expressed by means of *nomograms*. The two principal types of nomograms are *abacs*, or families of curves, and *alignment charts*. Only the latter will be discussed here. Before doing so, however, it is necessary to introduce some notions concerning scales for plotting.

It is often convenient to label a rectilinear scale with numbers proportional, not to the distance along the scale, but rather to a function of that distance. In order to plot a scale graduated in terms of some function $f(u)$, one sets the position x along the scale to

$$x = mf(u), \qquad (6\text{-}1)$$

where m is the *modulus*, or *scale factor*. If a scale is required, for example, to depict $f(u) - \log_{10} u$ for $0 \leq u \leq 100$, application of Eq. (6-1) yields $x = m \log u$ and $0 \leq x \leq 2m$. Supposing that 5 inches is to be the length of the scale, then the scale factor is found to be $m = 2.5$ inches/unit.

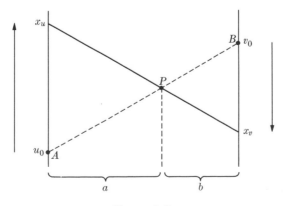

Figure 6–1

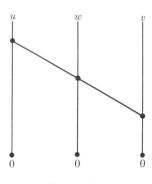

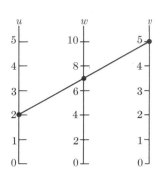

Figure 6–2   Figure 6–3

By graduating a single scale for two functions, $f(u)$ and $g(v)$, it is possible to express the correspondence between u and v implied by the equation $f(u) = g(v)$. Both scales must necessarily have the same modulus. If it is more convenient to use different moduli, the two scales can be separated, as in the general case represented in Fig. 6–1. From the figure it is seen that

$$x_u = m_u f(u), \qquad x_v = m_v g(v), \qquad \frac{x_u}{x_v} = \frac{AP}{PB} = \frac{a}{b} = \frac{m_u}{m_v}$$

because $f(u) = g(v)$. The last equality $a/b = m_u/m_v$ determines the horizontal placement of the projection *pole P*.

Suppose that the pole is itself allowed to move in correspondence with a third variable. The resulting diagram becomes one of the simplest forms of alignment chart, the three-parallel-line chart. For the chart shown in Fig. 6–2, with equidistant scales, $x_w = (x_u + x_v)/2$. By adjusting the scale factors as shown in Fig. 6–3, a chart for addition is obtained that yields $w = u + v$.

By suitable choice of the moduli and the spacing, the three-parallel-line chart may be made to yield generally $h(w) = f(u) + g(v)$. Consider the chart in Fig. 6–4. The following equations hold:

$$x_u = m_u f(u),$$

$$x_v = m_v g(v),$$

$$x_w = m_w h(w),$$

$$\frac{x_u - x_w}{a} = \frac{x_w - x_v}{b},$$

$$\frac{x_u}{a} - \frac{x_w}{a} = \frac{x_w}{b} - \frac{x_v}{b},$$

$$\frac{x_u}{a} + \frac{x_v}{b} = \frac{x_w}{a} + \frac{x_w}{b} = \frac{x_w}{ab/(a + b)},$$

$$\frac{m_u f(u)}{a} + \frac{m_v g(v)}{b} = \frac{m_w h(w)}{ab/(a + b)}.$$

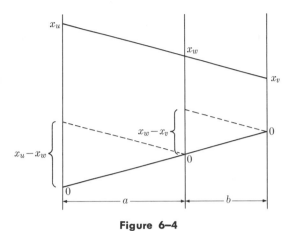

Figure 6–4

This can be valid for arbitrary functions f, g, h such that

$$f(u) + g(v) = h(w)$$

only if the three constant ratios

$$\frac{m_u}{a}, \qquad \frac{m_v}{b}, \qquad \text{and} \qquad \frac{m_w}{ab/(a+b)}$$

have the same value k. Therefore,

$$\frac{a}{b} = \frac{m_u}{m_v} \qquad \text{and} \qquad m_w = \frac{kab}{a+b} = \frac{kakb}{k(a+b)} = \frac{m_u m_v}{m_u + m_v}.$$

The design procedure consists of four steps. First, place the u- and v-scales as desired. Second, graduate them using the scale factors m_u and m_v. Third, place the w-scale so that $a/b = m_u/m_v$. Fourth, graduate the w-scale using $m_w = m_u m_v/(m_u + m_v)$. Let it be required, for example, to construct a nomo-

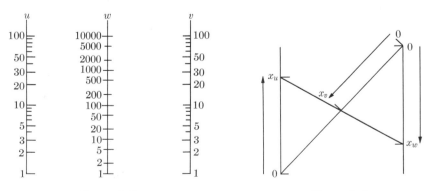

Figure 6–5　　　　　　　　　　　　**Figure 6–6**

gram for $\log u + \log v = \log w$, where u and v each range from 1 to 100, and $m_u = m_v = 1$.   It is found immediately that $a/b = m_u/m_v = 1$ and $m_w = 1/(1+1) = \frac{1}{2}$.   The derived chart, which has three nonlinear scales, is shown in Fig. 6–5.   It can of course be considered a chart for the function $w = uv$.

It is possible to perform multiplication directly with a chart that has two linear scales.   The type of chart that is required is called a Z-chart or N-chart from its shape and is represented in Fig. 6–6.   It is desired to produce $w = uv$ under the assumption that the u- and w-scales are linear.   Let a be the length of the diagonal between the two origins:

$$\frac{x_u}{x_w} = \frac{a - x_v}{x_v},$$

$$x_u = x_w \frac{a - x_v}{x_v},$$

$$x_w = m_w w,$$

$$x_u = m_u u,$$

$$m_u u = m_w w \frac{a - x_v}{x_v},$$

$$w = uv,$$

$$\frac{a - x_v}{x_v} = \frac{m_u}{m_w v},$$

$$x_v = \frac{m_w v a}{m_u + m_w v} = \frac{v a}{(m_u/m_w) + v}. \tag{6–2}$$

Equation (6–2) is not of the form $x_v = m_v v$, but it can nevertheless be used to graduate a scale for v.   In practice, the scale for v is most easily graduated by drawing lines between previously graduated u- and w-scales.   An example is given in Fig. 6–7. Z-charts can also be designed to yield $h(w) = f(u) \cdot g(v)$.

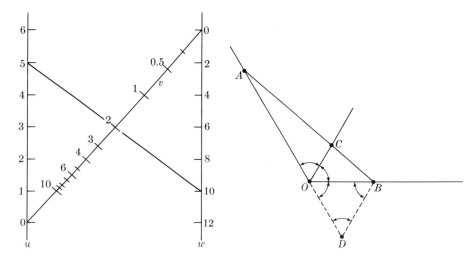

Figure 6–7   Figure 6–8

The last type of nomogram to be considered here is the three-concurrent-line diagram. Figure 6–8 illustrates the simple case of three identical linear scales intersecting at a common origin O with angular separations of 60°. The line AO may be extended as shown to the intersection D with the line BD constructed parallel to CO. Each marked angle measures 60°. It follows from the similarity of triangles ADB and AOC that $DB/OC = (OD + OA)/OA$. But DB and OD are both equal to OB, and the result may be rewritten as $OB/OC = (OB/OA) + 1$, from which it follows that

$$\frac{1}{OC} = \frac{1}{OA} + \frac{1}{OB}. \qquad (6\text{–}3)$$

Thus the diagram of Fig. 6–8 yields *harmonic* addition. On the original drawing, the lengths were $OA = 3.28$ and $OB = 1.62$ inches. The length OC was measured as 1.10 inches, in close agreement with the computed value 1.085 inches.

6–2 GRAPHICAL CALCULUS

Alignment charts were developed primarily for problems in algebra. For problems in analysis, where differentiation and integration are usually involved, they are less useful than the techniques about to be described. These techniques form only a part of the graphical calculus, which in its broadest sense also includes such subjects as nomography, analytic geometry, and two-dimensional vector calculus.

The basic construction is illustrated in Fig. 6–9, in which lines PB and OD are parallel. Two properties are to be noted. First, for a given base PA the height AB is proportional to the slope of PB. Second, it follows from the similarity of the two triangles that $PA/AB = OC/CD$, from which $CD = (AB \times OC)/PA$. This result can be interpreted as multiplication of the lengths AB and OC accompanied by a change of scale specified by the constant length PA.

Some modification of the foregoing construction will be used to solve the first three of the four following problems, in all of which $g(x)$ is the unknown function* to be constructed:

   (a) $g(x) = f'(x)$,

   (b) $g'(x) = f(x)$,

   (c) $g'(x) = f(g)$,

   (d) $g'(x) = f(x, g)$.

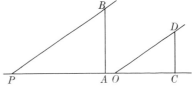

Figure 6–9

---

* The common notation $f'(x)$ is used for $\dfrac{d}{dx} f(x)$.

Problem (a) is that of differentiation; problem (b) is that of integration. Problems (b) through (d) are all *differential equations*, so-called because the derivative of the unknown function appears. Note that problems (b) and (c) are both special cases of problem (d). Both special cases will yield fairly easily to the graphical calculus, but the general differential equation will require yet more powerful techniques.

(a) Differentiation

Given a curve $y = f(x)$ it is required to develop the curve $y = g(x) = f'(x)$. It is generally desirable to use the same coordinate system for both curves, although possibly with a change of scale for y. The scale for x will remain unchanged. Ordinates proportional to the slope of $y = f(x)$ can be obtained, as in Fig. 6–9, by placing the pole P on the x-axis, at such a distance that the maximum slope will yield a height AB near the edge of the diagram.

An example is presented in Fig. 6–10. The pole P is placed at distance z from the y-axis, on which heights are measured. Because the slope $f'(x)$ equals h/z it follows that $h = zf'(x)$. A scale for the derivative curve is conveniently established by first choosing a height h corresponding to some given slope, greater than the maximum slope, and then drawing a line of that slope to intersect the x-axis, thus defining the point P. Usually h is selected to equal some round value of f as well as a round value of f', in order to permit the use

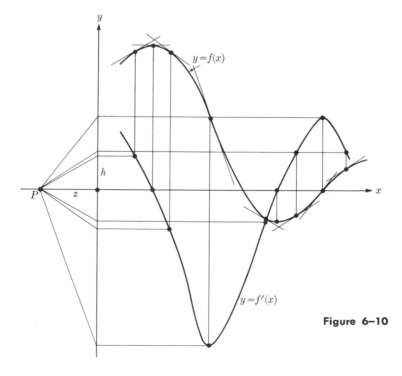

Figure 6–10

of the same graduations for the f- and f'-scales, with possibly different scale units. Alternatively, h can be selected at a height suitable for graduation in inches, centimeters, or other convenient units. The number of points along $y = f(x)$ at which tangents should be drawn depends on the nature of the given curve and the smoothness desired in the curve $y = g(x)$. In any case, it is wise to use all maxima, minima, and inflection points.

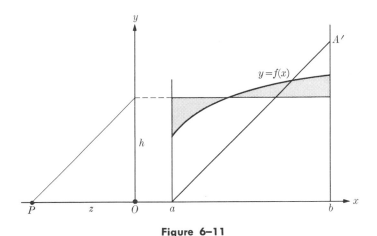

Figure 6–11

(b) Integration

Given a curve $y = f(x)$, it is required to develop a curve $y = g(x)$, where $g'(x) = f(x)$. It is again common to employ the same coordinate system for both curves, making any necessary change in the y-scale. The solution, or *integral curve*, $y = g(x)$ is not determined uniquely unless some point $[a, g(a)]$ on it is given. The task then reduces to the one of evaluating graphically the definite integral $A = \int_a^b f(x)\,dx = g(b) - g(a)$. The definite integral is represented by the area bounded by the straight lines $x = a$, $x = b$, $y = 0$, and the curve $y = f(x)$. It is convenient to replace the curve between $f(a)$ and $f(b)$ by a horizontal straight line so placed that the area under it is equal to the area under the curve. This construction is illustrated in Fig. 6–11, where the placement of the line has been estimated visually, much as that of tangents was done for differentiation. The placement of the horizontal line is such that the shaded areas are equal; its height is h. Through the point at height h on a fixed vertical line, here the y-axis, a polar ray from P is drawn. Parallel to this ray a line is drawn through the lower left-hand corner of the integration panel to intersect $x = b$ at the height A'. It follows immediately from the similarity of the triangles that $A' = h(b - a)/z = A/z$. The height A' is thus seen to be proportional to the area $A = \int_a^b f(x)\,dx$. The accuracy is dependent upon the ability to fix h so that the shaded areas are equal. This is improved by splitting the area into panels of suitable size over each of which integration

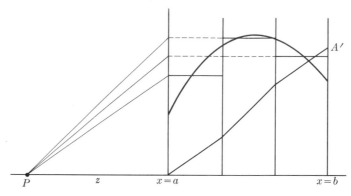

Figure 6–12

can be performed independently, as illustrated in Fig. 6–12. Observe that the line segment for each panel is drawn not from the corner of the panel, but from the endpoint of the segment for the previous panel. If the panels are small enough, the line segments constitute a good approximation to the integral curve $g(x)$ through the point $(a, 0)$. A smooth curve can also be passed through the endpoints of the line segments. By starting not at $(a, 0)$ but rather at an arbitrary point (a, k) on the line $x = a$, a curve $y = g(x)$ is obtained such that $g'(x) = f(x)$ and $g(a) = k$.

Two points are worth observing. The first is that errors are cumulative, in contradistinction to the situation in differentiation. The second is that it is possible to integrate around a closed curve. It is easily verified in such a case that for increasing x a positive $f(x)$ contributes positively to the area, whereas for decreasing x a positive $f(x)$ contributes negatively to the area.

(c) Differential Equations of the Form $y'(x) = f(y)$

In finding an integral curve $g(x)$ with the property $g'(x) = f(x)$, it was necessary to specify some point on the curve in order to select the desired member of the family of solutions. This is because, if $g_1(x)$ is a solution, so is $g_2(x) = g_1(x) + C$, where C is any constant. In evaluating $A = \int_a^b f(x)\, dx$, the equation $g'(x) = f(x)$ was solved subject to the *initial condition* $g(a) = 0$. Similarly, if $y_1(x)$ is a solution of the differential equation $y'(x) = f(y)$, then so is $y_2(x) = y_1(x) + C$. The problem is once again to find a solution or integral curve through a given point, that is, subject to a given initial condition.

The general method involves plotting $y'(x)$ not as a function of x (which is unknown anyway), but as the given function $f(y)$ of y. Values

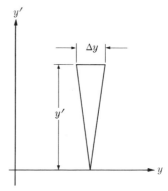

Figure 6–13

of x are then found that correspond to points chosen along the curve $y' = f(y)$. For each such point, values of x and y are then available and may be used to construct a curve for y as a function of x. The theoretical tool is the approximation $y' = \Delta y/\Delta x$, which may be solved for Δx to yield $\Delta x = \Delta y/y'$. An increment Δx in x is chosen, and held constant throughout the process. A triangle is drawn in the yy'-plane to show corresponding values of y' and Δy, as shown in Fig. 6–13. The base and altitude are set in the ratio $\Delta y/y' = \Delta x$. Parallels to the sides of this triangle are "bounced" off the y-axis. Figure 6–14 illustrates the solution by this method of the differential equation $y' = y/2$, subject to the initial condition $y(0) = 1$. Here $\Delta x = 0.2$. Note that a common y-axis is used for the yy'- and xy-planes.

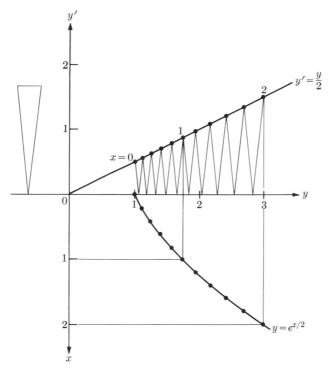

Figure 6–14

(d) Differential Equations of the Form $y'(x) = f(x, y)$

Although the bounce method of the preceding section can be extended to this general type of equation, its use will not be considered here because of the trial and error technique required. A more illuminating approach is offered by the *direction field*.

The first example will be of the special case $y'(x) = f(x)$. Let the differential equation be $y' = x^2$, whose solution is $y = \frac{1}{3}x^3 + C$. The direction field for

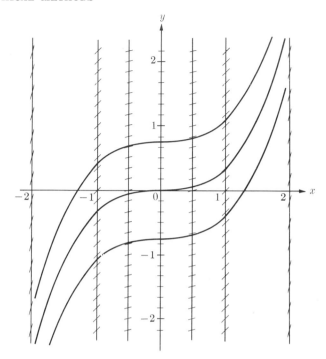

Figure 6–15

this equation is shown in Fig. 6–15, in which each short line segment at abscissa x has the slope x^2 specified in the differential equation. Each segment is actually tangent to an integral curve and constitutes an approximation to a portion of the integral curve. By joining the small segments as shown, one obtains for the entire region the integral curve through a given point. The vertical lines are loci of constant slope, called *isoclines*. The segments on each isocline are parallel to each other.

In the general case $y'(x) = f(x, y)$, the isoclines are specified by $f(x, y) = C$ (a constant). Consider the differential equation $y'(x) = y - 2x$, with the initial condition $y(0) = 1$. Although analytic techniques for solving all differential equations do not exist, methods are available for solving simple differential equations, such as this one. By their use, one can find $y(x) = -e^x + 2x + 2$ and verify that it is a solution:

$$y'(x) = -e^x + 2 = y - 2x,$$
$$y(0) = -e^0 + 2 \cdot 0 + 2 = -1 + 2 = 1.$$

It can be demonstrated that the solution is unique. The same solution, as well as those corresponding to different initial conditions, could have been obtained from the direction field shown in Fig. 6–16. The direction field was drawn by

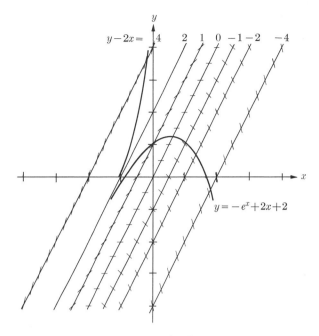

Figure 6–16

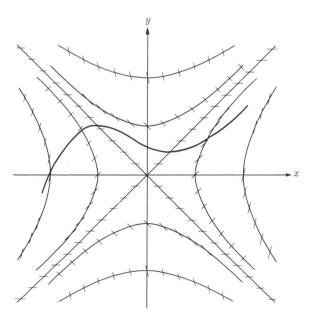

Figure 6–17

first constructing the isoclines $y - 2x = m$, on each of which the line segments have slope m. In this example the isoclines are straight lines, but not
parallel to the y-axis as they were in the preceding one. In the next example
(Fig. 6–17) they turn out to be curves. Here the differential equation is

$$y' = \tfrac{1}{2}(x^2 - y^2), \qquad y(-1) = 1,$$

and the isoclines are the equilateral hyperbolas $x^2 - y^2 = \pm m$.

Chapter 7

Computing Devices

The direction field does not directly yield a continuous line to represent the continuous variation of the dependent and independent variables. Line segments lying tangent to the same integral curve must be found and joined by visual estimation. Many mechanical and electrical devices, however, do afford a continuous representation of the variables. Some mechanical units are described first, in Section 7–1, primarily because their physical operation is easily explained in terms of familiar principles. The electronic units used in modern analog computers are described next. They are introduced in Section 7–2(a) as "black boxes" whose function is known but whose principle of operation is irrelevant. The physical details are presented for the interested reader in Section 7–2(b), which may however be omitted without loss of continuity.

7–1 MECHANICAL COMPONENTS

Linear and angular displacement are the most common mechanical analogs. Conversion from one to the other is easily effected by the rack and pinion illustrated in Fig. 7–1. The rack is constrained to slide along a fixed line; the pinion gear, to rotate about a fixed axis. By allowing the axis of the pinion to move linearly, and by incorporating a second rack, the adder of Fig. 7–2 is obtained. Let the horizontal displacements x and y of the two racks and z of the pinion axis all be zero for the reference position shown with dashed lines. Then the axis displacement z in the arbitrary position shown is given by $z = \frac{1}{2}(x + y)$. The signs of x, y, z correspond to the directions of the displacements from the reference position.

Angular addition is performed by the differential gear of Fig. 7–3. Again the equation $z = \frac{1}{2}(x + y)$ applies, where x and y are now the angular positions of the independent shafts and z is that of the cage. Subtraction is essentially addition with one input reversed in direction. Linear reversal is obtained by using an adder with the sum z fixed at zero. Angular reversal is provided simply by two meshing identical gears.

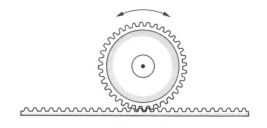

Figure 7–1

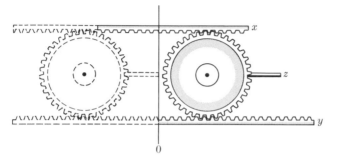

Figure 7–2

The factor $\frac{1}{2}$ inserted by the adders can be canceled through multiplication by two. Such multiplication by a constant is achievable by a train of gears or, for linear displacement, by a slotted lever arm. The latter device is illustrated in Fig. 7–4. The constant of multiplication becomes adjustable if the pivot is made movable; the fixed gear train can be replaced by a gear box and selector, as on an automobile.

The relation $xy = \int x\,dy + \int y\,dx$ suggests that the multiplication of two variables can be performed by the use of integrators. Although other devices, such as linkages, are available for multiplication, the integrator is of interest because it is applicable also to differential equations. The wheel and disk integrator is depicted in Fig. 7–5. A large disk rotates about a vertical axis. A small wheel of radius a, whose axis is horizontal and intersects that of the disk, is driven by the disk's rotation. The distance of the point of contact from

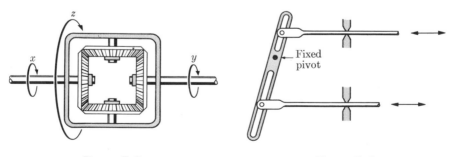

Figure 7–3

Figure 7–4

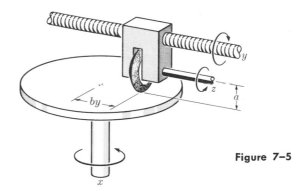

Figure 7–5

the center of the disk is controlled by a lead screw whose angular position is y. If b is the pitch of the screw (linear displacement per unit angular displacement), then by is the radius of the element of disk driving the wheel. An infinitesimal disk rotation dx displaces that element through $by\,dx$ and the wheel perimeter through $a\,dz$. If there is no slippage, the two displacements are equal: $by\,dx = a\,dz$. It follows that $dz = ky\,dx$, where the constant k equals b/a, or $z = k\int y\,dx$.

Mechanical integrators were first interconnected by Vannevar Bush in 1931 to solve differential equations, but they have been superseded by the faster, cheaper, and more rugged electronic integrators. The *planimeter*, related to the wheel and disk integrator, is still in use to measure areas enclosed by plane curves.

7–2 ELECTRONIC COMPONENTS

Electronic analog computers can be assembled from a variety of devices. A representative set of devices in which electrical voltage is the physical quantity measured will be described, first operationally and then physically. Numerical values quoted should be regarded as typical rather than universal.

(a) Operational Characteristics

The device whose introduction in 1940 made the modern analog computer possible is the *operational amplifier*, developed independently by Clarence Lovell and by George Philbrick. The operational amplifier is usually provided with controls to permit its use in any of several modes. Foremost among these is its use as an integrator, shown symbolically in Fig. 7–6(a). The output voltage e_o is the integral of the input voltage e_i with respect to time, inverted in sign and multiplied by a constant a associated with the amplifier. The initial value of the integrand must be presented as a constant input, assumed here to be inverted. The equation that describes the integrator is

$$e_o = e_o(\tau_0) - a\int_{\tau_0}^{\tau} e_i\,d\tau. \qquad (7\text{–}1)$$

The sign inversion is optional in some commercial amplifiers, but it will be assumed here to be mandatory, as it is in others. The independent variable τ is *real time*. Its variation is the actual passage of time that we measure daily, but cannot control. The units customarily employed are seconds for τ and for $1/a$ and volts for e_i and e_o.

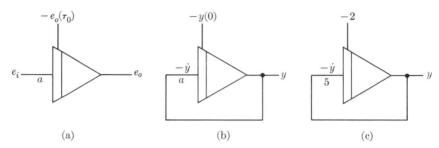

(a)   (b)   (c)

Figure 7–6

The use of an integrator to solve a differential equation is straightforward. Consider first the differential equation $dy/dx + 5y = 0$, subject to the initial condition $y(0) = 2$. The equation can be solved for the derivative to yield $\dot{y} = -5y$, where $\dot{y}$ is written in lieu of dy/dx. The computer solution is shown in outline in Fig. 7–6(b) and with numerical details supplied in Fig. 7–6(c). Real time τ is used to represent the independent variable x, and e_o to represent the dependent variable y. The constant a is seen to be 5. It effectively multiplies y to yield $-\dot{y}$.

Consider next the differential equation

$$4\frac{d^2y}{dt^2} + \frac{dy}{dt} + 9y = 0.$$

This can be solved for the highest-order derivative to yield $\ddot{y} = -\frac{1}{4}\dot{y} - \frac{9}{4}y$, where each dot over the dependent variable symbolizes differentiation once with respect to the independent variable. It is clear that the implementation of the equation presupposes means of performing sign inversion, summation, and multiplication by a constant.

The operational amplifier can be controlled to perform sign inversion and constant multiplication without integration. In this mode the equation of operation is

$$e_o = -ae_i. \tag{7–2}$$

The symbol for such an *inverter* is obtained from that for an integrator by removing the vertical bar within the triangle that represents the amplifier. Both symbols are shown in Fig. 7–7.

Most operational amplifiers are provided with several inputs e_j, each with its multiplicative constant a_j. When the amplifier is connected as an inverter,

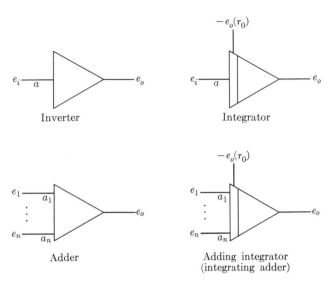

Figure 7–7

its operation is the weighted addition of the several inputs according to the equation

$$e_o = - \sum_{j=1}^{n} a_j e_j. \tag{7-3}$$

When the amplifier is connected as an integrator, both summation and integration are performed. The governing equation is

$$e_o = e_o(\tau_0) - \sum_{j=1}^{n} a_j \int_{\tau_0}^{\tau} e_j \, d\tau = e_o(\tau_0) - \int_{\tau_0}^{\tau} \left(\sum_{j=1}^{n} a_j e_j \right) d\tau. \tag{7-4}$$

The symbols used for multiple inputs are also shown in Fig. 7–7.

The multiplicative constants a_j are normally built into the amplifier, one being associated with each input line. One widely used amplifier has seven input lines, of which three have $a = 1$, two have $a = 5$, and two have $a = 10$. Multiplication by 2 can be achieved by connecting one input voltage to two of the $a = 1$ lines. The limits of this approach are soon reached, however, and another device is needed. The *attenuator*, symbolized in Fig. 7–8, performs multiplication by any constant not exceeding unity, but without inversion. Its equation is

$$e_o = \alpha e_i, \tag{7-5}$$

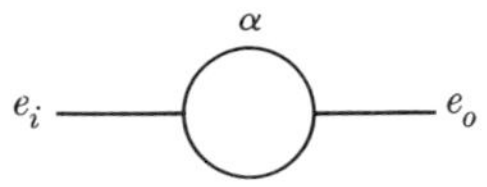

Figure 7–8

where α is continuously adjustable from 0 to 1. Values of α will be quoted to four decimal places, the normal limit of accuracy for such devices. Arbitrary input multiples are obtained by combining a variable attenuator with one of

Figure 7–9

the fixed input multiples. Thus multiplication of an amplifier input by four is shown in Fig. 7–9(a) and by $\frac{1}{2}$ in Fig. 7–9(b). Note the customary omission of a if $a = 1$.

(b) Physical Operation

The attenuator, as well as the different modes of the operational amplifier, will now be explained by the use of elementary physical principles, which will first be reviewed.

A *resistor*, shown symbolically in Fig. 7–10(a), is a device for dissipating electrical energy. It has been verified experimentally that the ratio of *voltage* drop e across a resistor to *current* i through the resistor is a constant, known as the *resistance* $R = e/i$ ($e = Ri$, $i = e/R$). Corresponding units for e, i, and R are *volts*, *amperes*, and *ohms*, respectively.

A *capacitor*, shown symbolically in Fig. 7–10(b), is a device for storing energy. It has been verified experimentally that the ratio of *charge* q on a capacitor to voltage drop e across the capacitor is a constant, known as the *capacitance* $C = q/e$ ($q = Ce$, $e = q/C$). Corresponding units for q, e, and C are *coulombs*, *volts*, and *farads*, respectively.

Electrical current i is defined as the rate of change of electrical charge q with respect to time τ, and it follows that $i = dq/d\tau$ and $q = \int_{-\infty}^{\tau} i \, d\tau$. The voltage e can therefore be written as $e = (1/C)\int_{-\infty}^{\tau} i \, d\tau$. Kirchhoff's law states that the total current leaving an electrical junction must equal the current entering the junction. In other words, charge within a circuit cannot accumulate at a point.

An *amplifier*, shown symbolically in Fig. 7–11, is a device for the controlled amplification of energy. Unlike the resistor and capacitor, which are two-terminal devices, the amplifier possesses four terminals, two of which are shown connected to a reference voltage known as *ground* and taken to equal zero. The amplifier is itself composed of various devices so chosen that the over-all operation is described by the equation $e_0 = B - Ae_g$, where A is a positive constant. Amplifiers used in analog computers have been specially designed to obtain $B = 0$, usually at the expense of requiring stabilization and delicate adjustment (symbolized in Fig. 7–11 by the small box with the arrow), and to incorporate very high *amplification* A. For many computers A is of the order of 10^8 or 10^9. Amplifier operation will henceforth be described by the equation $e_o = -Ae_g$.

Consider now the circuit shown in Fig. 7–12 and composed of a resistor in series with the combination of a capacitor and amplifier in parallel with each other. The two ground terminals of the amplifier have been omitted for the sake of simplicity. The voltage across the capacitor is given by

$$e = e(\tau_0) + \frac{1}{C}\int_{\tau_0}^{\tau} i_2 \, d\tau.$$

Upon substituting $e = e_g - e_o$, $i_2 = i_1 - i_3$, $i_1 = (e_i - e_g)/R$, and $e_g = -e_o/A$, the equation becomes

$$-\frac{e_o}{A} - e_o = -\frac{e_o(\tau_0)}{A} - e_o(\tau_0) + \frac{1}{C}\int_{\tau_0}^{\tau} \left(\frac{e_i + (e_o/A)}{R} - i_3\right) d\tau.$$

Because A is such a large denominator, e_o/A can be neglected in comparison with either e_o or e_i. Moreover, in a well-built amplifier the grid current i_3 is very nearly zero, and can be neglected relative to e_i/R. Elimination of these very small quantities yields the sufficiently accurate simple equation

$$e_o = e_o(\tau_0) - \frac{1}{RC}\int_{\tau_0}^{\tau} e_i \, d\tau. \tag{7–6}$$

Three points should be remarked about Fig. 7–12 and Eq. (7–6). First, the circuit performs integration of the input voltage e_i with respect to *real time* τ (and no other independent variable), together with sign inversion and reduction by the scale factor RC. Second, the product RC must have the dimensions of time. In fact, 1 ohm times 1 farad is 1 second. Using more common units,

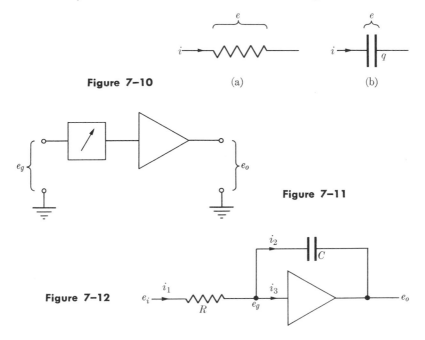

Figure 7–10   (a)   (b)

Figure 7–11

Figure 7–12

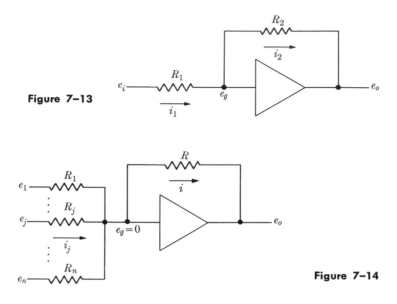

Figure 7–13

Figure 7–14

1 megohm (10^6 ohms) times 1 microfarad (10^{-6} farad) is 1 second. Comparison with Eq. (7–1) identifies the constant a as $1/RC$. Third, the initial condition of the integrator is $e_o(\tau_0)$, the voltage due to the initial charge on the capacitor.

In order to omit the detail of Fig. 7–12, an integrator is usually symbolized as in Fig. 7–7. The initial condition is shown with the sign reversed because, for one widely used computer, a further reversal is incorporated in the starting procedure.

The inverter of Fig. 7–7 is realized as in Fig. 7–13. Here, since $e_g = 0$, then $e_i/R_i = i_1 = i_2 = -e_o/R_2$, from which it follows that

$$e_o = -\frac{R_2}{R_1} e_i. \tag{7–7}$$

Comparison with Eq. (7–2) identifies the constant a in that case as the dimensionless ratio R_2/R_1.

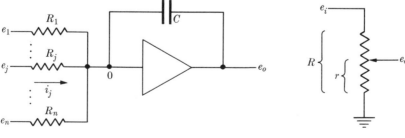

Figure 7–15

Figure 7–16

The summation mode of the operational amplifier is embodied in the circuit of Fig. 7–14. Here $e_j/R_j = i_j$ and the sum of the i_j must equal i. Hence, $-e_o/R = \sum(e_j/R_j)$, and it follows that $e_o = -\sum(R/R_j)e_j$.

Use of the input resistor network of Fig. 7–14 together with the feedback capacitor of Fig. 7–12 yields the circuit for the integration of sums, shown schematically in Fig. 7–15. The reader is invited to derive the circuit equation and compare it with Eq. (7–4).

The attenuator is simply a resistor grounded at one end and provided with a movable electric contact. Let the attenuator, shown in Fig. 7–16, have total resistance R, of which r is between the adjustable contact and the end connected to ground. Then, if no current is drawn by the output circuit, the current i flowing into the resistor is measured by e_i/R or by e_o/r. Since these quantities are equal, $e_o = (r/R)e_i$, where $r \leq R$.

Chapter 8

Automatic Computation

An analog computer is essentially a collection of the foregoing devices, with their terminals brought out to a plugboard, and with a mechanism for starting the solution at any desired τ_0. The computer user must set attenuators and must interconnect the various devices by means of patch cords inserted into the plugboard. Specification of the required interconnections is known as programming the analog computer. The plugboard wiring is often done directly from diagrams of which Fig. 7–6(c) is a simple example.

8–1 ELEMENTARY SOLUTIONS

A solution to the differential equation $\ddot{y} = -\frac{1}{4}\dot{y} - \frac{9}{4}y$ presented earlier can now be diagramed as in Fig. 8–1. The numbers $\frac{9}{4}$ and $\frac{1}{4}$ indicate the constant multipliers to be selected for the summing amplifier. If the initial conditions $y(0)$ and $\dot{y}(0)$ are represented by the correct initial voltages, and the independent variable is represented by real time τ, then the output y of the second integrator will represent the solution as a function of time. Since the diagram represents a closed circuit, it appears at first sight that the operation is akin to lifting one's self by one's bootstraps. This is not the case, for energy is being

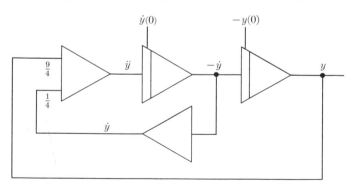

Figure 8–1

supplied continually in the amplifiers. The closed circuit paths merely embody constraints on the simultaneous variation of the several quantities represented by the circuit.

The method used to design the circuit of Fig. 8–1 is of general applicability, and is summarized in the four following steps:

(1) assume the existence of the derivative of highest order;

(2) integrate that derivative successively to obtain lower-order derivatives up to and including that of zero order, i.e., the dependent variable;

(3) reconstitute the previously assumed derivative from the lower ones according to the differential equation;

(4) specify the initial conditions.

In preparing an analog computer solution to a differential equation, the machine user must remain within voltage and other limits imposed by the machine. A convenient technique is the use of normalized variables, because it grants the programmer a certain measure of independence of the particular computer to be used. An estimate is first made, by means to be elaborated later, of the maximum values of all variables that appear in the solution of the differential equation. Each variable is then normalized with respect to its assumed maximum value, so that the maximum of each normalized variable is unity. This maximum can later be made to correspond to the maximum voltage of the computer.

If the differential equation of Fig. 8–1, $4\ddot{y} + \dot{y} + 9y = 0$, is accompanied by the initial conditions $y(0) = 4$ and $\dot{y}(0) = -\frac{3}{4}$, then it can be shown that $y_m = |y|_{\max} = 4$, $\dot{y}_m = |\dot{y}|_{\max} = 6$, and $\ddot{y}_m = |\ddot{y}|_{\max} = 9$ are upper bounds on the maximum magnitudes of the variables. Rewriting the equation in terms of the normalized variables y/y_m, $\dot{y}/\dot{y}_m$, and $\ddot{y}/\ddot{y}_m$ yields

$$36\left(\frac{\ddot{y}}{9}\right) + 6\left(\frac{\dot{y}}{6}\right) + 36\left(\frac{y}{4}\right) = 0,$$

$$\left(\frac{\ddot{y}}{9}\right) = -\frac{1}{6}\left(\frac{\dot{y}}{6}\right) - \left(\frac{y}{4}\right),$$

and the initial conditions

$$\left(\frac{y(0)}{4}\right) = 1, \qquad \left(\frac{\dot{y}(0)}{6}\right) = -\frac{1}{8}.$$

A diagram of the solution, thus *scaled* to the assumed maxima, is shown in Fig. 8–2, which should be compared with Fig. 8–1. The multiplicative factors of $\frac{3}{2}$ at the integrator inputs are required to implement the relations

$$\frac{\dot{y}}{6} = \frac{3}{2}\int\frac{\ddot{y}}{9}\,dt, \qquad \frac{y}{4} = \frac{3}{2}\int\frac{\dot{y}}{6}\,dt.$$

A completely scaled diagram of a solution to the differential equation of Fig. 8–1 is displayed in Fig. 8–3. It has been assumed that fixed voltage sources are available only for the maximum values of ± 1 unit. If $\ddot{y}$ is not needed explicitly,

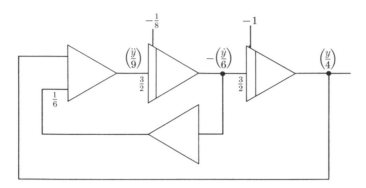

Figure 8–2

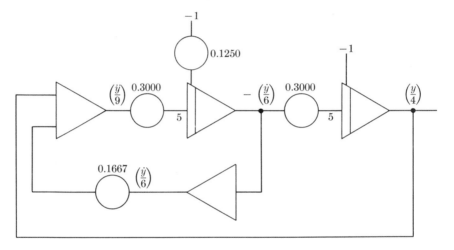

Figure 8–3

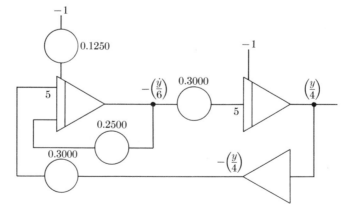

Figure 8–4

the summation of $y/4$ and $\dot{y}/6$ can be performed together with the integration that yields $\dot{y}/6$. The multiplicative factors, or voltage *gains*, supplied for each summand must still be supplied in the resulting solution. This is still $\frac{3}{2}$ for $y/4$, but for $\dot{y}/6$ it is $(\frac{1}{6})(\frac{3}{2}) = \frac{1}{4}$. The corresponding diagram is given in Fig. 8–4. Note that an inverter is now needed for y but not for $\dot{y}$. Only three amplifiers are required, as opposed to four in the previous solution. Amplifier performance is adversely affected by the use of multiple inputs, but the degradation is normally less for amplifiers used as integrators than for those used only as summers. The programmer must therefore choose between the greater simplicity of the solution of Fig. 8–4 and the higher accuracy of the solution of Fig. 8–3.

The solution of the differential equation occurs as a function of time after capacitors, whose voltages represent initial conditions, are disconnected from their original voltages by the computer starting mechanism. All voltages in the circuit are constrained to vary according to the differential equation modeled by the circuit (or describing its behavior), and the solution can be observed by either of two common methods. One is to use the selected voltage(s) to drive the pen of a line plotter over a sheet of graph paper. The other is to drive an oscilloscope with the voltage(s), normally in conjunction with an automatic device that simultaneously restarts both the computer solution and the oscilloscope sweep. If the repetition rate is high enough, the persistence of the image will cause it to appear stationary, thus permitting both measurement and photographic recording. Two common pairs of coordinates are $\dot{y}$ and y, which yield a so-called *phase plane* plot, and y and t. In the latter case t may be generated, if it is not otherwise available, by integrating a constant voltage.

Scaling must be established not only for the dependent variable and its derivatives, but also for the independent variable t, which is represented by real time τ. It can be shown mathematically, or found from an analog computer, that the differential equation of Figs. 8–1 through 8–4 has a damped sinusoidal solution, whose period is about four seconds. Let it be required, for example, to display the solution on an oscilloscope at the rate of about one period per second. If one period corresponds to problem time $t = 4$ and to real (computer) time $\tau = 1$, then $\tau = 0.25t$ and the computer solution is faster than the problem by a factor of 4. In general, if $\tau = \beta t$, the computer solution will be faster by $1/\beta$ for $\beta < 1$ and slower by β for $\beta > 1$.

By making the substitution $\tau = \beta t$ in the integrator equation

$$e_o(\tau) = e_o(\tau_0) - \frac{1}{RC} \int_{\tau_0}^{\tau} e_i(\tau)\, d\tau,$$

one obtains

$$e_o(\beta t) = e_o(\beta t_0) - \frac{1}{RC} \int_{\beta t_0}^{\beta t} e_i(\beta t)\, d(\beta t),$$

$$e_o(\beta t) = e_o(\beta t_0) - \frac{\beta}{RC} \int_{\beta t_0}^{\beta t} e_i(\beta t)\, dt.$$

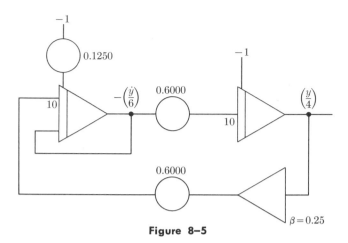

Figure 8–5

The integrator operation can therefore be regarded as integration with respect to problem time t, together with multiplication by β. A compensating factor $1/\beta$ must therefore be introduced in scaling if the computer solution is to represent the given problem. If $\beta < 1$, the gain of each amplifier input must be increased by $1/\beta$. If $\beta > 1$, each must be attenuated by $1/\beta$. This modification must not be made for adder inputs. The several computer variables may be regarded as functions either of τ or of t. Their initial and maximum values remain unchanged.

For the differential equation of Fig. 8–4 an extra gain of 4 must be provided for each integrator input, since $\beta = 0.25$. The resulting diagram, labeled with the corresponding value of β (which will henceforth be assumed to be unity unless otherwise shown), is presented in Fig. 8–5.

8–2 CLASSIFICATION OF DIFFERENTIAL EQUATIONS

It is convenient at this point to introduce some of the terminology used in the classification of differential equations. An *ordinary* differential equation has only one independent variable; a *partial* differential equation has more than one. Attention will be restricted here to ordinary differential equations. The *order* of a differential equation is the order of the highest derivative that appears in it. For example, the differential equation solved by the diagram of Fig. 8–5 is of second order. A *linear* differential equation is one expressible in the form

$$f_n(x)\frac{d^n y}{dx^n} + f_{n-1}(x)\frac{d^{n-1} y}{dx^{n-1}} + \cdots + f_1(x)\frac{dy}{dx} + f_0(x)y = f(x).$$

If $f_i(x)$ is a constant for every i, the equation is said to have *constant coefficients*; otherwise, it has *variable coefficients*. The function $f(x)$ is often termed the *forcing function*. If $f(x) = 0$, the equation is said to be *homogeneous*. A *nonlinear* differential equation is one that is not linear.

In order to specify the solution of an nth-order differential equation, n conditions must be given. This number corresponds precisely to the number of integrators required in the general solution method for integrating the nth derivative. The conditions required by that method are the initial values of the dependent variable and its first $n - 1$ derivatives.

8–3 ESTIMATION OF MAXIMUM VALUES

The process of scaling is dependent on the judicious determination of maximum values of the variables. The normal procedure is to make guesses, more or less educated, of the maximum values and to use them in diagraming the solution and interconnecting the amplifiers. If a guess is too small, at least one amplifier will overload and the solution will be incorrect. In this event, an alarm is normally given by the computer, but no damage occurs. If a guess is excessively high, the full range of the corresponding amplifier will not be used, and a given absolute error in the voltage will cause a greater relative error. This condition, in which the solution is less accurate than it could be, can be detected by a voltmeter, usually incorporated in the computer.

If the first guess is poor, the programmer need merely make another guess. The only loss is that of time. When a physical system is being modeled by a differential equation, often the system will furnish clues as to the maxima. It should be noted incidentally that it is not algebraic maxima, but rather maximum magnitudes (absolute values), that are of interest for scaling.

Rules for estimating maximum values will now be stated without proof for three commonly encountered types of differential equations. The rules can be justified rigorously for the first two types; for the third, no formal justification exists, but the rule appears to work in general in practice, despite the existence of at least one known exception.

(1) *Second-order linear homogeneous differential equations with constant coefficients.* Let the differential equation be written as

$$a\ddot{y} + b\dot{y} + cy = 0. \tag{8–1}$$

Corresponding to (8–1) is the *characteristic equation*

$$ay^2 + by + c = 0.$$

The nature of the solution is closely related to the roots of the characteristic equation. Three cases can be distinguished:

(a) If $b^2 - 4ac > 0$, the characteristic equation has two distinct real roots α_1 and α_2. It can be verified by direct substitution in Eq. (8–1) that the solution of the differential equation is

$$y = Ae^{\alpha_1 t} + Be^{\alpha_2 t},$$

where A and B are arbitrary constants. Maximum values of y and $\dot{y}$ are easily estimated from a knowledge of the signs and relative magnitudes of α_1 and α_2, and of the maximum desired value of t.

(b) If $b^2 - 4ac = 0$, the characteristic equation has a double real root α, and the differential equation solution is

$$y = e^{\alpha t}(A + Bt).$$

Usually it is not difficult to determine which term predominates in the specified range of t.

(c) If $b^2 - 4ac < 0$, the characteristic equation has conjugate complex roots $\alpha \pm i\omega$. This case is frequently encountered in practice, because the oscillating systems fall in this category. Substitution in Eq. (8–1) verifies that the solution is

$$y = e^{\alpha t}(A \sin \omega t + B \cos \omega t).$$

If $\alpha \leq 0$, the solution is sinusoidal (damped if $\alpha < 0$), and estimates which are never too small are provided by

$$y_m = \{[y(0)]^2 + [\dot{y}(0)/\omega_0]^2\}^{1/2},$$

$$\dot{y}_m = \omega_0 y_m,$$

$$\ddot{y}_m = \omega_0^2 y_m,$$

where $\omega_0 = (c/a)^{1/2}$ is an approximation to the exact

$$\omega = \frac{1}{2a}(-b^2 + 4ac)^{1/2}.$$

(2) *Second-order linear differential equations with constant coefficients and constant forcing function.* Let the equation be written as

$$a\ddot{y} + b\dot{y} + cy = F. \tag{8–2}$$

The trivial solution $y = F/c$ is easily found. Direct substitution in Eq. (8–2) shows that $y = \tilde{y} + (F/c)$ is a solution whenever $\tilde{y}$ satisfies the homogeneous equation (8–1):

$$a\ddot{y} + b\dot{y} + cy = a(\ddot{\tilde{y}} + \ddot{F}/c) + b(\dot{\tilde{y}} + \dot{F}/c) + c(\tilde{y} + F/c)$$

$$= a\ddot{\tilde{y}} + b\dot{\tilde{y}} + c\tilde{y} + F$$

$$= F.$$

For the important case $b^2 - 4ac < 0$ and $\alpha \leq 0$, $\tilde{y}$ is oscillatory, and suitable estimates of the maximum values are

$$y_m = \tilde{y}_m + |F/c|, \qquad \dot{y}_m = \omega_0 \tilde{y}_m, \qquad \ddot{y}_m = \omega_0^2 \tilde{y}_m,$$

where $\tilde{y}_m$ is given by

$$\tilde{y}_m = \{[y(0) - (F/c)]^2 + [\dot{y}(0)/\omega_0]^2\}^{1/2}.$$

(3) *Equal-coefficient rule.* This rule applies to linear differential equations of any order, with constant coefficients and constant forcing function, and with initial conditions all zero:

$$a_n y^{(n)} + \cdots + a_1 y^{(1)} + a_0 y = C,$$

$$y(0) = y^{(1)}(0) = \cdots = y^{(n-1)}(0) = 0.$$

The rule gives maxima of

$$y_m = 2C/a_0, \qquad y_m^{(i)} = C/a_i,$$

but is applicable *only* if the sequence of maxima thus specified is monotone (nondecreasing or nonincreasing). The name of the rule comes from the fact that coefficients of the derivatives in the normalized equation will be equal.

8–4 METHODS OF SOLUTION

(a) Linear Differential Equations with Constant Coefficients and Constant Forcing Function

Let the equation be

$$\dddot{\theta} + 3\ddot{\theta} + 5\dot{\theta} + 12\theta = 24, \qquad \theta(0) = \dot{\theta}(0) = \ddot{\theta}(0) = 0.$$

Applying the equal-coefficient rule,

$$\theta_m = 2\tfrac{24}{12} = 4,$$

$$\dot{\theta}_m = \tfrac{24}{5} = 4.8,$$

$$\ddot{\theta}_m = \tfrac{24}{3} = 8,$$

$$\dddot{\theta}_m = \tfrac{24}{1} = 24.$$

Since the sequence is monotone, it will serve. It might be convenient for ease of measuring $\dot{\theta}$ to replace 4.8 by the more conservative limit 5, but the method will be illustrated without this modification. The equality of the coefficients is observed in the normalized differential equation

$$24\left(\frac{\dddot{\theta}}{24}\right) + 24\left(\frac{\ddot{\theta}}{8}\right) + 24\left(\frac{\dot{\theta}}{4.8}\right) + 48\left(\frac{\theta}{4}\right) = 24,$$

$$\left(\frac{\dddot{\theta}}{24}\right) = -\left(\frac{\ddot{\theta}}{8}\right) - \left(\frac{\dot{\theta}}{4.8}\right) - 2\left(\frac{\theta}{4}\right) + 1.$$

Let it be required to display three cycles in about four seconds. It is permissible to speak of cycles in this case because an analysis (omitted here) or a trial computer run shows a dominating sinusoidal component in the solution. An approximate frequency is obtained, by neglecting the first and third derivatives, as $\omega = \sqrt{\frac{12}{3}} = 2$. (This approximation is surprisingly accurate, for $\omega = 2.0808$ is the actual frequency of the oscillation.) Since $\sin \omega t$ has period 2π, the time to complete three cycles is given by $\omega t = 6\pi$, or $t = 3\pi$ if $\omega = 2$. This is approximately $t = 10$, which yields, in view of the requirement $\tau = 4$, the time scale factor $\beta = 0.4$ since $\tau = 0.4t$. An extra gain of $1/\beta = 2.5$ is therefore required at each input to an integrator. Total gains required are as follows:

$$\text{Amplifier yielding } \theta/4: \quad \frac{4.8}{4} \times 2.5 = 3;$$

$$\text{Amplifier yielding } \dot{\theta}/4.8: \quad \frac{8}{4.8} \times 2.5 = 4.1667;$$

$$\text{Amplifier yielding } \ddot{\theta}/8: \quad \frac{24}{8} \times 2.5 = 7.5.$$

The complete diagram for $\theta(0.4t)$ is presented in Fig. 8–6. Note that the constant term, corresponding to the forcing function, is obtained from a constant voltage source.

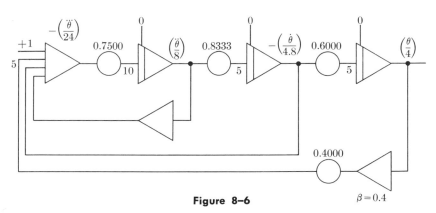

Figure 8–6

(b) Linear Differential Equations with Constant Coefficients and Variable Forcing Function

The general form of the differential equation is

$$\sum_{i=1}^{n} a_i \frac{d^i x}{dt^i} + a_0 x = f(t).$$

The standard technique is to generate $f(t)$ as the solution of a differential equation auxiliary to the given one. The time scales for both the given and auxiliary differential equations must be the same. Consider the differential equation

$$4\ddot{y} + \dot{y} + 9y = 3 \cos 2t, \qquad y(0) = 4, \qquad \dot{y}(0) = -\tfrac{3}{4}.$$

The corresponding homogeneous equation is one whose computer solution has previously been developed. The same maxima as before can be assumed to hold for y, $\dot{y}$, $\ddot{y}$. The maximum value of $\cos 2t$ is 1. The normalized equation is then

$$36 \left(\frac{\ddot{y}}{9}\right) + 6 \left(\frac{\dot{y}}{6}\right) + 36 \left(\frac{y}{4}\right) = 3 \left(\frac{\cos 2t}{1}\right),$$

$$-\left(\frac{\ddot{y}}{9}\right) = \frac{1}{6} \left(\frac{\dot{y}}{6}\right) + \left(\frac{y}{4}\right) - \frac{1}{12} \cos 2t,$$

$$\frac{y(0)}{4} = 1, \qquad \frac{\dot{y}(0)}{6} = -\frac{1}{8}.$$

The provision of an input $-\tfrac{1}{12} \cos 2t$ to the leftmost summing amplifier of Fig. 8–3 would yield the required solution. The factor $\tfrac{1}{12}$ is obtained from an attenuator; the $-\cos 2t$ can be generated as the solution to an auxiliary dif-

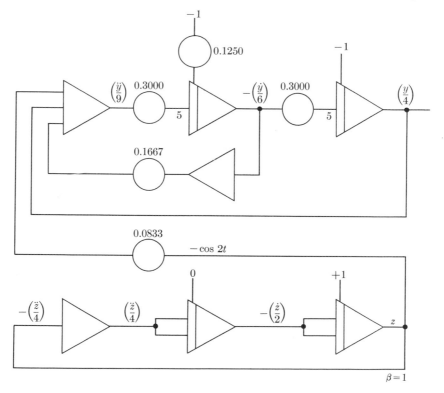

Figure 8–7

ferential equation. The easiest way to find an appropriate differential equation is to list the function whose synthesis is desired, along with its first few derivatives, and to scan the list for relationships which permit the easy specification of a differential equation. For the present example,

$$z = -\cos 2t, \qquad z_m = 1,$$
$$\dot{z} = 2 \sin 2t, \qquad \dot{z}_m = 2,$$
$$\ddot{z} = 4 \cos 2t, \qquad \ddot{z}_m = 4.$$

The required equation is easily seen to be

$$\ddot{z} + 4z = 0, \qquad z(0) = -1, \qquad \dot{z}(0) = 0,$$

or

$$\left(\frac{\ddot{z}}{4}\right) + z = 0, \qquad z(0) = -1, \qquad \frac{\dot{z}(0)}{2} = 0.$$

A *real-time solution* ($\beta = 1$) of the given differential equation is provided by the interconnections shown in Fig. 8–7, the bottom section of which produces the auxiliary differential equation. If it is desired to change the time scale, the inputs to *all four integrators* must be multiplied by the same factor $1/\beta$.

(c) Linear Differential Equations with Variable Coefficients

The general form of the equation is

$$\frac{d^n x}{dt^n} + f_{n-1}(t)\frac{d^{n-1}x}{dt^{n-1}} + \cdots + f_1(t)\frac{dx}{dt} + f_0(t)x = f(t).$$

The leading coefficient $f_n(t)$ has been assumed to be unity in order to avoid division in solving for the highest-order derivative. A technique has already been presented for generating the functions $f_i(t)$ by the use of auxiliary differential equations. It is now further required to provide for their multiplication by the corresponding derivatives. The symbol in Fig. 8–8(a) will be used to represent a multiplier. Different types of multipliers exist in analog computers, and their physical operation will not be described here.

If a multiplier had inputs x and y, each of which had a maximum value of 100 volts, an unscaled multiplication could yield a product xy of 10,000 volts, which would be highly unreasonable. Consequently, it is customary to build multipliers that incorporate a multiplicative factor (equal to 1/100 in this example) equal to the reciprocal of the maximum amplifier voltage. The re-

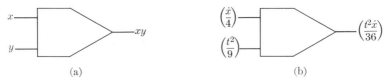

(a)   (b)

Figure 8–8

sulting maximum multiplier output is then equal to the maximum amplifier output. If computer diagrams are labeled with the normalized variables x/x_m and y/y_m, whose maximum values are unity, the maximum product $xy/x_m y_m$ will also be unity, and no multiplier scaling will be necessary. Figure 8–8(b) presents an example of multiplier labeling.

Consider Mathieu's equation

$$\ddot{x} + (a - 2\theta \cos \omega t)x = 0,$$

which arises in the study of frequency modulation oscillations. Let the parameters be such as to yield the equation

$$\ddot{x} + (4 - 1.2 \cos 1.5t)x = 0, \qquad x(0) = 4, \qquad \dot{x}(0) = 0.$$

If the differential equation had $\theta = 0$, the solution would be $x = 4 \cos 2t$. The effect of the periodic coefficient is not obvious, and the assumption $x_m = 4$ could lead to difficulties. Instead, assume the following maxima:

$$x_m = 5,$$
$$\dot{x}_m = 5(2) = 10,$$
$$\ddot{x}_m = 5(2)^2 = 20,$$
$$(\cos 1.5t)_m = 1.$$

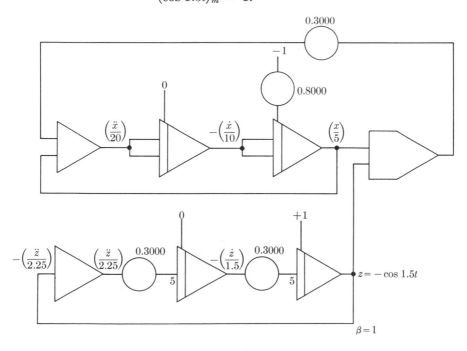

Figure 8–9

Normalization yields

$$20\left(\frac{\ddot{x}}{20}\right) + (4 - 1.2\cos 1.5t)5\left(\frac{x}{5}\right) = 0,$$

$$-\left(\frac{\ddot{x}}{20}\right) = \left(\frac{x}{5}\right) - 0.3\left(\frac{x}{5}\right)\cos 1.5t,$$

$$\left(\frac{x(0)}{5}\right) = 0.8 \qquad \left(\frac{\dot{x}(0)}{10}\right) = 0.$$

A real-time solution is diagramed in Fig. 8–9. An auxiliary differential equation provides $z = -\cos 1.5t$, and multiplication by 2 for each main differential equation integrator and by 1.5 for each auxiliary differential equation integrator is required to adjust for the ratios of maximum values.

Note that the multiplier output is fed to an inverter and not to an integrator. For technical reasons this is preferable, and an inverter should be added if necessary to secure this feature. If the time scale is changed, it should of course be done consistently for all four integrators.

(d) Explicit Nonlinearity

Nonlinear differential equations have either explicit nonlinear terms in $y^{(i)}$ or coefficients that are functions of the dependent rather than of the independent variable. An example of the former situation is van der Pol's equation

$$\ddot{y} + \lambda(y^2 - 1)\dot{y} + y = 0.$$

The equation may be rewritten as

$$\ddot{y} = -(y - \lambda\dot{y} + \lambda y^2\dot{y}),$$

in which the last term on the right-hand side is the nonlinear term. The solution

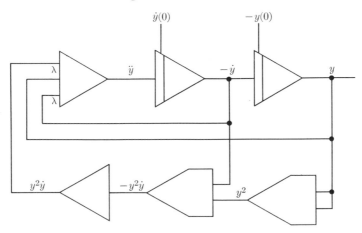

Figure 8–10

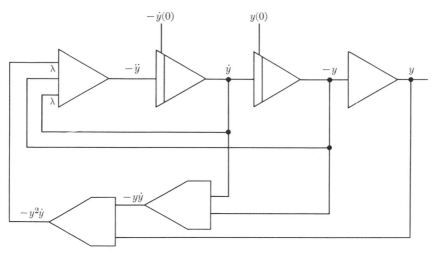

Figure 8–11

requires the use of multipliers in a manner similar to that used in the previous section. An unscaled diagram for this differential equation is shown in Fig. 8–10. An alternative arrangement is shown in Fig. 8–11, in which the two multipliers have a common factor. This is a useful feature for certain types of multipliers, even though the factor appears here once with each sign.

(e) Implicit Nonlinearity

If one of the coefficients of a differential equation is a function of the dependent variable, the auxiliary differential equation used to generate the coefficient has as its independent variable the dependent variable of the given differential equation. Thus the given and auxiliary differential equations have different independent variables. This is a matter of concern because the single independent variable in the computer, real time, cannot simultaneously represent two different problem variables. The technique for circumventing this difficulty is based upon the relation

$$\int u \, dv = \int u \frac{dv}{dt} \, dt. \tag{8-3}$$

Integration with respect to the variable v can be performed, if both dv/dt and a multiplier are available, by an integrator whose variable of integration is t. When the desired variable of integration is the dependent variable of the given differential equation, its first derivative with respect to t is normally available, at least with a negative sign.

The angular position θ of a simple two-foot pendulum released from rest at an angle of 1 radian from the vertical is given by the following differential equation:

$$\ddot{\theta} + 16 \sin \theta = 0, \qquad \theta(0) = 1, \qquad \dot{\theta}(0) = 0.$$

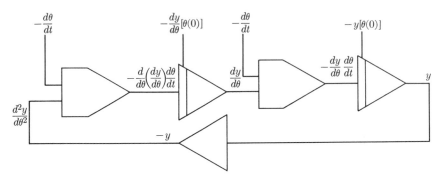

Figure 8–12

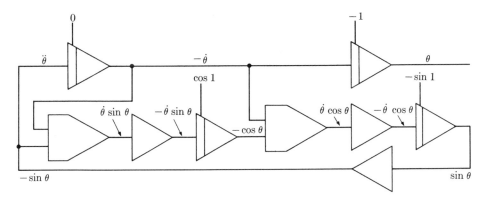

Figure 8–13

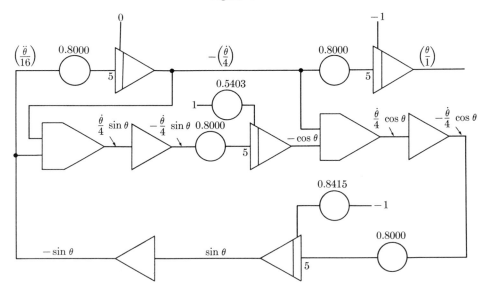

Figure 8–14

It is necessary to produce the function $y = \sin \theta$, which is a solution of the auxiliary differential equation $d^2y/d\theta^2 + y = 0$. In this case $v = \theta$, and $-d\theta/dt$ will be available from the solution of the given differential equation. An unscaled diagram for $y = \sin \theta$ is given in Fig. 8–12. This diagram is not quite proper, however, because each multiplier should drive an inverter rather than an integrator. The omission of the two inverters does not alter the over-all sign change, and it focuses attention on the application of Eq. (8–3). If the inverters are inserted and integrators for the original differential equation are connected, the solution of Fig. 8–13 results.

Magnitude scaling can be performed by considering the simplified equation

$$\ddot{\theta} + 16\theta = 0, \qquad \theta(0) = 1, \qquad \dot{\theta}(0) = 0.$$

The solution to this is $\theta = \cos 4t$, with maxima $\theta_m = 1$, $\dot{\theta}_m = 4$, $\ddot{\theta}_m = 16$. Replacement of θ by $\sin \theta$ in the simplified equation would yield a smaller value of $|\ddot{\theta}|$ and hence of $|\dot{\theta}|$, because $|\sin \theta| < |\theta|$. The assumed maxima therefore constitute conservative estimates. Since the maximum values of $\sin \theta$ and $\cos \theta$ are unity, maxima of $\dot{\theta} \sin \theta$ and similar expressions will equal 4. In normalized variables the differential equation becomes

$$\frac{\ddot{\theta}}{16} + \sin \theta = 0, \qquad \theta(0) = 1, \qquad \frac{\dot{\theta}(0)}{4} = 0.$$

A word on initial conditions is in order. In the realization of the function $y = \sin \theta$, the initial conditions are the values of the function and its derivative, not for *zero* θ, but for *initial* θ. Since the initial value of θ is $\theta(0) = 1$, the required values are $\cos 1 = 0.5403$ and $\sin 1 = 0.8415$. A fully scaled real-time solution is diagramed in Fig. 8–14.

8–5 OUTPUT PLOTTING

In plotting $\dot{y}$ as a function of y, both quantities are available from the computer hookup for the differential equation. If it is desired to plot y as a function of t, however, the latter must usually be produced separately. Since t satisfies the differential equation $\dot{t} = 1$, the diagram in Fig. 8–15(a) indicates the method used.

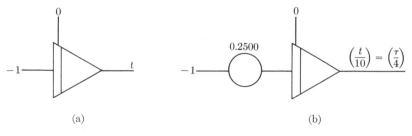

(a)   (b)

Figure 8–15

In general, both magnitude *and time* scaling must be provided. Consider the problem in Section 8–4(a), in which 10 units of the problem variable t are to be displayed in 4 seconds of real time τ. Here $1/\beta = 2.5$ and $t_m = 10$. The normalized variable is $t/10$ and the over-all multiplication required is $2.5 \times 0.1 = 0.25$. The resulting scaled time integrator is diagramed in Fig. 8–15(b).

References for Part III

ASHLEY, J. R., *Introduction to Analog Computation*. New York: Wiley, 1963.

BERKELEY, E. C., and L. WAINWRIGHT, *Computers: Their Operation and Applications*. New York: Reinhold, 1956. Section III.

DOUGLASS, R. D., and D. P. ADAMS, *Elements of Nomography*. New York: McGraw-Hill, 1947.

FORD, L. R., *Differential Equations*. New York: McGraw-Hill, 1933. Chapter I.

HANDEL, P. VON, ed., *Electronic Computers*. Englewood Cliffs: Prentice-Hall, 1961. Chapter 3.

JACKSON, A. S., *Analog Computation*. New York: McGraw-Hill, 1960. Chapters 3 and 4.

JOHNSON, C. L., *Analog Computer Techniques*. 2nd ed. New York: McGraw-Hill, 1963. Chapter 3.

JOHNSON, L. H., *Nomography and Empirical Equations*. New York: Wiley, 1952.

KAPLAN, W., *Ordinary Differential Equations*. Reading: Addison-Wesley, 1958. Chapter 1.

KARPLUS, W. J., and W. W. SOROKA, *Analog Methods*. 2nd ed. New York: McGraw-Hill, 1959.

LEVENS, A. S., *Nomography*. 2nd ed. New York: Wiley, 1948.

MACKEY, C. O., *Graphical Solutions*. 2nd ed. New York: Wiley, 1944.

Exercise Set for Part III

1. Calculate the scale factors m_V, m_K, and m_F and the scale positions for a nomogram for the equation $F = V + K$. The variable V is to vary between 2120 and 4240, and K between -860 and -686. The height of the scales is to be 10 inches, and the V- and K-scales are to be 7 inches apart.

2. Using the results of Exercise 1, construct a nomogram for the evaluation of f as a function of U and T from the empirical formula $S = 0.212(1 - 21.2/R)$, where

   $S = fd/U$ (Strouhal number, nondimensional),
   $R = Ud/\nu$ (Reynolds number, nondimensional),
   $\nu = (0.0055T + 1.25) \times 10^{-4}$ (kinematic viscosity of fluid, feet^2/second),
   T is temperature of fluid (°F),
   f is frequency at which vortices form on one side of the wake of a cylinder moving through a fluid (second^{-1}),
   d is diameter of cylinder (feet),
   U is velocity of cylinder (feet/second).

The scale for U should vary from 10 to 20 in increments of 2. The scale for T should vary from 50 to 120 in increments of 10. These two scales are each to be 10 inches high and 7 inches apart. The scale for f is to be graduated in increments of 500. The diameter d is the constant 0.012 *inch.*

3. (a) With the aid of a table, plot carefully one period of the curve $y = \sin x$. Differentiate it graphically to obtain the curve $y = \cos x$. [*Hint:* A small mirror aids in drawing accurate normals to the curve, whose tangents can then easily be constructed. Hold the mirror perpendicular to the paper at a point where the tangent is desired. Rotate the mirror until the curve and its reflection appear to form a single smooth curve. The mirror will then be normal to the curve.]

   (b) Copy your cosine curve onto another sheet of tracing paper, and there integrate it graphically. Compare the result with your original sine curve.

4. Solve graphically the differential equation $dy/dx - 0.2y^2 = 0$, subject to the initial condition $y(0) = 1.5$, for x in the range $0 \le x \le 1$. Obtain at least 6 points on the integral curve $y = f(x)$. Draw a half-parabola first.

5. Solve graphically the differential equation $dy/dx = \frac{3}{2}\sqrt{y}$, subject to the initial condition $y(0) = \frac{1}{2}$, for x in the range $0 \le x \le 2$.

6. Prepare a direction field for the differential equation $dy/dx + 5y = 0$. Determine the integral curve through the point $(0, 2)$.

7. Program an analog computer to solve the differential equation

$$dy/dx = 2y + x^2,$$

subject to the initial condition $y(0) = 1$. Assume that y must be displayed as a function of x for $0 \le x \le 1$ in 0.5 second and that $y \le 8$ over the interval.

8. Program an analog computer to plot the variable A as a function of z, where A is the area bounded by the curves $y = e^{-x}$, $y = 0$, $x = 0$, and $x = z$, for $0 \le z \le 4$.

9. Program an analog computer to solve the differential equation

$$\dddot{x} + 3\ddot{x} + 3\dot{x} + 6x = 3,$$

subject to the initial conditions

$$x(0) = 2, \qquad \dot{x}(0) = 1, \qquad \ddot{x}(0) = -3$$

by plotting four complete cycles of x as a function of t in about 10 seconds. Be sure to provide for the generation of t. For purposes of scaling, suitable bounds on the magnitudes of the variables may be obtained in this particular case by neglecting the first and third derivatives and considering instead the simplified equation

$$3\ddot{x} + 6x = 3,$$

which is satisfied, together with the stated conditions, by

$$x = \frac{\sqrt{2}}{2} \sin \sqrt{2}\, t + \tfrac{3}{2} \cos \sqrt{2}\, t + \tfrac{1}{2}.$$

10. Program an analog computer to solve the differential equation $\dddot{y} + 4\ddot{y} + 6\dot{y} + 16y = 24$, subject to the initial conditions $\ddot{y}(0) = \ddot{y}(0) = \dot{y}(0) = 0$. Provide for the display of three cycles of the solution in about 5 seconds. Estimate the natural frequency by ignoring the first and third derivatives.

11. Multiplication can be performed by a *quarter-squares* multiplier, which implements the equation

$$xy = \tfrac{1}{4}[(x + y)^2 - (x - y)^2].$$

Explain how a mechanical integrator can be used to perform the necessary squaring. Explain why an electronic integrator cannot be so used.

12. Program an analog computer to solve the differential equation

$$\frac{d^2 y}{dx^2} + (1 - k \sin x)y = 0 \qquad \text{for } x \geq 0,$$

subject to the conditions $y(0) = 0$ and $dy/dx(0) = 1$. Scale the solution for $k = 0.1$, and a display of 10 units of x per second. In estimating maximum values of the variables, make the simplifying approximation $k = 0$.

13. Program an analog computer to solve the differential equation

$$\ddot{x} + \lambda e^{-t}\dot{x} + 9x = 0$$

for the parameter range $0 \leq \lambda \leq 6$, subject to the initial conditions $x(0) = 4$ and $\dot{x}(0) = -9$. Provide for the plotting of two complete cycles of x as a function of t in about 8 seconds. Use 5 as the maximum value of $|x|$ and obtain magnitude scaling for the derivatives, and time scaling for all integrators, by considering the simplified equation with $\lambda = 0$. Label all amplifier inputs and outputs, and indicate initial conditions, attenuator settings, and the scale factor for time. [*Hint:* Perform scaling in terms of the normalized parameter $\lambda/6$.]

14. Program an analog computer to solve the differential equation $dy/dx = x - y^2$, subject to the initial condition $y(0) = 2$. Assume that it is required to display y as a function of x for $0.0 \leq x \leq 0.4$ in 0.1 second, and that the maximum value of y over the interval is 2.

15. Program an analog computer to solve the differential equation

$$\frac{d^3 y}{dx^3} + y\frac{d^2 y}{dx^2} = 0 \qquad \text{for } 1 \leq x \leq 10,$$

subject to the initial conditions $y(1) = 3$, $dy/dx(1) = -3$, and $d^2y/dx^2(1) = 6$. Scaling may be omitted.

16. Program for $x \geq 0$ the solution of the van der Pol equation

$$\frac{d^2 y}{dx^2} + \lambda(y^2 - 1)\frac{dy}{dx} + y = 0,$$

where $\lambda > 0$, subject to the conditions $y(0) = \sqrt{2}/2$ and $dy/dx(0) = \sqrt{2}/2$. Scale the solution for real time and for $\lambda = 0.1$. In estimating maximum values of the variables, make the simplifying approximation $\lambda = 0$, and allow for possible negative damping by doubling the estimates thus obtained.

17. The motion of a damped simple pendulum is described by the equation

$$\frac{d^2\theta}{dt^2} + k\frac{d\theta}{dt} + \frac{g}{r}\sin\theta = 0.$$

Program a solution for the case in which the parameters are $k = \frac{1}{2}$ second^{-1}, $g = 32$ feet/second^2, $r = 8$ feet, the initial conditions are $\theta(0) = \pi/3$ and $\dot{\theta}(0) = 0$, and it is desired to represent five complete oscillations in 1 second.

Part IV

Numerical Methods

Automatic digital computers are usually provided with means of performing the four elementary arithmetical operations of addition, subtraction, multiplication, and division, as well as some sort of decision operation. Most mathematical problems, such as the evaluation of a definite integral or the extraction of the roots of a polynomial, are not couched in terms of these operations. In order to make use of the computational power of automatic machines, it is therefore essential to develop methods of reducing the solution of mathematical problems to finite sequences of the elementary operations. Such numerical methods are often the only ones by which problems can be attacked.

This part will attempt neither a survey of the vast literature of numerical analysis, nor a comprehensive treatment of any portion of it. Instead, an elementary discussion will be presented of five classes of problems frequently encountered in practice.

The solution of an algebraic equation in a single variable is discussed in Chapter 9. Simultaneous algebraic equations are examined in Chapter 10, but the development is restricted to linear equations. Polynomials, a special class of the functions of Chapter 9, are introduced in Chapter 11. They serve as the basis of some of the techniques developed in Chapter 12 for the elementary operations of analysis. Differential equations, already considered in Part III from the point of view of analog computation, are attacked by digital techniques in Chapter 13.

Chapter 9

Algebraic Equations

A basic problem of algebra is to solve an equation or, equivalently, to find a zero of a function. If a function $f(x)$ can be expressed in the form

$$f(x) = \sum_{i=0}^{n} a_i x^i, \qquad (9\text{--}1)$$

where the a_i are constants, then $f(x)$ is said to be a *polynomial*. Many special methods take advantage of the properties of polynomials. Their presentation will be deferred, however, until after the introduction of several iterative techniques which enjoy more general applicability. These methods may be used to find zeros not only of polynomials, but also of *transcendental* functions, such as those involving logarithms, exponentials, trigonometric, or hyperbolic functions.

Iterative methods require an initial approximation x_0 to a zero, or root, X of a function $f(x)$. The procedure refines the approximation further and further, and may be terminated whenever two successive approximations are sufficiently close that one of them may be considered to give a numerical value of the root. The value of the initial approximation is often most easily obtained graphically, although methods can be devised to scan the real-number axis or the complex plane for the neighborhood of a root.

9–1 GENERAL ITERATION METHOD

If the function $f(x)$ is expressible as the difference of two functions, $f(x) = g(x) - h(x)$, it follows from $f(X) = 0$ for a root X that $g(X) = h(X)$. Substitution of the initial approximation x_0 for X in $h(X)$ leads to the equation $g(x) = h(x_0)$, which may be solved for x to yield x_0'. Substitution of this value in the left-hand member yields the equation $h(x) = g(x_0')$, which may be solved for a new approximation x_1. The process is then repeated, and may be summarized in the equation

$$x_{i+1} = g^{-1}[h(x_i)]. \qquad (9\text{--}2)$$

Example 9–1
$$f(x) = e^x + x - 5,$$
$$e^x - (5 - x) = 0,$$
$$x_{i+1} = \ln(5 - x_i),$$
$$x_0 = 1 \quad \text{(obtained graphically).}$$

i	x_i	$5 - x_i$	$\ln(5 - x_i)$
0	1.0	4.0	1.3863
1	1.3863	3.6137	1.2847
2	1.2847	3.7153	.
3	1.3125	3.6875	.
4	1.3049	3.6951	.
5	1.3070	3.6930	
6	1.3064	3.6936	
7	1.3066	3.6934	
8	1.30654	3.69346	
9	1.306558	3.693442	
10	1.3065584		

A graphical representation of the general case is shown in Fig. 9–1. The abscissa of intersection of the curves $g(x)$ and $h(x)$ is X. It is intuitively clear that for convergence to take place, the relation

$$|h'(x)| < |g'(x)| \tag{9–3}$$

must hold at X and in the neighborhood of X that includes x_0. It can be proved that this condition leads to convergence of the process to a zero of $f(x)$. For the function of the example

$$g(x) = e^x, \qquad g'(x) = e^x \doteq 3.7 \quad \text{at } x = X,$$
$$h(x) = 5 - x, \qquad h'(x) = -1.$$

Here $|h'(x)| = 1 < 3.7 = |g'(x)|$ and the condition is satisfied. The oscillation of x_i about X is due to the fact that the slopes are of opposite signs, as illustrated in Fig. 9–2.

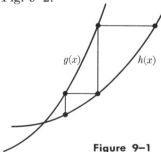

Figure 9–1

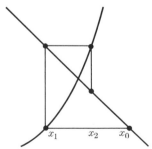

Figure 9–2

9–2 FALSE POSITION METHOD

The method of false position (*regula falsi*) is a very old one, which obviates the necessity of splitting the function into two additive parts, and avoids the calculation of an inverse function. However, it requires two starting approximations instead of one. The method is derived geometrically in Fig. 9–3. A secant is passed through the points corresponding to x_i and x_j on the curve $f(x)$, and the intersection of the secant with the x-axis yields the new approximation x_{i+1}. The slope λ_{ij} of the secant is given by

$$\lambda_{ij} = \frac{f(x_i) - f(x_j)}{x_i - x_j} = \frac{f(x_i)}{x_i - x_{i+1}}. \tag{9-4}$$

Solution of Eq. (9–4) for x_{i+1} yields the false-position method formula

$$x_{i+1} = x_i - f(x_i)\frac{x_i - x_j}{f(x_i) - f(x_j)}. \tag{9-5}$$

Once a third point has been obtained, the question of selecting a pair for the next iteration arises. Different choices are possible.

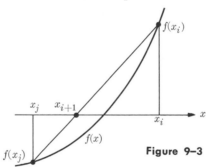

Figure 9–3

Variation 1. Choose $j = i - 1$. This variation is easily programmed, and will often move the limits in from both sides, yielding rapid convergence. It should be used with caution, however, because it is unsafe in many cases. Figure 9–4 shows a function and initial approximations for which the variation converges to the wrong root. Cases also exist for which the variation diverges.

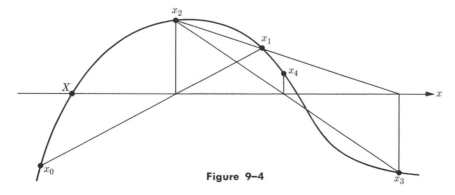

Figure 9–4

Variation 2. Choose i, j in such a manner that the root is always bracketed. Use the signs of the $f(x_i)$ to determine bracketing, and retain the most recent approximation on either side of the root. If the initial approximations lie on the same side of the root, there is of course no guarantee that any subsequent approximation will lie on the opposite side. However, the method cannot diverge, once the root is bracketed. Convergence is most rapid when the curvature of $y = f(x)$ changes sign in the interval near the root, as in Fig. 9–5.

Program 9–1

$$x_k \leftarrow x_i - y_i \frac{x_i - x_j}{y_i - y_j}$$

$$y_k \leftarrow f(x_k)$$

$$y_k : 0$$

$$x_i \leftarrow x_k$$

$$y_i \leftarrow y_k$$

$$x_j \leftarrow x_k$$

$$y_j \leftarrow y_k$$

This variation requires a slightly more complex program than does Variation 1. The heart of the process is presented as Program 9–1, in which $y_i = f(x_i)$ is assumed to be positive and $y_j = f(x_j)$, negative.

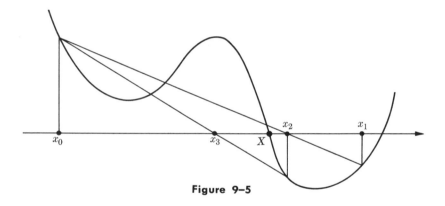

Figure 9–5

Example 9–2. *Variation* 1.

$$f(x) = e^x + x - 5. \quad x_0 = 1, x_1 = 2.$$

i	x_i	e^{x_i}	$f(x_i)$	i, j	x_{i+1}
0	1.00	2.72	-1.28		
1	2.00	7.39	$+4.39$	0, 1	1.226
2	1.226	3.41	-0.364	1, 2	1.285
3	1.285	3.615	-0.100	2, 3	1.308
4	1.308	3.699	$+0.007$	3, 4	1.3065
5	1.3065	3.6932	-0.0003	4, 5	1.30656
6	1.30656	3.69344	0.00000		

9–3 CONSTANT-SLOPE METHOD

Equation (9–5), the formula for the false-position method, can be rewritten as

$$x_{i+1} = x_i - \frac{f(x_i)}{\lambda}, \tag{9–6}$$

where λ is the slope of the line used to locate the next approximation. Ideally, λ should be the slope of the line through the points (x_i, y_i) and $(X, 0)$. The value of X is of course unknown, and an appropriate value of λ must be obtained without knowledge of X. In the constant-slope method, Eq. (9–6) is used with a constant value of λ. The simplest choices for λ are λ_{01} of the false-position method and $f'(x_0)$. The latter is the more common, and leads to the formula

$$x_{i+1} = x_i - \frac{f(x_i)}{f'(x_0)}, \tag{9–7}$$

whose use is illustrated graphically in Fig. 9–6 and numerically in Example 9–3.

Example 9–3

$$f(x) = e^x + x - 5,$$
$$f'(x) = e^x + 1,$$
$$x_0 = 1,$$
$$f'(x_0) = 3.7183 = \lambda.$$

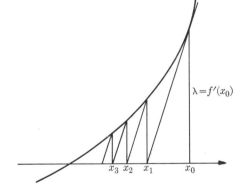

Figure 9–6

i	x_i	e^{x_i}	$f(x_i)$	$\dfrac{f(x_i)}{\lambda}$
0	1.00	2.7183	−1.2817	−0.3447
1	1.3447	3.8370	+0.1717	+0.0462
2	1.2985	3.6638	−0.0477	−0.0128
3	1.3113	3.7110	+0.0223	+0.0060
4	1.3053	3.6888	−0.0059	−0.0015
5	1.3068	3.6943	+0.0011	+0.0003
6	1.3065	3.6932	−0.0003	−0.00008
7	1.30658	3.69344	+0.00010	

9–4 NEWTON-RAPHSON METHOD

The powerful Newton-Raphson method may be viewed as the result of using each new approximation to X to obtain a better value of λ. After x_i has been obtained, λ is set equal to $f'(x_i)$ rather than to $f'(x_0)$, yielding the formula

$$x_{i+1} = x_i - \frac{f(x_i)}{f'(x_i)}. \tag{9–8}$$

The Newton-Raphson formula is illustrated graphically in Fig. 9–7 and numerically in Example 9–4.

Example 9–4

$$f(x) = e^x + x - 5,$$

$$f'(x) = e^x + 1,$$

$$x_{i+1} = x_i - \frac{e^{x_i} + x_i - 5}{e^{x_i} + 1}$$

$$= \frac{(x_i - 1)e^{x_i} + 5}{e^{x_i} + 1}.$$

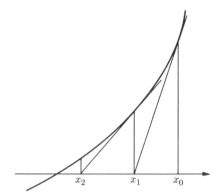

Figure 9–7

i	x_i	e^{x_i}	Numerator	Denominator
0	1.	2.7183	5.0000	3.7183
1	1.3447	3.8370	6.3226	4.8370
2	1.3071	3.6954	6.1349	4.6954
3	1.30658	3.69344	6.13233	4.69344
4	1.306575	3.693500	6.132335	4.693500
5	1.306559			

Note that the Newton-Raphson method converges much more rapidly than the methods described previously. The rapid convergence is obtained at the expense of more elaborate computation. Two limitations of the Newton-Raphson method are that convergence is slower if $f'(X)$ is near zero, and that a poor initial approximation may lead to divergence. The latter condition is illustrated in Fig. 9–8.

The rates of convergence of the iterative processes discussed thus far can be described in terms of a simple definition. The quantity a is said to be *of the order of* b^n if $\lim_{b \to 0} (a/b^n)$ is finite. This is generally written as $a = 0(b^n)$. The *order of convergence* of the iterative processes under discussion is defined in terms of

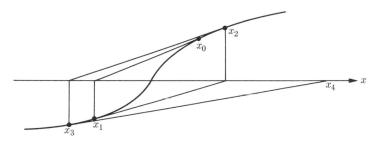

Figure 9–8

the errors ϵ_i and ϵ_{i+1} in successive approximations. These are given by the equation $X = x_i + \epsilon_i = x_{i+1} + \epsilon_{i+1}$. A process has kth order convergence if k is the greatest integer such that $\epsilon_{i+1} = 0(\epsilon_i^k)$.

Example 9–5

$$f(x) = x^2 - N,$$

$$f'(x) = 2x,$$

$$x_{i+1} = x_i - \frac{x_i^2 - N}{2x_i} = \frac{1}{2}\left(x_i + \frac{N}{x_i}\right).$$

This is the process used in Section 2–1(b) for square-root extraction, and it was shown in Exercise II–21 that it had second-order convergence.

It can be proved in general that the Newton-Raphson process exhibits second-order convergence, and that the methods of general iteration, false position, and constant slope generally exhibit first-order convergence. As a consequence, the number of correct digits beyond the radix point should approximately double with each iteration of the Newton-Raphson process. With first-order convergence, the number of significant digits should increase by about the same amount on each iteration.

Further iterative methods are also available. In some cases convergence is accelerated by the use of Eq. (9–6) with a value of λ equal to the mean of the false-position and Newton-Raphson slopes. Orders of convergence higher than the second are obtainable from formulas based on approximating $f(x)$ by a polynomial. Presentation of such formulas will be omitted, because of their relative infrequency of use and because of the need for Taylor series in most derivations.

Chapter 10

Systems of Linear Equations

A *linear* algebraic equation is one in which each variable appears, if at all, raised only to the first power, and multiplied by no other variable. A system of three linear equations in three variables is the following.

$$\begin{aligned} 2x - 4y + z &= 11, \\ 4x - 5y - 2z &= 7, \\ -2x - 5y + z &= 4. \end{aligned} \qquad (10\text{--}1)$$

Systems of this kind arise frequently in such diverse fields of study as electrical circuits, spectrographic analysis, and economic activity. The solution of differential equations, especially the partial differential equations of mathematical physics, often leads to the use of systems of linear algebraic equations.

Any one of the equations (10–1) clearly has many solutions x, y, z. The classic problem is to determine whether there exist any triples x, y, z that satisfy all three equations (10–1) simultaneously. It will be seen that when the number of equations equals the number of variables, there usually exists exactly one solution, although one must guard against exceptions, and the problem becomes the determination of that solution. The theory of systems of linear algebraic equations and the practice of solving such systems will be developed together.

10–1 GAUSS ELIMINATION

The existence of equivalent linear systems (systems which, although composed of different equations, have the same solution) has led to the development of *elimination* methods of solution. These methods proceed by multiplying equations by constants and adding equations together. Each equation is thus transformed into another equation which is satisfied by the solution of the original set. Gauss elimination is the easiest to follow of the several methods in common use. The following worksheet illustrates the solution of the system (10–1) by Gauss elimination. To the right of each equation is an identifying number and, for the equations derived from the first three, a summary of the derivation. The correctness of the results in the last three equations can be verified by substitution in the first three.

Example 10–1

$$
\begin{array}{llll}
\textcircled{$+2$}x & -4y & +1z = & 11 & (1,1) \\
+4x & -5y & -2z = & 7 & (2,1) \\
-2x & -5y & +1z = & 4 & (3,1) \\[4pt]
0 & \textcircled{$+3$}y & -4z = & -15 & (2,2) = (2,1) - \tfrac{4}{2}(1,1) \\[4pt]
0 & -9y & +2z = & 15 & (3,2) = (3,1) - \dfrac{-2}{2}(1,1) \\[4pt] \hline
0 & 0 & \textcircled{-10}z = & -30 & (3,3) = (3,2) - \dfrac{-9}{3}(2,2) \\[4pt]
+1x & -2y & +\tfrac{1}{2}z = & \tfrac{11}{2} & (1,4) = \tfrac{1}{2}(1,1) \\
0 & +1y & -\tfrac{4}{3}z = & -5 & (2,4) = \tfrac{1}{3}(2,2) \\
0 & 0 & 1z = & 3 & (3,4) = -\tfrac{1}{10}(3,3) \\[4pt] \hline
 & & z = & 3 & (3,5) = (3,4) \\[4pt]
 & y & = & -1 & (2,5) = (2,4) - (-\tfrac{4}{3})(3,5) \\[4pt]
x & & = & 2 & (1,5) = (1,4) - (-2)(2,5) - \tfrac{1}{2}(3,5)
\end{array}
$$

For any number of equations the process consists of three phases. The first, *triangularization*, eliminates the variables successively. An appropriate multiple of the first equation is subtracted from each of the remaining equations, yielding equations in which the coefficients of x are zero. Equation $(2, 2)$ is produced by subtracting from equation $(2, 1)$ the equation $(1, 1)$ multiplied by $\tfrac{4}{2}$. The multiplier $\tfrac{4}{2}$ is simply the ratio of the coefficients of x in $(2, 1)$ and $(1, 1)$. Equation $(3, 2)$ is similarly obtained. An appropriate multiple of $(2, 2)$ is then subtracted from each remaining equation in the second set (in this case only one equation), yielding $(3, 3)$, in which the coefficient of y is 0. If there were more equations, the process would be continued until only one new equation was produced. The resulting equations (i, i), if written on successive lines, would display zero coefficients in the lower left triangle of terms. The second phase is *normalization*, in which each equation (i, i) is multiplied by the reciprocal of its first nonzero coefficient. In the third phase, that of *back substitution*, the resulting equations are then solved successively for the variables. Because the normalization has reduced the first nonzero coefficient of each equation to unity, the back substitution requires no division by coefficients, as do the two preceding phases.

    The only operations performed are the multiplication of an equation by a constant and the addition to one equation of a constant multiple of another. The multipliers are determined only by numbers on the left-hand sides of the equations, and are independent of those on the right-hand sides. The process could therefore be carried out for several sets of right-hand sides simultaneously. The circled coefficients are known as *pivots*, and are used as divisors, that is, their reciprocals serve as multipliers. If a zero pivot is developed, the process cannot continue. This situation is examined in the following worksheets. The names of the variables and the equal signs are omitted for convenience.

Example 10–2

②	-1	3	-8	$(1, 1)$
4	-2	1	-6	$(2, 1)$
3	5	2	19	$(3, 1)$
0	⓪	-5	10	$(2, 2)$
0	$6\frac{1}{2}$	$-2\frac{1}{2}$	31	$(3, 2)$

A zero pivot appears in $(2, 2)$. This zero pivot can be avoided by permuting the first three rows, that is, by listing the given equations in a different order.

Example 10–3

②	-1	3	-8	$(1, 1)$
3	5	2	19	$(2, 1)$
4	-2	1	-6	$(3, 1)$
0	⑥½	$-2\frac{1}{2}$	31	$(2, 2)$
0	0	⊖5	10	$(3, 3) = (3, 2)$
1	$-\frac{1}{2}$	$1\frac{1}{2}$	-4	$(1, 4)$
0	1	$-\frac{5}{13}$	$\frac{62}{13}$	$(2, 4)$
0	0	1	-2	$(3, 4)$
			$z = -2$	$(3, 5)$
	y		4	$(2, 5)$
x			1	$(1, 5)$

Unfortunately, one does not generally know in advance what row interchanges will be required. Consider next the following two systems of equations.

Example 10–4

②	1	-1	0
1	2	1	0
-1	1	2	0
0	①½	$1\frac{1}{2}$	0
0	$1\frac{1}{2}$	$1\frac{1}{2}$	0
0	0	⓪	0

In this system, any value of z will satisfy the last equation, because $0z = 0$ for all z. For any arbitrarily chosen z, the other equations yield $x = z$ and

$y = -z$. There is thus an infinite family of solutions to the system of equations. In the next system it will be seen that there is no solution at all.

Example 10–5

$$
\begin{array}{cccc}
② & 1 & -1 & 1 \\
1 & 2 & 1 & 2 \\
2 & 4 & 2 & 3 \\
\hline
0 & (1\tfrac{1}{2}) & 1\tfrac{1}{2} & 1\tfrac{1}{2} \\
0 & 3 & 3 & 2 \\
\hline
0 & 0 & ⓪ & -1
\end{array}
$$

The two systems just presented are examples of *singular* systems. In each case, an unavoidable zero pivot appeared.

10–2 MATRIX NOTATION

Consider next the general system of m linear algebraic equations in n unknowns

$$
\begin{aligned}
a_{11}x_1 + a_{12}x_2 + \cdots + a_{1n}x_n &= b_1, \\
a_{21}x_1 + a_{22}x_2 + \cdots + a_{2n}x_n &= b_2, \\
&\ \vdots \\
a_{m1}x_1 + a_{m2}x_2 + \cdots + a_{mn}x_n &= b_m.
\end{aligned}
\tag{10–2}
$$

The system (10–2) can be represented in condensed notation as $\mathbf{Ax} = \mathbf{b}$, where $\mathbf{A}$ is a two-dimensional array, or *matrix*, of mn elements and $\mathbf{x}$ and $\mathbf{b}$ are one-dimensional arrays, or (column) *vectors*, of n and m elements, respectively. The arrays may be written as

$$
\mathbf{A} =
\begin{pmatrix}
a_{11} & a_{12} & \cdots & a_{1n} \\
a_{21} & a_{22} & \cdots & a_{2n} \\
\vdots & & & \vdots \\
a_{m1} & a_{m2} & \cdots & a_{mn}
\end{pmatrix},
\qquad
\mathbf{x} =
\begin{pmatrix}
x_1 \\ x_2 \\ \vdots \\ x_n
\end{pmatrix},
\qquad
\mathbf{b} =
\begin{pmatrix}
b_1 \\ b_2 \\ \vdots \\ b_m
\end{pmatrix}.
$$

One may also write $\mathbf{A} = \{a_{ij}\}$, where i is the *row index* and j the *column index* of the general element a_{ij}. Similarly $\mathbf{x} = \{x_j\}$ and $\mathbf{b} = \{b_i\}$. It is also customary to write $[\mathbf{A}]_{ij} = a_{ij}$. The ith equation of the system (10–2) may be written as

$$
\sum_{j=1}^{n} a_{ij}x_j = b_i.
\tag{10–3}
$$

The matrix $\mathbf{A}$ is said to be of dimensions m by n, and the vectors $\mathbf{x}$ and $\mathbf{b}$ can be considered to be matrices of a single column, with dimensions n by 1 and

m by 1, respectively. For the multiplication $\mathbf{Ax} = \mathbf{b}$, the dimensions may be written side by side as

$$(m \text{ by } n)(n \text{ by } 1) = (m \text{ by } 1),$$

and the inner dimensions are seen to cancel. The original system of equations (10–1) may be written in the matrix notation, together with the solution, as

$$\begin{pmatrix} 2 & -4 & 1 \\ 4 & -5 & -2 \\ -2 & -5 & 1 \end{pmatrix} \begin{pmatrix} x \\ y \\ z \end{pmatrix} = \begin{pmatrix} 11 \\ 7 \\ 4 \end{pmatrix}, \qquad \begin{pmatrix} x \\ y \\ z \end{pmatrix} = \begin{pmatrix} 2 \\ -1 \\ 3 \end{pmatrix}.$$

The solution can be verified by using Eq. (10–3) to perform the multiplication.

$$\begin{pmatrix} 2 & -4 & 1 \\ 4 & -5 & -2 \\ -2 & -5 & 1 \end{pmatrix} \begin{pmatrix} 2 \\ -1 \\ 3 \end{pmatrix} = \begin{pmatrix} 11 \\ 7 \\ 4 \end{pmatrix}.$$

The element $b_2 = 7$ is obtained from

$$b_2 = \sum_{j=1}^{3} a_{2j} x_j = (4)(2) + (-5)(-1) + (-2)(3) = 8 + 5 - 6 = 7.$$

Suppose that $\mathbf{y} = \mathbf{Bx}$ and $\mathbf{z} = \mathbf{Ay}$, where $\mathbf{A}$, $\mathbf{B}$ are matrices and $\mathbf{x}$, $\mathbf{y}$, $\mathbf{z}$ are column vectors. Then $\mathbf{z} = \mathbf{A(Bx)}$. Presumably there exists some matrix $\mathbf{C}$ such that $\mathbf{z} = \mathbf{Cx}$. A multiplication of matrices will now be defined so that $\mathbf{Cx} = \mathbf{A(Bx)}$ and it will therefore be possible to write $\mathbf{C} = \mathbf{AB}$ or $\mathbf{z} = (\mathbf{AB})\mathbf{x}$.

The dimensions of the various matrices and vectors will be as shown in Table 10–1. Equation (10–3) will then be applied to the various products in question:

$$z_i = \sum_{j=1}^{n} a_{ij} y_j, \qquad y_j = \sum_{k=1}^{p} b_{jk} x_k;$$

therefore,

$$z_i = \sum_{j=1}^{n} a_{ij} \sum_{k=1}^{p} b_{jk} x_k = \sum_{k=1}^{p} \left(\sum_{j=1}^{n} a_{ij} b_{jk} \right) x_k,$$

but

$$z_i = \sum_{k=1}^{p} c_{ik} x_k;$$

therefore,

$$c_{ik} = \sum_{j=1}^{n} a_{ij} b_{jk} \tag{10–4}$$

defines

$$\mathbf{C} = \mathbf{AB}.$$

Table 10–1

Matrix	Dimension	Reason
x	$p \times 1$	Assumption
B	$n \times p$	Deduce p, assume n
y	$n \times 1$	Deduce n
A	$m \times n$	Deduce n, assume m
z	$m \times 1$	Deduce m
C	$m \times p$	Deduce m, p

Example 10–6

$$A = \begin{pmatrix} -1 & -2 \\ 1 & 3 \end{pmatrix}, \quad B = \begin{pmatrix} 2 & -1 \\ 1 & 3 \end{pmatrix}, \quad x = \begin{pmatrix} -2 \\ 1 \end{pmatrix},$$

$$y = Bx = \begin{pmatrix} 2 & -1 \\ 1 & 3 \end{pmatrix}\begin{pmatrix} -2 \\ 1 \end{pmatrix} = \begin{pmatrix} -5 \\ 1 \end{pmatrix},$$

$$z = Ay = \begin{pmatrix} -1 & -2 \\ 1 & 3 \end{pmatrix}\begin{pmatrix} -5 \\ 1 \end{pmatrix} = \begin{pmatrix} 3 \\ -2 \end{pmatrix},$$

$$C = AB = \begin{pmatrix} -1 & -2 \\ 1 & 3 \end{pmatrix}\begin{pmatrix} 2 & -1 \\ 1 & 3 \end{pmatrix} = \begin{pmatrix} -4 & -5 \\ 5 & 8 \end{pmatrix},$$

$$Cx = \begin{pmatrix} -4 & -5 \\ 5 & 8 \end{pmatrix}\begin{pmatrix} -2 \\ 1 \end{pmatrix} = \begin{pmatrix} 3 \\ -2 \end{pmatrix} = z.$$

The matrices used in the example are square, but this is not necessary. It is required only that the pairs of matrices being multiplied be *conformable*. This means that the number of columns of the left-hand factor is equal to the number of rows of the right-hand factor. If a column vector or row vector (a single horizontal row of elements) is considered a special case of a matrix, then the conformability requirement holds for all products among vectors and matrices. Five common situations are summarized in Table 10–2.

Table 10–2

Left factor	Right factor	Product
Square matrix	Column vector	Column vector
Square matrix	Square matrix	Square matrix
Row vector	Square matrix	Row vector
Row vector	Column vector	Single element (1×1 matrix)
Column vector	Row vector	Matrix

10–3 ELEMENTARY PROPERTIES

Some of the properties of matrix multiplication will now be investigated. It is natural to inquire whether matrix multiplication is *commutative*, that is whether $\mathbf{AB} = \mathbf{BA}$ holds in general. The two products both exist only if $\mathbf{A}$ has dimensions m by n and $\mathbf{B}$ has dimensions n by m. Because the two products can be of the same dimensions only if $m = n$, it makes sense only for square matrices even to speak of commutativity. It is easily verified for the matrices of Example 10–6 that

$$\mathbf{AB} = \begin{pmatrix} -4 & -5 \\ 5 & 8 \end{pmatrix} \quad \text{and} \quad \mathbf{BA} = \begin{pmatrix} -3 & -7 \\ 2 & 7 \end{pmatrix}.$$

Matrix multiplication is therefore not commutative. Every square matrix does commute, however, with the *unit matrix* $\mathbf{I}$ of the same dimension. The unit matrix is a square matrix with elements 1 on the *main diagonal* and 0 elsewhere.

$$[\mathbf{I}]_{ij} = \begin{cases} 1 & \text{for } i = j, \\ 0 & \text{for } i \neq j. \end{cases}$$

It is easily verified by application of Eq. (10–4) that $\mathbf{AI} = \mathbf{A} = \mathbf{IA}$ for all square matrices $\mathbf{A}$. For example,

$$\begin{pmatrix} 1 & 2 \\ 1 & 1 \end{pmatrix}\begin{pmatrix} 1 & 0 \\ 0 & 1 \end{pmatrix} = \begin{pmatrix} 1 & 2 \\ 1 & 1 \end{pmatrix} = \begin{pmatrix} 1 & 0 \\ 0 & 1 \end{pmatrix}\begin{pmatrix} 1 & 2 \\ 1 & 1 \end{pmatrix}.$$

The unit matrix $\mathbf{I}$ is said to be an *identity* for the operation of matrix multiplication, because it leaves any other matrix unchanged, or *invariant*. It can be shown that it is the only identity. The columns of the unit matrix are the unit (column) vectors,

$$\mathbf{e}^1 = \begin{pmatrix} 1 \\ 0 \\ \vdots \\ 0 \end{pmatrix}, \quad \mathbf{e}^2 = \begin{pmatrix} 0 \\ 1 \\ \vdots \\ 0 \end{pmatrix}, \dots, \quad \mathbf{e}^n = \begin{pmatrix} 0 \\ 0 \\ \vdots \\ 1 \end{pmatrix},$$

each of which has all components equal to 0 except one component equal to 1.

The multiplication of real or complex numbers is *associative*, because $(xy)z = x(yz)$ for any three numbers x, y, z. It is easily shown that matrix multiplication, although not commutative, is indeed associative, as has actually been shown already for the case in which the rightmost matrix is a column vector. Equation (10–4) is applied to the general case as follows:

$$[(\mathbf{AB})\mathbf{C}]_{ij} = \sum_l \left(\sum_k a_{ik}b_{kl} \right) c_{lj},$$

$$[\mathbf{A}(\mathbf{BC})]_{ij} = \sum_k a_{ik} \left(\sum_l b_{kl}c_{lj} \right).$$

The two expressions are seen to be equal, and it follows immediately that $(\mathbf{AB})\mathbf{C} = \mathbf{A}(\mathbf{BC})$. The product may therefore be unambiguously written $\mathbf{ABC}$.

Two matrices $\mathbf{A}$ and $\mathbf{B}$ of the same dimensions are said to be *equal* if and only if $a_{ij} = b_{ij}$. This definition has been tacitly assumed in the foregoing discussion. *Addition* of two matrices of the same dimensions is defined by $[\mathbf{A} + \mathbf{B}]_{ij} = a_{ij} + b_{ij}$. *Scalar multiplication* of a matrix $\mathbf{A}$ by a scalar, or single element, α is defined by $[\alpha\mathbf{A}]_{ij} = \alpha a_{ij}$. Scalar multiplication by α is equivalent to matrix multiplication by $\alpha\mathbf{I}$. The result of scalar multiplication by $\alpha = 0$ is the zero matrix $\mathbf{0}$. This matrix is one whose every element is 0 and it is the unique identity for the operation of addition, because $\mathbf{A} + \mathbf{0} = \mathbf{A} = \mathbf{0} + \mathbf{A}$.

10–4 INVERSES

By a *right inverse* of the matrix $\mathbf{A}$ is meant a matrix $\mathbf{A}_r^{-1}$ such that $\mathbf{AA}_r^{-1} = \mathbf{I}$. By a *left inverse* is meant a matrix $\mathbf{A}_l^{-1}$ such that $\mathbf{A}_l^{-1}\mathbf{A} = \mathbf{I}$. A given matrix may or may not have a right or left inverse.

Example 10–7. The matrix

$$\mathbf{A} = \begin{pmatrix} 0.2 & 0.0 & 0.2 \\ 0.2 & 0.4 & 0.0 \end{pmatrix}$$

has a right inverse

$$\mathbf{A}_r^{-1} = \begin{pmatrix} 4 & 1 \\ -2 & 2 \\ 1 & -1 \end{pmatrix}$$

because

$$\begin{pmatrix} 0.2 & 0.0 & 0.2 \\ 0.2 & 0.4 & 0.0 \end{pmatrix}\begin{pmatrix} 4 & 1 \\ -2 & 2 \\ 1 & -1 \end{pmatrix} = \begin{pmatrix} 1 & 0 \\ 0 & 1 \end{pmatrix}.$$

It is easily verified that $\mathbf{A}_r^{-1}$ is not a left inverse of $\mathbf{A}$.

Theorem 10–1. A right inverse of a square matrix is also a left inverse.

Proof: Let $\mathbf{A}_r^{-1}$ be a right inverse of $\mathbf{A}$. By the squareness of $\mathbf{A}$ and associativity, one may write

$$\mathbf{A}(\mathbf{A}_r^{-1}\mathbf{A}) = (\mathbf{AA}_r^{-1})\mathbf{A} = \mathbf{IA} = \mathbf{A}.$$

Thus $(\mathbf{A}_r^{-1}\mathbf{A})$ is a multiplicative identity matrix for $\mathbf{A}$. But $\mathbf{A}$ is arbitrary and the only identity for an arbitrary matrix is $\mathbf{I}$. Therefore $\mathbf{A}_r^{-1}\mathbf{A} = \mathbf{I}$ and $\mathbf{A}_r^{-1}$ is seen to be a left inverse of $\mathbf{A}$ as well. As a result one customarily writes merely $\mathbf{A}^{-1}$ as an *inverse* of $\mathbf{A}$.

Example 10–8. The matrix

$$\mathbf{B} = \begin{pmatrix} -1 & 2 \\ 4 & 2 \end{pmatrix}$$

has an inverse

$$\mathbf{B}^{-1} = \begin{pmatrix} -0.2 & 0.2 \\ 0.4 & 0.1 \end{pmatrix}.$$

The reader should verify that $\mathbf{BB}^{-1} = \mathbf{I} = \mathbf{B}^{-1}\mathbf{B}$.

If a square matrix has no inverse, it is said to be *singular*. Otherwise its inverse is unique, as proved in the following theorem.

Theorem 10–2. A square matrix has at most one inverse.

Proof: Let $\mathbf{B}$ be some inverse of $\mathbf{A}$, which has inverse $\mathbf{A}^{-1}$.

$$\mathbf{AB} = \mathbf{I},$$
$$\mathbf{A}^{-1}\mathbf{AB} = \mathbf{A}^{-1}\mathbf{I},$$
$$\mathbf{IB} = \mathbf{A}^{-1}\mathbf{I},$$
$$\mathbf{B} = \mathbf{A}^{-1}.$$

10–5 DETERMINANTS

With every square matrix $\mathbf{A}$ is associated an important number known as its *determinant* and usually designated $|\mathbf{A}|$. It is defined as

$$|\mathbf{A}| = \Sigma(-1)^{\sigma} a_{1\alpha} a_{2\beta} \ldots a_{n\nu}, \tag{10–5}$$

where $\alpha, \beta, \ldots, \nu$ is a permutation of $1, 2, \ldots, n$, the summation is over all $n!$ permutations, and σ equals 1 for odd* permutations and 0 for even permutations.

Example 10–9

$$\mathbf{A} = \begin{pmatrix} 2 & -4 & 1 \\ 4 & -5 & -2 \\ -2 & -5 & 1 \end{pmatrix}.$$

$\alpha\ \beta\ \gamma$	$a_{1\alpha}$	$a_{2\beta}$	$a_{3\gamma}$	$(-1)^{\sigma}$	Product
1 2 3	2	-5	1	$+1$	-10
1 3 2	2	-2	-5	-1	-20
2 1 3	-4	4	1	-1	$+16$
2 3 1	-4	-2	-2	$+1$	-16
3 1 2	1	4	-5	$+1$	-20
3 2 1	1	-5	-2	-1	-10
				$|\mathbf{A}| =$	-60

---

* A permutation is said to be odd or even accordingly as the number of interchanges of adjacent elements required to restore the original order is odd or even.

A method commonly taught for the evaluation of determinants is the following. All columns except the last are written in the original order to the right of the complete matrix.

$$\begin{array}{rrr|rr} 2 & -4 & 1 & 2 & -4 \\ 4 & -5 & -2 & 4 & -5 \\ -2 & -5 & 1 & -2 & -5. \end{array}$$

Products of elements along all 45° diagonals of length equal to the order of the matrix are then taken. Terms contributed by diagonals sloping down to the right are added positively; those contributed by diagonals sloping up to the right are added negatively. The resulting sum is the determinant. It is not always realized that this method is valid *only* for $n = 3$. For larger n, evaluation from the definition (10–5) is extremely cumbersome. Other methods will be developed after the following proofs of several properties of determinants.

Theorem 10–3. Interchanging two rows of $\mathbf{A}$ reverses the sign of $|\mathbf{A}|$.

Proof: Let $\mathbf{A}'$ be the result of interchanging rows k, l of $\mathbf{A}$. To every term

$$(-1)^\sigma a_{1\alpha} \ldots a_{k\kappa} \ldots a_{l\lambda} \ldots a_{n\nu}$$

in the expansion (10–5) of $|\mathbf{A}|$ corresponds the term

$$(-1)^{\sigma'} a_{1\alpha} \ldots a_{l\lambda} \ldots a_{k\kappa} \ldots a_{n\nu}$$

in the expansion of $|\mathbf{A}'|$. The matrix elements in the two terms are identical, but $\sigma' = 1 - \sigma$ because the interchange of κ, λ alone is always an odd permutation. Therefore the two terms have equal magnitude and opposite sign, and so must their sums $|\mathbf{A}|$ and $|\mathbf{A}'|$.

Theorem 10–4. If two rows of $\mathbf{A}$ are identical, $|\mathbf{A}| = 0$.

Proof: By Theorem 10–3, interchange of the identical rows yields $|\mathbf{A}| = -|\mathbf{A}|$, which is satisfied only by $|\mathbf{A}| = 0$.

Theorem 10–5. The addition to one row of $\mathbf{A}$ of a multiple of another row leaves $|\mathbf{A}|$ invariant.

Proof: Let $\mathbf{B}$ be obtained from $\mathbf{A}$ by replacing a_{lj} by $a_{lj} + k a_{mj}$.

$$|\mathbf{B}| = \Sigma(-1)^\sigma a_{1\alpha} \ldots (a_{l\lambda} + k a_{m\lambda}) \ldots a_{m\mu} \ldots a_{n\nu}$$
$$= \Sigma(-1)^\sigma a_{1\alpha} \ldots a_{l\lambda} \ldots a_{m\mu} \ldots a_{n\nu} + k\Sigma(-1)^\sigma a_{1\alpha} \ldots a_{m\lambda} \ldots a_{m\mu} \ldots a_{n\nu}$$
$$= |\mathbf{A}| + 0 = |\mathbf{A}|,$$

because the second term is the determinant of a matrix with two equal rows. Similar theorems can be proved for the corresponding column operations.

10–6 COMPUTATIONAL METHODS

The use of the Gauss elimination process to compute the determinant of a matrix is now easily described. In the triangularization phase of the process, the only operation performed is the addition of a multiple of one row to another row. At any intermediate stage, therefore, the determinant of the resulting matrix $\mathbf{A}'$ is equal to that of the original matrix $\mathbf{A}$. After elimination has been performed on the first k rows, the resulting matrix has the following partitioned form.

$$
\mathbf{A}' =
\left(
\begin{array}{cccc:c}
\textcircled{x} & x & \cdots & x & \\
0 & \textcircled{x} & \cdots & x & \\
\vdots & & & \vdots & \mathbf{M}' \\
0 & 0 & \cdots & \textcircled{x} & \\
\hdashline
& & 0 & & \mathbf{M}
\end{array}
\right).
$$

The upper left-hand submatrix is a triangular k by k matrix with pivots on the main diagonal. The lower right-hand submatrix $\mathbf{M}$ is an $n - k$ by $n - k$ matrix whose elements are those of $\mathbf{A}$. As a result, every nonzero term in $|\mathbf{A}'|$ must have the form

$$
(-1)^{\sigma} a'_{11} a'_{22} \ldots a'_{kk} a_{k+1,\mu} \ldots a_{n\nu},
$$

where μ through ν are a permutation of $k + 1$ through n, and a'_{ij} is an element of $\mathbf{A}'$ only, but a_{ij} is an element of both $\mathbf{A}$ and $\mathbf{A}'$. It follows that

$$
\begin{aligned}
|\mathbf{A}'| &= \Sigma(-1)^{\sigma} a'_{11} a'_{22} \ldots a'_{kk} a_{k+1,\mu} \ldots a_{n\nu} \\
&= a'_{11} a'_{22} \ldots a'_{kk} \Sigma(-1)^{\sigma} a_{k+1,\mu} \ldots a_{n\nu} \\
&= a'_{11} a'_{22} \ldots a'_{kk} |\mathbf{M}|.
\end{aligned}
$$

The exponent σ is unchanged by factoring out the a'_{ii}, because they contribute no interchanges. Inasmuch as the a'_{ii} are the pivots and $|\mathbf{A}'| = |\mathbf{A}|$, the foregoing development constitutes a proof of Theorem 10–6.

> **Theorem 10–6.** At any intermediate stage of the solution of $\mathbf{Ax} = \mathbf{b}$ by Gauss elimination, the product of the pivots already found and the determinant of the remaining square submatrix of $\mathbf{A}$ is $|\mathbf{A}|$.

It is clear that at the end of the triangularization phase the product of all n pivots is the determinant. This observation provides the most convenient method for obtaining the determinant of a large matrix.

> **Theorem 10–7.** $\mathbf{Ax} = \mathbf{b}$ has a unique solution if and only if $\mathbf{A}$ is nonsingular (that is, if and only if $\mathbf{A}^{-1}$ exists).

Proof of "if" statement: If A^{-1} exists, then $x = A^{-1}b$ is a solution, because

$$Ax = A(A^{-1}b) = (AA^{-1})b = Ib = b.$$

The solution x is unique, because $Ay = b$ implies that

$$y = Iy = (A^{-1}A)y = A^{-1}(Ay) = A^{-1}b = x.$$

Proof of "only if" statement: If b is set equal in turn to the unit column vectors $e^1, \ldots, e^n$, then unique solutions $x^1, \ldots, x^n$ are obtained. These solutions can then be juxtaposed to form the matrix $X = x^1 \mid x^2 \mid \ldots \mid x^n$. Then

$$
\begin{aligned}
AX &= A(x^1 \mid x^2 \mid \ldots \mid x^n), \\
&= Ax^1 \mid Ax^2 \mid \ldots \mid Ax^n, \\
&= e^1 \mid e^2 \mid \ldots \mid e^n = I,
\end{aligned}
$$

and X is therefore the inverse of A.

The last part of the proof of Theorem 10–7 gives a method for inverting a matrix. The entire Gauss elimination process can be carried out simultaneously for all n unit vectors as b, as illustrated in Example 10–10.

Example 10–10

1	0	1	1	0	0	$(1, 1)$
1	2	0	0	1	0	$(2, 1)$
0	1	2	0	0	1	$(3, 1)$
0	2	-1	-1	1	0	$(2, 2) = (2, 1) - (1, 1)$
0	0	-5	-1	1	-2	$(3, 3) = (2, 2) - 2(3, 1)$
1	0	1	1	0	0	$(1, 4) = (1, 1)$
0	1	2	0	0	1	$(2, 4) = (3, 1)$
0	0	1	0.2	-0.2	0.4	$(3, 4) = -\frac{1}{5}(3, 3)$
1	0	0	0.8	0.2	-0.4	$(1, 5) = (1, 4) - (3, 4)$
0	1	0	-0.4	0.4	0.2	$(2, 5) = (2, 4) - 2(3, 4)$
0	0	1	0.2	-0.2	0.4	$(3, 5) = (3, 4)$

The inverse of $\begin{pmatrix} 1 & 0 & 1 \\ 1 & 2 & 0 \\ 0 & 1 & 2 \end{pmatrix}$ is thus found to be $\frac{1}{5}\begin{pmatrix} 4 & 1 & -2 \\ -2 & 2 & 1 \\ 1 & -1 & 2 \end{pmatrix}$,

as can easily be verified.

Theorem 10–8. $\mathbf{Ax} = \mathbf{b}$ has a unique solution if and only if $|\mathbf{A}| \neq 0$.

Proof: Consider the Gauss elimination process. If no zero pivots occur, then back substitution yields a unique solution and the product of the pivots is a nonzero $|\mathbf{A}|$. If a zero pivot occurs, it may be possible to eliminate it by row interchanges (changing the order of the equations) or column interchanges* (changing the order of the variables). Either change may reverse the sign of $|\mathbf{A}|$, but the determinant will remain zero or nonzero. If nonzero pivots can be found each time, then the earlier discussion applies. If no nonzero pivot is obtainable, then the reduced matrix $\mathbf{M}$ is $\mathbf{0}$ and the intermediate results have this form:

$$
\left(
\begin{array}{cccc|c}
a'_{11} & x & \cdots & x & \\
0 & a'_{22} & \cdots & x & \mathbf{M'} \\
\vdots & & & \vdots & \\
0 & 0 & \cdots & a'_{kk} & \\
\hline
& & \mathbf{0} & & \mathbf{0}
\end{array}
\right)
\left(
\begin{array}{c}
x_1 \\
x_2 \\
\vdots \\
x_k \\
\hline
x_{k+1} \\
\vdots \\
x_n
\end{array}
\right)
=
\left(
\begin{array}{c}
b'_1 \\
b'_2 \\
\vdots \\
b'_k \\
\hline
b'_{k+1} \\
\vdots \\
b'_n
\end{array}
\right).
$$

Here $|\mathbf{A}| = |\mathbf{A'}| = 0$ because $|\mathbf{M}| = 0$. If $\mathbf{y}$ is defined as the column vector whose components are $x_{k+1}, \ldots, x_n$ and $\mathbf{c}$ as the column vector with components $b'_{k+1}, \ldots, b'_n$, then the last $n - k$ equations may be written as $\mathbf{0y} = \mathbf{c}$. If $\mathbf{c} = \mathbf{0}$, then $\mathbf{y}$ is arbitrary and there exists, not a unique solution, but an $(n - k)$-fold infinity of solutions. If $\mathbf{c} \neq \mathbf{0}$, then the equations are inconsistent and there is no solution at all.

A direct consequence of Theorems 10–7 and 10–8 is the following theorem.

Theorem 10–9. $\mathbf{A}$ is nonsingular if and only if $|\mathbf{A}| \neq 0$.

10–7 ACCURACY

A useful diagnostic check against errors in computation is provided by the incorporation of a check column. For the given equations, the element in this column is set equal to the negative of the sum of the other elements in its row. The sum of all row elements will therefore equal zero. The computations are then carried out on the array with the check column included. The elements of each newly generated row, obtained by adding to one row a multiple of another, must also sum to zero. The use of the check column is illustrated in Example 10–11, which incorporates the worksheet of Example 10–10. A final check is provided, of course, by substitution in the original equation.

---

* Each column interchange must be accompanied by the corresponding interchange of elements of $\mathbf{b}$.

Example 10–11

1	0	1	1	0	0	-3
1	2	0	0	1	0	-4
0	1	2	0	0	1	-4

0	2	-1	-1	1	0	-1
0	0	-5	-1	1	-2	7

1	0	1	1	0	0	-3
0	1	2	0	0	1	-4
0	0	1	0.2	-0.2	0.4	-1.4

1	0	0	0.8	0.2	-0.4	-1.6
0	1	0	-0.4	0.4	0.2	-1.2
0	0	1	0.2	-0.2	0.4	-1.4

In considering the accuracy of a presumed solution to the problem of inverting a matrix, care should be taken to distinguish the *error* from the *residual*.
Let $\mathbf{X}_n$ be an approximate solution of the equation $\mathbf{AX} = \mathbf{I}$, whose exact solution is $\mathbf{X} = \mathbf{A}^{-1}$. The residual is defined as $\mathbf{R}_n = \mathbf{I} - \mathbf{AX}_n$ and the error is
defined as $\mathbf{E}_n = \mathbf{A}^{-1} - \mathbf{X}_n$. The error is the amount by which the approximate
solution differs from the (unknown) exact solution. The residual is the amount
by which the product of the given matrix by the approximate solution differs
from the (known) unit matrix. It can be verified from the definitions that the
residual and error are related by the equations $\mathbf{R}_n = \mathbf{AE}_n$ and $\mathbf{E}_n = \mathbf{A}^{-1}\mathbf{R}_n$.
Thus the error can be estimated from a knowledge of the residual, provided
that a good approximation to $\mathbf{A}^{-1}$ is available.

For well-behaved matrices, a small residual is a good indication of a small
error. However, if $|\mathbf{A}|$ is nonzero but nearly equal to zero, $\mathbf{A}^{-1}$ will contain
very large elements. In such a case, a small residual may conceal a large error.
A matrix $\mathbf{A}$ with this property is said to be *ill-conditioned*. For example, consider the approximation
$$\begin{pmatrix} 102 & -101 \\ -101 & 101 \end{pmatrix}$$
to the inverse of
$$\mathbf{A} = \begin{pmatrix} 1 & 1 \\ 1 & 1.01 \end{pmatrix}.$$
It is easily found that the residual is only
$$\begin{pmatrix} 0 & 0 \\ 0.01 & -0.01 \end{pmatrix}$$
but that the error is
$$\begin{pmatrix} -1 & 1 \\ 1 & -1 \end{pmatrix}.$$
The value of $|\mathbf{A}|$ is only 0.01.

10-8 ITERATIVE IMPROVEMENTS

Given an approximation $\mathbf{X}_n$ to $\mathbf{A}^{-1}$, an improved approximation $\mathbf{X}_{n+1}$ can be obtained by the following method:

$$\mathbf{A}^{-1} = \mathbf{X}_n + \mathbf{E}_n,$$
$$\mathbf{A}^{-1} = \mathbf{X}_n + \mathbf{A}^{-1}\mathbf{R}_n,$$
$$\mathbf{X}_{n+1} = \mathbf{X}_n + \mathbf{X}_n\mathbf{R}_n \qquad \text{(using } \mathbf{X}_n \text{ as the best value for } \mathbf{A}^{-1}\text{)},$$
$$\mathbf{X}_{n+1} = \mathbf{X}_n + \mathbf{X}_n(\mathbf{I} - \mathbf{A}\mathbf{X}_n),$$
$$\mathbf{X}_{n+1} = 2\mathbf{X}_n - \mathbf{X}_n\mathbf{A}\mathbf{X}_n = \mathbf{X}_n(2\mathbf{I} - \mathbf{A}\mathbf{X}_n).$$

The last form of the equation corresponds to the Newton-Raphson formula $x_{n+1} = x_n(2 - Nx_n)$ for improving an approximation to the reciprocal (multiplicative inverse) of a real number N. It can be shown that the matrix form of the Newton-Raphson process has second-order convergence, as does the other form.

An iterative method frequently used for systems of the form $\mathbf{Ax} = \mathbf{b}$ is that of Seidel. The ith equation of the system,

$$\sum_{j=1}^{n} a_{ij}x_j = b_i, \tag{10-3}$$

is solved for x_i by substituting for each x_j $(j \neq i)$ the latest approximation obtained. Thus, if $x_j^{(k)}$ is the kth approximation to x_j, then

$$x_i^{(k+1)} = \frac{1}{a_{ii}}\left[b_i - \sum_{j=1}^{i-1} a_{ij}x_j^{(k+1)} - \sum_{j=i+1}^{n} a_{ij}x_j^{(k)} \right]. \tag{10-6}$$

There is no assurance in general that the process will converge, and the known conditions for convergence are not easily tested in practice. Moreover, convergence is of the first order at best, and is often irregular. Because of the division by a_{ii} in Eq. (10-6), it is helpful to arrange the equations so that the pivots are large in magnitude. For example,

the system   may be rewritten as

$$\begin{pmatrix} 1 & 2 & 3 \\ 2 & -1 & -3 \\ 4 & 1 & 1 \end{pmatrix} \mathbf{x} = \begin{pmatrix} 5 \\ -3 \\ 5 \end{pmatrix} \qquad \begin{pmatrix} 4 & 1 & 1 \\ 1 & 2 & 3 \\ 2 & -1 & -3 \end{pmatrix} \mathbf{x} = \begin{pmatrix} 5 \\ 5 \\ -3 \end{pmatrix}.$$

These equations, written in full as

$$4x_1 + 1x_2 + 1x_3 = 5,$$
$$1x_1 + 2x_2 + 3x_3 = 5,$$
$$2x_1 - 1x_2 - 3x_3 = -3,$$

yield the relations

$$x_1 = \tfrac{1}{4}(5 - x_2 - x_3),$$
$$x_2 = \tfrac{1}{2}(5 - x_1 - 3x_3),$$
$$x_3 = \tfrac{1}{3}(3 + 2x_1 - x_2).$$

It follows that

$$x_1^{(k+1)} = \tfrac{1}{4}(5 - x_2^{(k)} - x_3^{(k)}),$$
$$x_2^{(k+1)} = \tfrac{1}{2}(5 - x_1^{(k+1)} - 3x_3^{(k)}),$$
$$x_3^{(k+1)} = \tfrac{1}{3}(3 + 2x_1^{(k+1)} - x_2^{(k+1)}).$$

The Seidel method may be used either to refine an approximate solution obtained by another method, or to solve $\mathbf{Ax} = \mathbf{b}$ from an arbitrary initial approximation. The work is terminated as soon as two successive values for each x_i differ by less than a preassigned tolerance. If $\mathbf{x} = \mathbf{0}$ is chosen as an initial approximation, and computations are carried to three places beyond the decimal point, the following successive vectors $\mathbf{x}^{(k)}$ are obtained.

Example 10–12

k	$x_1^{(k)}$	$x_2^{(k)}$	$x_3^{(k)}$	k	$x_1^{(k)}$	$x_2^{(k)}$	$x_3^{(k)}$
0	0.000	0.000	0.000	14	0.992	−0.957	1.980
1	1.250	1.875	1.208	15	0.994	−0.967	1.985
2	0.479	0.499	1.166	16	0.996	−0.976	1.989
3	0.844	0.329	1.453	17	0.997	−0.982	1.992
4	0.805	−0.082	1.564	18	0.998	−0.987	1.994
5	0.880	−0.286	1.682	19	0.998	−0.990	1.995
6	0.901	−0.474	1.825	20	0.999	−0.992	1.997
7	0.912	−0.694	1.839	21	0.999	−0.995	1.998
8	0.964	−0.741	1.890	22	0.999	−0.997	1.998
9	0.963	−0.817	1.914	23	1.000	−0.997	1.999
10	0.976	−0.859	1.937	24	1.000	−0.999	2.000
11	0.981	−0.896	1.953	25	1.000	−1.000	2.000
12	0.986	−0.923	1.965	26	1.000	−1.000	
13	0.990	−0.943	1.974				

The Seidel method can be extended to the refinement of inverses, but for this task it is inferior to the Newton-Raphson process. Both methods, as well as other iterative methods generally, are better suited to automatic than to hand computation. The Seidel method, in particular, is very easily programmed. For hand computation, there is usually less labor in carrying out an explicit solution to the desired precision.

Chapter 11

Polynomials

11-1 THEORY

The highly developed theory of polynomial equations makes possible the derivation of special methods for evaluating polynomials and for locating their roots. The relevant portions of the theory will now be presented. Consider the polynomial

$$P_n(x) = a_n x^n + a_{n-1} x^{n-1} + \cdots + a_1 x^1 + a_0.$$

Unless explicitly stated otherwise, it will be assumed throughout that the coefficients a_i are real numbers. The variable x may or may not be restricted to the reals. The polynomial $P_n(x)$ is said to be equal to the polynomial

$$Q_n(x) = b_n x^n + b_{n-1} x^{n-1} + \cdots + b_1 x^1 + b_0$$

if and only if $P_n(x) = Q_n(x)$ for all x. A necessary consequence of this equality is that $a_i = b_i$ for all i (See Exercise IV–19). The *degree* of $P_n(x)$ is the greatest integer i such that $a_i \neq 0$, and is often written as a subscript on the name of the polynomial. A *root* r of a polynomial is a real or complex number such that $P_n(r) = 0$.

Theorem 11–1 (*The Division Algorithm*). Given polynomials $P_n(x)$ of degree n and $D_m(x)$ of degree $m \leq n$, then there exist unique polynomials $Q_{n-m}(x)$ and $R_k(x)$ such that

(a) $k < m$;

(b) $P = DQ + R.$

Proof: The existence of the polynomials Q and R follows from the customary long division of P by D. No higher power of x than x^{n-m} can occur in Q, but that power must occur in order to yield the term $a_n x^n$ in the product DQ. If the degree of R were as great as m, then R could be further divided by D.

The uniqueness of Q and R is shown by assuming that polynomials Q' and R' of the appropriate degrees exist such that

$$P = DQ' + R' = DQ + R,$$
$$D(Q - Q') = R - R'.$$

If $Q \neq Q'$, the left-hand side is a polynomial of degree at least m and the right-hand side is a polynomial of degree not exceeding $k < m$. But two polynomials of different degrees cannot be equal, and it follows therefore that $Q = Q'$ and $R = R'$.

If $R = 0$, then Q is said to be a *factor* of P and P is said to be *divisible* by Q.

Theorem 11–2 (*The Remainder Theorem*). If $D(x) = x - b$, then $R = P_n(b)$.

Proof: By Theorem 11–1,

$$P_n(x) = (x - b)Q_{n-1}(x) + R_0.$$

The substitution $x = b$ yields

$$P_n(b) = R_0.$$

It should be clear that $P_n(b)$ is not a polynomial of degree n, but rather the number obtained by substituting b for x in $P_n(x)$ and carrying out the indicated operations. The polynomial $R_0(x)$ is of degree zero, that is, a constant, and is shown by the remainder theorem to be equal to that number.

Theorem 11–3 (*The Fundamental Theorem of Algebra*). Given a polynomial $P_n(x)$ of degree $n > 0$ whose coefficients a_i are *complex* numbers, there exists a *complex* number r such that $P_n(r) = 0$.

The proof of this theorem is beyond the scope of this book, and may be found in any textbook of function theory or higher algebra. The theorem states that *every* nonconstant polynomial with complex coefficients has a complex root. Inasmuch as real numbers may be viewed as complex, Corollary 1 follows immediately.

Corollary 1. Given a polynomial $P_n(x)$ of degree $n > 0$ whose coefficients a_i are *real* numbers, there exists a *complex* number r such that $P_n(r) = 0$.

Henceforth only polynomials with real coefficients will be considered. Designate r_1 as the root of $P_n(x)$ whose existence is guaranteed by Corollary 1. By the remainder theorem, one has

$$P_n(x) = (x - r_1)Q_{n-1}(x).$$

But $Q_{n-1}(x)$ has, by the fundamental theorem, a root r_2 if $n > 1$, and by the remainder theorem one may write for Q_{n-1} and its successors

$$Q_{n-1}(x) = (x - r_2)Q_{n-2}(x),$$
$$\vdots$$
$$Q_1(x) = (x - r_n)Q_0(x).$$

Substituting each equation in the preceding one, one obtains

$$P_n(x) = (x - r_1)(x - r_2) \cdots (x - r_n)Q_0(x),$$

and finds further, by equating coefficients of x^n, that $a_n = Q_0(x)$. The polynomial can therefore be expressed in terms of its roots as

$$P_n(x) = a_n \prod_{k=1}^{n} (x - r_k). \tag{11–1}$$

If a factor $(x - r_k)$ occurs m times, the root r_k is said to have *multiplicity m*. Equation (11–1) proves the following corollary.

Corollary 2. A polynomial of degree $n > 0$ has exactly n roots (counting m times each root of multiplicity m).

The relation between the coefficients and roots of $P_n(x)$ is easily determined. Upon rewriting Eq. (11–1) as

$$a_n x^n + a_{n-1}x^{n-1} + \cdots + a_1 x^1 + a_0 = a_n(x - r_1)(x - r_2) \cdots (x - r_n)$$

and equating coefficients of like powers of x, one obtains

$$-\frac{a_{n-1}}{a_n} = \Sigma r_k,$$
$$+\frac{a_{n-2}}{a_n} = \Sigma r_j r_k,$$
$$-\frac{a_{n-3}}{a_n} = \Sigma r_i r_j r_k,$$
$$\vdots$$
$$(-1)^n \frac{a_0}{a_n} = \Pi r_k.$$

Each summation is over all distinct products of the number of roots shown, with multiple roots counted multiply. The location of the roots is restricted by the next theorem, of which two proofs will be given, and by its corollaries.

Theorem 11–4. The roots r_k of the polynomial $P_n(x)$ with real coefficients are real or occur in complex conjugate pairs.

First Proof: Let $P_n(x)$ have the roots $r_1, \ldots, r_n$. Construct the polynomial $\mathcal{P}_n(x)$ with leading coefficient a_n and roots $\bar{r}_1, \ldots, \bar{r}_n$. The coefficient α_i of x_i in $\mathcal{P}_n(x)$ is determined as

$$\alpha_i = (-1)^{n-i} a_n \sum \underbrace{\bar{r}_j \cdots \bar{r}_k}_{n-i \text{ factors}}$$

and is equal to $\bar{a}_i$ because $\overline{z_1 + z_2} = \bar{z}_1 + \bar{z}_2$ and $\overline{z_1 z_2} = \bar{z}_1 \cdot \bar{z}_2$ and

$$\alpha_i = (-1)^{n-i} a_n \sum \underbrace{r_j \cdots r_k}_{n-i \text{ factors}}.$$

But $a_i = \bar{a}_i$ because a_i is real, and therefore $\mathcal{P}_n(x) = P_n(x)$.

Second Proof:

$$\begin{aligned}
P_n(x + iy) &= a_n(x + iy)^n + a_{n-1}(x + iy)^{n-1} + \cdots + a_1(x + iy) + a_0 \\
&= b_n i^n + b_{n-1} i^{n-1} + \cdots + b_1 i + b_0 \\
&= X + iY, \\
P_n(x - iy) &= b_n(-i)^n + b_{n-1}(-i)^{n-1} + \cdots + b_1(-i) + b_0 \\
&= X - iY.
\end{aligned}$$

If $X + iY$ vanishes, so does $X - iY$.

Corollary 1. The number of complex roots is even.

Corollary 2. If n is odd, $P_n(x)$ has at least one real root.

Corollary 3. $P_n(x)$ can be factored into real linear and quadratic factors.

Proof of the first two corollaries is omitted. The third follows from the observation that the coefficients of the product

$$[x - (a + bi)][x - (a - bi)] = [x^2 - 2ax + (a^2 + b^2)]$$

are real. The polynomial can therefore be written as

$$P_n(x) = a_n \prod_{k=1}^{p} (x - b_k) \prod_{j=1}^{q} (x^2 + \alpha_j x + \beta_j),$$

where $p + 2q = n$ and b, α, β are all real.

Several criteria for further localizing the roots of a polynomial are listed in any book on the theory of equations. One particularly convenient criterion is stated here without proof.

Theorem 11–5 (*Descartes Rule of Signs*). Let p be the number of sign changes in the sequence a_n, a_{n-1}, $\ldots$, a_1, a_0. Then the number of real positive roots is $p - 2k$, that is, less than or equal to p and of the same parity.

Corollary. The number of real negative roots is less than or equal to the number of sign changes in the sequence $a_n, -a_{n-1}, \ldots, (-1)^{n-1}a_1, (-1)^n a_0$ and of the same parity.

11–2 EVALUATION

The evaluation of $P_n(b)$ can be effected by carrying out the operations indicated in the expansion

$$P_n(b) = a_n b^n + a_{n-1} b^{n-1} + \cdots + a_1 b^1 + a_0.$$

To obtain b^2 through b^n, $n - 1$ multiplications are required, and n more are needed to produce the $a_i b^i$. A total of n additions and $2n - 1$ multiplications are required by this procedure. Only n multiplications and n additions are needed if the polynomial is written in the factored form

$$P_n(b) = (\cdots((a_n b + a_{n-1})b + a_{n-2})b + \cdots + a_1)b + a_0.$$

Moreover, the intermediate results are significant. Consider the remainder theorem, which can be used to evaluate $P_n(b)$.

$$P_n(x) = (x - b)Q_{n-1}(x) + R_0,$$
$$a_n x^n + a_{n-1} x^{n-1} + \cdots + a_0 = (x - b)(\alpha_{n-1} x^{n-1} + \cdots + \alpha_0) + R_0. \quad (11\text{–}2)$$

Equating coefficients of like powers in Eq. (11–2), one obtains:

$$
\begin{aligned}
a_n &= \alpha_{n-1}, & \alpha_{n-1} &= a_n, \\
a_{n-1} &= \alpha_{n-2} - b\alpha_{n-1}, & \alpha_{n-2} &= a_{n-1} + b\alpha_{n-1}, \\
&\;\;\vdots & &\;\;\vdots \\
a_{i-1} &= \alpha_{i-2} - b\alpha_{i-1}, & \alpha_{i-2} &= a_{i-1} + b\alpha_{i-1}, \\
&\;\;\vdots & &\;\;\vdots \\
a_1 &= \alpha_0 - b\alpha_1, & \alpha_0 &= a_1 + b\alpha_1, \\
a_0 &= R_0 - b\alpha_0, & R_0 &= a_0 + b\alpha_0.
\end{aligned}
$$

The computation can be conveniently laid out in the following two-column format.

b	0
a_n	α_{n-1}
a_{n-1}	α_{n-2}
a_{n-2}	α_{n-3}
$\vdots$	$\vdots$
a_1	α_0
a_0	R_0

Each α_i (or R_0) is obtained by multiplying the number above it by b and then adding the number to the left. Because the method yields the coefficients of $Q_{n-1}(x)$, as well as $R_0 = P_n(b)$, it is termed *synthetic division*. Program 11–1 for the evaluation is derived from the foregoing format; Program 11–2 is a slightly more efficient version.

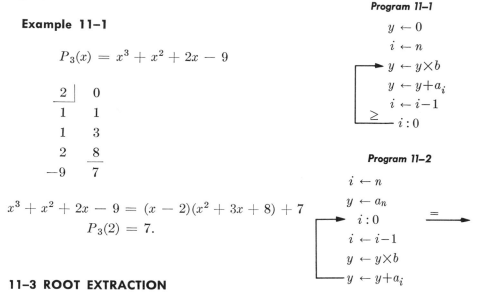

Program 11–1

Example 11–1

$$P_3(x) = x^3 + x^2 + 2x - 9$$

$$
\begin{array}{c|c}
2 & 0 \\
1 & 1 \\
1 & 3 \\
2 & 8 \\
-9 & 7
\end{array}
$$

$$x^3 + x^2 + 2x - 9 = (x - 2)(x^2 + 3x + 8) + 7$$
$$P_3(2) = 7.$$

Program 11–2

11–3 ROOT EXTRACTION

The Newton-Raphson method is easily applied to the calculation of the roots of a polynomial, with the aid of synthetic division in evaluating the two polynomials in the Newton-Raphson formula

$$x_{i+1} = x_i - \frac{P_n(x_i)}{P'_n(x_i)}. \tag{11-3}$$

In this equation, $P'_n(x)$ is the derivative, with respect to x, of $P_n(x)$ and is of course of degree $n - 1$.

$$P_n(x) = (x - b)Q_{n-1}(x) + R_0,$$
$$P'_n(x) = (x - b)Q'_{n-1}(x) + Q_{n-1}(x),$$
$$P'_n(b) = Q_{n-1}(b).$$

The denominator in Eq. (11–3) is seen to be $Q_{n-1}(x_i)$, the remainder after the division of $Q_{n-1}(x)$ by $(x - x_i)$. The synthetic division of $P_n(x)$ by $(x - x_i)$ yields not only the remainder $P_n(x_i)$ but also the quotient $Q_{n-1}(x)$. A second synthetic division by $(x - x_i)$ yields $P'_n(x_i) = Q_{n-1}(x_i)$. The resulting process is called the *Birge-Vieta* method. The extraction of the roots of a cubic will now be illustrated.

Example 11–2. $P_3(x) = x^3 + x^2 + 2x - 9,$ $x_0 = 2.$

$$
\begin{array}{r|rr}
2 & 0 & 0 \\
1 & 1 & 1 \\
1 & 3 & \underline{5} \\
2 & 8 & 18 \\
-9 & \underline{7} &
\end{array}
$$

$$x_1 = 2 - \tfrac{7}{18} = 1.6$$

$$
\begin{array}{r|rr}
1.6 & 0 & 0 \\
1 & 1 & 1 \\
1 & 2.6 & \underline{4.2} \\
2 & 6.16 & 12.88 \\
-9 & \underline{0.86} &
\end{array}
$$

$$x_2 = 1.6 - \frac{0.86}{12.88} = 1.533$$

$$
\begin{array}{r|rr}
1.533 & 0 & 0 \\
1 & 1 & 1 \\
1 & 2.533 & \underline{4.066} \\
2 & 5.883 & 12.116 \\
-9 & \underline{0.019} &
\end{array}
$$

$$x_3 = 1.533 - \frac{0.019}{12.116} = 1.5314$$

$$
\begin{array}{r|rr}
1.5314 & 0 & 0 \\
1 & 1 & 1 \\
1 & 2.5314 & \underline{4.0628} \\
2 & 5.8766 & 12.0984 \\
-9 & \underline{-0.00057} &
\end{array}
$$

$$x_4 = 1.5314 + \frac{0.00057}{12.0984} = 1.531447.$$

Note how quickly $P'_n(x_i)$ stabilizes.   After the first few iterations the latest value of $P'_n(x_i)$ can be used in subsequent iterations, turning the method into a constant-slope process.   The Birge-Vieta procedure diverges from points too far from a root, and the most difficult problem is the selection of an initial approximation, especially for complex roots.

Once the first root has been extracted, the next can be extracted from the quotient polynomial. In the example, this is of degree two, and the quadratic formula can be applied instead. In general, error will be accumulated by using successive quotient polynomials. Each value so obtained may be improved, however, by iterating on the original polynomial $P_n(x)$. If the a_i or x_i are complex, it is possible to carry complex numbers in the worksheet, and various layouts have been devised for this.

A convenient way to avoid dealing with complex numbers until the very end is the quadratic-factor method. This involves the extraction of a real quadratic (rather than linear) factor. The coefficients of x^1 and x^0 in the factor are unknown, and a two-dimensional version of the Newton-Raphson process is required to improve the approximation. Division by the quadratic factor can be performed synthetically. Details are available in textbooks on numerical analysis.

Other methods for extracting roots of polynomials are Horner's, which is especially suited to desk calculators, and Graeffe's, which requires no initial value.

11–4 INTERPOLATION

(a) The Interpolating Polynomial

Given a table of function values, a common problem is to find a value that does not correspond to the tabular points. The most basic approach is to approximate the tabulated function, which may be arbitrary, even empirically obtained, by a polynomial, which is always tractable. Evaluation of the polynomial yields an approximation to the desired function value. Many methods have been developed for obtaining an approximating polynomial and many formulas exist, most of which are based on the use of differences (cf. Section 1–2). The approach that will be adopted here is often simpler intuitively, although it may be more complex in practice.

> **Theorem 11–6.** There exists a unique polynomial $P_n(x)$ of degree at most n such that $P_n(x_j) = y_j$ for $j = 0, \ldots, n$, where x_j, y_j are preassigned numbers with the x_j distinct.

Proof of existence: Consider the so-called Lagrange polynomial

$$L_j^n(x) = \prod_{\substack{k=0 \\ k \neq j}}^{n} \frac{x - x_k}{x_j - x_k}. \tag{11–4}$$

This is a polynomial of degree exactly n, and has the properties that $L_j^n(x_k) = 0$ for $k \neq j$ because one of the numerators is $x_k - x_k = 0$, and that $L_j^n(x_j) = 1$

because each factor has the form $(x_j - x_k)/(x_j - x_k)$. Each of the $n + 1$ Lagrange polynomials $L_0^n(x), \ldots, L_n^n(x)$ therefore equals unity at one of the specified abscissas and zero at each of the others. The polynomial

$$P_n(x) = \sum_{j=0}^{n} y_j L_j^n(x) \qquad (11\text{–}5)$$

clearly assumes the value y_j for $x = x_j$. The addition of the Lagrange polynomials, each weighted by y_j, may result in the annihilation of the coefficients of one or more of the highest powers of x, and $P_n(x)$ may therefore be of degree less than n. The interpolating polynomial can be written as

$$P_n(x) = \sum_{j=0}^{n} y_j \prod_{\substack{k=0 \\ k \neq j}}^{n} \frac{x - x_k}{x_j - x_k}. \qquad (11\text{–}6)$$

Proof of uniqueness: Let $P_n(x)$ and $Q_n(x)$ both satisfy the conditions of the theorem. Form $S_n(x) = P_n(x) - Q_n(x)$. Then $S_n(x_j) = 0$ for $j = 0, \ldots, n$. Unless $S_n(x)$ is everywhere zero, $S_n(x)$ is a polynomial of degree at most n with $n + 1$ roots. But this contradicts Corollary 2 to Theorem 11–3, whence it follows that $S_n(x) = 0$ and $P_n(x) = Q_n(x)$.

Consideration will henceforth be restricted to the case of equally spaced arguments. One may in this case write $x_j = x_0 + jh$, where h is the increment or *mesh* of the table of numbers. Making the substitution one obtains

$$\frac{x - x_k}{x_j - x_k} = \frac{x - (x_0 + kh)}{(x_0 + jh) - (x_0 + kh)}$$

$$= \frac{[(x - x_0)/h]h - kh}{(j - k)h} = \frac{[(x - x_0)/h] - k}{j - k}.$$

A new variable can be defined by

$$s = \frac{x - x_0}{h}, \qquad x = x_0 + hs, \qquad dx = h \, ds, \qquad (11\text{–}7)$$

yielding

$$L_j^n(x) = \prod_{\substack{k=0 \\ k \neq j}}^{n} \frac{[(x - x_0)/h] - k}{j - k} = \prod_{\substack{k=0 \\ k \neq j}}^{n} \frac{s - k}{j - k}. \qquad (11\text{–}8)$$

If the polynomial $P_n(x)$ is required to fit the function $f(x)$ at the arguments x_j, for which $f(x_j) = f_j$, substitution of Eq. (11–8) into Eq. (11–5) yields

$$P_n(x_0 + hs) = \sum_{j=0}^{n} f_j \prod_{\substack{k=0 \\ k \neq j}}^{n} \frac{s - k}{j - k}. \qquad (11\text{–}9)$$

Although $f(x_j) = P_n(x_j)$ for the interpolation points, one must in general write

$$f(x) = P_n(x) + R(x).$$ (11–10)

The error function $R(x)$ can be shown by the use of advanced techniques to equal

$$R(x) = \frac{f^{(n+1)}(\xi)}{(n+1)!} \prod_{k=0}^{n} (x - x_k)$$

or

$$R(x_0 + hs) = \frac{h^{n+1}f^{(n+1)}(\xi)}{(n+1)!} \prod_{k=0}^{n} (s - k),$$ (11–11)

where ξ is a function $\xi(x)$ of x with value in the range $\{x_0, \ldots, x_n, x\}$.

Example 11–3. $f(x) = x^3$. $P_1(x)$ is to coincide with $f(x)$ at $x_0 = 1$, $x_1 = 2$.

$$P_1(x) = \sum_{j=0}^{1} f(x_j) \prod_{\substack{k=0 \\ k \neq j}}^{1} \frac{x - x_k}{x_j - x_k} = 1\left(\frac{x-2}{1-2}\right) + 8\left(\frac{x-1}{2-1}\right) = 7x - 6.$$

$$f(x) = P_n(x) + R(x) = P_1(x) + \frac{f''(\xi)}{2}(x - x_0)(x - x_1),$$

$$x^3 = 7x - 6 + \frac{6\xi}{2}(x - 1)(x - 2),$$

$$\xi = \frac{x^3 - 7x + 6}{3(x - 1)(x - 2)} = 1 + \frac{x}{3},$$

which indeed lies in the range $\{1, 2, x\}$.

(b) Polynomial Interpolation

Linear interpolation in a table is performed by choosing a polynomial of degree one (a straight line), usually through the tabular points bracketing the desired value. Higher-order interpolation requires the use of a polynomial of higher degree, and therefore of more tabular points. Both linear and quadratic interpolation will be illustrated with respect to the function $f(x) = 1/x$, which is tabulated for $x = 3.0(0.1)3.4$ (from $x = 3.0$ to $x = 3.4$ in increments of 0.1) in Table 11–1.

Table 11–1

x	$f(x)$	s
3.0	0.33333	0
3.1	0.32258	1
3.2	0.31250	2
3.3	0.30303	3
3.4	0.29118	4

Example 11–4. Find $f(3.17)$ from Table 11–1.
Linear interpolation:

$$f(3.17) = 0.32258 + \frac{0.07}{0.10}(0.31250 - 0.32258) = 0.31552.$$

Quadratic interpolation:

$$s = \frac{x - x_0}{h} = \frac{3.17 - 3.00}{0.10} = 1.7.$$

$j = 1$	2	3
$L_j^n = \dfrac{(s-2)(s-3)}{(1-2)(1-3)}$	$\dfrac{(s-1)(s-3)}{(2-1)(2-3)}$	$\dfrac{(s-1)(s-2)}{(3-1)(3-2)}$
$L_j^n = \dfrac{(-0.3)(-1.3)}{(-1)(-2)}$	$\dfrac{(0.7)(-1.3)}{(1)(-1)}$	$\dfrac{(0.7)(-0.3)}{(2)(1)}$
$L_j^n = +0.195$	$+0.910$	-0.105
$f_j = \quad 0.32258$	0.31250	0.30303

$$P_2(3.17) = (0.195)(0.32258) + (0.910)(0.31250) - (0.105)(0.30303) = 0.31546.$$

Note that the sum of the values of L_j^n is unity. It is readily verified that $f(3.17) = 0.31546$. Quadratic interpolation gives a result correct to the full precision of Table 11–1; linear interpolation yields an error of 6 in the last place. The layout of the quadratic interpolation should be changed if more than one value is to be computed. In that case the coefficients of $P_2(x_0 + hs)$ are best calculated explicitly to permit easy evaluation for the several arguments.

Inverse interpolation is the determination of the argument value corresponding to a given function value. Upon interchanging the roles of argument and function, inverse interpolation becomes normal interpolation. Two difficulties arise. First, the inverse of the tabulated function may not be single-valued, thus preventing the definition of a suitable polynomial. Second, the new argument (old function) values are generally not equally spaced, and Eq. (11–6) may not be replaceable by the simpler form (11–9).
An alternative approach to inverse interpolation is to approximate the original function by a polynomial and then to solve for the desired argument, instead of evaluating the function. Thus quadratic inverse interpolation based

on the three central values of Table 11–1 would use the equation

$$P_2(3 + 0.1s) = 0.32258 \frac{(s-2)(s-3)}{(1-2)(1-3)}$$

$$+ 0.31250 \frac{(s-1)(s-3)}{(2-1)(2-3)} + 0.30303 \frac{(s-2)(s-3)}{(1-2)(1-3)}$$

$$= 0.000305s^2 - 0.01100s + 0.33327.$$

The argument corresponding to the function value 0.318 is one of the roots of the equation

$$0.318 = 0.000305s^2 - 0.011s + 0.33327.$$

Inverse linear interpolation has already been encountered in the method of false position.

(c) Bivariate Interpolation

Interpolation is easily performed for a function of two variables. A formula for such *bivariate* interpolation will now be derived. By viewing $f(x, y)$ for fixed x as a function of y alone, one may write from Eq. (11–5)

$$f(x, y) = \sum_{j=0}^{n} f(x, y_j)L_j^n(y). \tag{11–12}$$

But $f(x, y_j)$ is a function of x alone and may be written as

$$f(x, y_j) = \sum_{i=0}^{m} f(x_i, y_j)L_i^m(x). \tag{11–13}$$

Substitution of Eq. (11–13) into Eq. (11–12) yields

$$f(x, y) = \sum_{i=0}^{m} \sum_{j=0}^{n} L_i^m(x)f(x_i, y_j)L_j^n(y), \tag{11–14}$$

which may be rewritten as

$$f(x, y) = \mathbf{u}\mathbf{A}\mathbf{v}, \tag{11–15}$$

where $\mathbf{u}$ is the row vector $[L_0^m(x), \ldots, L_m^m(x)]$, $\mathbf{v}$ is the column vector whose elements are $L_0^n(y), \ldots, L_n^n(y)$, and $\mathbf{A}$ is the $m+1$ by $n+1$ matrix of function values

$$\mathbf{A} = \begin{pmatrix} f_{00} & f_{01} & \cdots & f_{0n} \\ f_{10} & f_{11} & \cdots & f_{1n} \\ \vdots & & & \vdots \\ f_{m0} & f_{m1} & \cdots & f_{mn} \end{pmatrix}.$$

The product $\mathbf{uAv}$ must have dimensions

$$(1 \text{ by } m + 1)(m + 1 \text{ by } n + 1)(n + 1 \text{ by } 1) = (1 \text{ by } 1)$$

and therefore be a single number. That Eq. (11–15) is a correct formulation of Eq. (11–14) is seen from the following calculation:

$$[\mathbf{uA}]_j = \sum_{i=0}^{m} \mathbf{u}_i[\mathbf{A}]_{ij},$$

$$\mathbf{uAv} = (\mathbf{uA})\mathbf{v} = \sum_{j=0}^{n} [\mathbf{uA}]_j \mathbf{v}_j,$$

$$= \sum_{j=0}^{n} \sum_{i=0}^{m} \mathbf{u}_i[\mathbf{A}]_{ij} \mathbf{v}_j$$

$$= \sum_{i=0}^{m} \sum_{j=0}^{n} L_i^m(x) f_{ij} L_j^n(y).$$

Example 11–5. Find $f(\frac{1}{2}, \frac{1}{2})$ from the table below.

x \ y	0	1	2
0	0	1	4
1	1	4	9
2	4	9	16

Here $m = n = 2$ and

$$L_0^2\left(\frac{1}{2}\right) = \frac{(1/2 - 1)(1/2 - 2)}{(0 - 1)(0 - 2)} = \frac{3}{8}.$$

Similarly $L_1^2(\frac{1}{2}) = \frac{3}{4}$ and $L_2^2(\frac{1}{2}) = -\frac{1}{8}$.

$$f(\tfrac{1}{2}, \tfrac{1}{2}) = (\tfrac{3}{8} \ \tfrac{3}{4} \ -\tfrac{1}{8})\mathbf{A}\begin{pmatrix} \frac{3}{8} \\ \frac{3}{4} \\ -\frac{1}{8} \end{pmatrix}$$

$$= \tfrac{1}{64}(3 \ 6 \ -1)\begin{pmatrix} 0 & 1 & 4 \\ 1 & 4 & 9 \\ 4 & 9 & 16 \end{pmatrix}\begin{pmatrix} 3 \\ 6 \\ -1 \end{pmatrix} = 1,$$

which is in accord with the defining function $f = (x + y)^2$.

Chapter 12

Numerical Calculus

12–1 DIFFERENTIATION

The derivative of $f(x)$ is defined as

$$f'(x) = \lim_{h \to 0} \frac{f(x + h) - f(x)}{h}.$$

For numerical computation, a first approximation to the derivative is given by the quotient

$$f'(x_0) = \frac{f(x_1) - f(x_0)}{h} = \frac{f_1 - f_0}{h}. \tag{12–1}$$

The error in formula (12–1) can be shown to be $0(h)$. A second approximation is the mean of the first approximations taken in both directions from the point in question:

$$f'(x_1) = \frac{1}{2}\left[\frac{f_2 - f_1}{h} + \frac{f_1 - f_0}{h}\right] = \frac{f_2 - f_0}{2h}. \tag{12–2}$$

The error in Eq. (12–2) is $0(h^2)$. Both approximations are obviously exact for $f(x) = P_1$, a straight line. The second formula is exact for $f(x) = P_2$ also, as is illustrated in Example 12–1. This exactness is a result of the symmetry of the formula about x_1.

Example 12–1
$$f(x) = x^2 + 3x + 2,$$
$$f'(x) = 2x + 3,$$

x	$f(x)$	$f'(x)$
-1	0	1
0	2	3
1	6	5
2	12	7

$$f'(1) = \frac{f(2) - f(0)}{2 - 0} = \frac{12 - 2}{2} = 5.$$

A more general approach to numerical differentiation is provided by the use of the interpolating polynomial. Differentiation of Eq. (11–10) yields

$$f'(x) = P'_n(x) + R'(x).$$

If $R(x)$ is well behaved, $P'_n(x)$ can be used as a good approximation to $f'(x)$. A general formula for $P'_n(x)$ can be obtained by differentiation of Eq. (11–9), but it is rather lengthy and cumbersome to use. Families of differentiation formulas can be obtained easily by first constructing a particular polynomial from Eq. (11–9), then differentiating it, and evaluating the derivative at various points. It should be noted that Eq. (11–9) expresses P_n as a function of s, but that differentiation is desired with respect to x instead. Thus

$$\frac{d}{dx} P_n(x_0 + hs) = \frac{d}{ds} P_n(x_0 + hs) \frac{ds}{dx}.$$

Substituting $ds/dx = 1/h$ from Eq. (11–7) into Eq. (11–9), one obtains

$$P'_n(x_0 + hs) = \frac{1}{h} \sum_{j=0}^{n} f_j \frac{d}{ds} \left(\prod_{\substack{k=0 \\ k \neq j}}^{n} \frac{s-k}{j-k} \right). \tag{12-3}$$

Example 12–2

$$P_2(x_0 + sh) = \frac{(s-1)(s-2)}{(0-1)(0-2)} f_0 + \frac{(s-0)(s-2)}{(1-0)(1-2)} f_1 + \frac{(s-0)(s-1)}{(2-0)(2-1)} f_2,$$

$$hP'_2(x_0 + sh) = \frac{s-2+s-1}{(-1)(-2)} f_0 + \frac{s-2+s-0}{(1)(-1)} f_1 + \frac{s-1+s-0}{(2)(1)} f_2$$

$$= \frac{2s-3}{2} f_0 + \frac{2s-2}{-1} f_1 + \frac{2s-1}{2} f_2.$$

Setting $s = 0$, $P'(x_0) = \dfrac{1}{2h} (-3f_0 + 4f_1 - f_2);$

setting $s = 1$, $P'(x_1) = \dfrac{1}{2h} (-f_0 \qquad + f_2);$

setting $s = 2$, $P'(x_2) = \dfrac{1}{2h} (\quad f_0 - 4f_1 + 3f_2).$

x	$f(x) = \sin x$	$f'(x) = \cos x$	$P'_2(x)$	R'
0.750	0.6816 3876	0.731689	0.731695	−0.000006
0.751	0.6823 7011	0.731007	0.731005	+0.000002
0.752	0.6831 0077	0.730324	0.730315	+0.000009

The error is generally least in the center of the range that defines the polynomial.

12–2 QUADRATURE

Two general problems of integration will be described below. The problem of *antidifferentiation* is to find a *function* $y(x)$ such that dy/dx is equal to some given function $f(x)$. The problem of *quadrature* is to find a *number* N such that

$$N = \int_a^b f(x)\, dx = y(b) - y(a).$$

Numerical quadrature permits N to be evaluated without finding an antiderivative $y(x)$ explicitly. This is a great advantage in two situations. In the first, the antiderivative cannot be expressed in closed form. An example is $\int e^{-x^2}\, dx$. In the other, the antiderivative is too complicated to be easily evaluated. For example,

$$\int \frac{dx}{a^3 + x^3} = \frac{1}{6a^2} \ln \frac{(a+x)^2}{a^2 - ax + x^2} + \frac{1}{a\sqrt{3}} \tan^{-1} \frac{2x - a}{a\sqrt{3}}.$$

The definite integral may be defined as

$$\int_{x_0}^{x_1} f(x)\, dx = \lim_{\substack{n \to \infty \\ h \to 0 \\ nh = x_1 - x_0}} \sum_{i=0}^{n-1} hf(x_0 + ih).$$

By using a finite sum rather than the limit, one obtains the Euler integration formula

$$\int_{x_0}^{x_0 + h} f(x)\, dx = hf(x_0), \qquad (12\text{–}4)$$

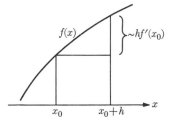

Figure 12–1

which is illustrated in Fig. 12–1. The rectangle represents the area reckoned by the formula, and the curvilinear triangle above it represents the error. Since the base of the triangle is h and its height approximately $hf'(x_0)$, the error may be estimated as $\frac{1}{2}h^2 f'(x_0)$. It can be proved that the error is $\frac{1}{2}h^2 f'(\xi)$ for some ξ in the interval $(x_0, x_0 + h)$. The Euler formula, or rectangular rule, is essentially the integration of $P_0(x)$ through the point $[x_0, f(x_0)]$.

A general method for integration is the use of the integral of the polynomial P_n as an approximation to the desired one. The error in this approximation is the integral of the error in the approximation of $f(x)$ by $P_n(x)$:

$$\int_a^b f(x)\, dx = \int_a^b P_n(x)\, dx + \int_a^b R(x)\, dx. \qquad (12\text{–}5)$$

Methods for estimating the error will be deferred until later. Two methods will now be presented for deriving quadrature formulas. The formulas, like the differentiation formulas, are expressed in terms of the ordinates, or function values.

Some of the types of formulas will be named first for later ease of reference. The interval between adjacent argument values is often called a *panel*. The Adams formulas integrate over a single panel, located just beyond the last argument value for an *open* formula, and just within it for a *closed* formula. The *n*-point Newton-Cotes formulas integrate over the $n + 1$ panels enclosing those points for an open formula, and over the $n - 1$ panels within those points for a closed formula. These four types of formulas are illustrated schematically in Fig. 12–2. Many other types of formulas have also been developed.

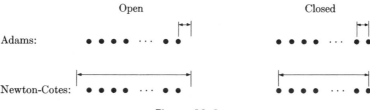

Figure 12–2

A standard method of deriving integration formulas is to carry out the integration of $P_n(x)$ over some range. The derivation of three representative formulas will illustrate this method.

Example 12–3. Two-point closed Adams (or Newton-Cotes) formula:

$$P_1(x_0 + hs) = \sum_{j=0}^{1} f_j \prod_{\substack{k=0 \\ k \neq j}}^{1} \frac{s - k}{j - k}$$

$$= f_0 \frac{s - 1}{0 - 1} + f_1 \frac{s - 0}{1 - 0} = (f_1 - f_0)s + f_0,$$

$$\int_{x_0}^{x_1} P_1 \, dx = h \int_0^1 P_1 \, ds = h \int_0^1 [(f_1 - f_0)s + f_0] \, ds$$

$$= h \left[\frac{f_1 - f_0}{2} s^2 + f_0 s \right]_0^1$$

$$= \frac{h}{2} (f_0 + f_1). \tag{12–6}$$

Formula (12–6) is also known as the trapezoidal rule, because it gives the area in the trapezoid defined as in Fig. 12–3 by the straight line P_1 through the two points of interpolation.

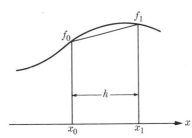

Figure 12–3

Example 12–4. Three-point closed Newton-Cotes formula. A parabola $P_2(x)$ is passed through three points and integrated over two panels.

$$P_2(x_0 + hs) = \sum_{j=0}^{2} f_j \prod_{\substack{k=0 \\ k \neq j}}^{2} \frac{s-k}{j-k}$$

$$= f_0 \frac{(s-1)(s-2)}{(0-1)(0-2)} + f_1 \frac{(s-0)(s-2)}{(1-0)(1-2)} + f_2 \frac{(s-0)(s-1)}{(2-0)(2-1)}$$

$$= f_0 \frac{(s-1)(s-2)}{2} + f_1 \frac{s(s-2)}{-1} + f_2 \frac{s(s-1)}{2},$$

$$\int_{x_0}^{x_1} P_2 \, dx = h \int_0^2 P_2 \, ds$$

$$= \frac{h}{2} \int_0^2 [f_0(s^2 - 3s + 2) - 2f_1(s^2 - 2s) + f_2(s^2 - s)] \, ds$$

$$= \frac{h}{2} \left[f_0 \left(\frac{s^3}{3} - \frac{3s^2}{2} + 2s \right) - 2f_1 \left(\frac{s^3}{3} - s^2 \right) + f_2 \left(\frac{s^3}{3} - \frac{s^2}{2} \right) \right]_0^2$$

$$= \frac{h}{2} [f_0(\tfrac{8}{3} - \tfrac{12}{2} + 4) - 2f_1(\tfrac{8}{3} - 4) + f_2(\tfrac{8}{3} - 2)]$$

$$= \frac{h}{3} (f_0 + 4f_1 + f_2). \tag{12–7}$$

Formula (12–7) is widely known as Simpson's one-third rule, or Simpson's rule.

Example 12–5. Three-point open Newton-Cotes formula. The desired form is

$$\int_{x_0}^{x_4} f(x) \, dx = \sum_{j=1}^{3} a_j f_j,$$

$$P_2(x_0 + hs) = f_1 \frac{(s-2)(s-3)}{(1-2)(1-3)} + f_2 \frac{(s-1)(s-3)}{(2-1)(2-3)} + f_3 \frac{(s-1)(s-2)}{(3-1)(3-2)},$$

$$\int_{x_0}^{x_4} P_2 \, dx = h \int_0^4 P_2 \, ds = \frac{4h}{3} (2f_1 - f_2 + 2f_3).$$

It may be observed that if f is set equal to a constant in each of the last three examples, the formulas derived reduce to hf for the trapezoidal rule, $2hf$ for Simpson's rule, and $4hf$ for the last formula. These correspond to the integrations over 1, 2, and 4 panels.

12–3 UNDETERMINED COEFFICIENTS

Another process for deriving numerical calculus formulas is the method of undetermined coefficients. For quadrature, the form

$$\int_{x_0}^{x_0+nh} f(x)\, dx = h \sum_i a_i f_i$$

is assumed, and coefficients are determined which render the formula exact whenever $f(x)$ is a polynomial of any degree less than the number of ordinates f_i used.

Example 12–6. Three-point closed Adams formula. Assume

$$\int_{x_0}^{x_1} f(x)\, dx = af_{-1} + bf_0 + cf_1,$$

and evaluate the formula for $f = 1, f = x - x_0$, and $f = (x - x_0)^2$:

$$\int_{x_0}^{x_1} 1\, dx = x \Big|_{x_0}^{x_1} = h = \quad a + b + \quad c,$$

$$\int_{x_0}^{x_1} (x - x_0)\, dx = \frac{(x - x_0)^2}{2}\Big|_{x_0}^{x_1} = \frac{h^2}{2} = -ha \quad\quad + hc,$$

$$\int_{x_0}^{x_1} (x - x_0)^2\, dx = \frac{(x - x_0)^3}{3}\Big|_{x_0}^{x_1} = \frac{h^3}{3} = h^2 a \quad\quad + h^2 c.$$

This leads to the linear system:

$$a + b + c = h,$$
$$-a \quad\quad + c = h/2,$$
$$a \quad\quad + c = h/3,$$

which has the solution $a = -h/12,\ b = 2h/3,\ c = 5h/12$. The desired formula is therefore:

$$\int_{x_0}^{x_1} f(x)\, dx = \frac{h}{12}\,(-f_{-1} + 8f_0 + 5f_1).$$

Example 12–7. Simpson's rule (second derivation). Evaluate

$$\int_{x_0}^{x_2} f(x)\, dx = af_0 + bf_1 + cf_2$$

for $f = 1$, $f = x - x_1$, and $f = (x - x_1)^2$.

$$\int_{x_0}^{x_2} 1\, dx = 2h = \quad a + b + \quad c,$$

$$\int_{x_0}^{x_2} (x - x_1)\, dx = \quad 0 = -ha \quad + hc,$$

$$\int_{x_0}^{x_2} (x - x_1)^2\, dx = \frac{2h^3}{3} = h^2 a \quad + h^2 c.$$

The resulting linear system has the solution $a = h/3$, $b = 4h/3$, $c = h/3$, whence the formula already found in Example 12–4 is reproduced.

The method of undetermined coefficients can easily be used to derive differentiation formulas.

Example 12–8. The coefficients in the formula

$$f'(x_0) = af_0 + bf_1 + cf_2$$

are found by substitution of the following values of $f(x)$:

$f(x)$	$f'(x)$
1	0
$x - x_1$	1
$(x - x_1)^2$	$2(x - x_1)$

into the assumed formula, yielding the system:

$$0 = \quad a + b + \quad c,$$
$$1 = -ha \quad + hc,$$
$$-2h = \quad h^2 a \quad + h^2 c,$$

which has the solution $a = -3/2h$, $b = 2/h$, $c = -1/2h$. The resulting formula is therefore

$$f'(x_0) = \frac{1}{2h}(-3f_0 + 4f_1 - f_2),$$

which was previously obtained in Example 12–2.

12–4 ERROR ANALYSIS

The foregoing formulas are all subject to error. The errors depend both on the mesh size h and on the smoothness of $f(x)$ as compared with that of the interpolating polynomial. The smoothness is most readily measured by the magnitude of one of the derivatives of $f(x)$. A simple method for estimating the error in quadrature formulas will now be presented. Justification of its validity is, however, beyond the scope of this book. If a quadrature formula derived from the integrating polynomial is exact for $f(x)$, a polynomial of degree n but no higher, then the error is of the form

$$E = \alpha h^{n+2} f^{(n+1)}(\xi).$$

The coefficient α can be determined by applying the integration formula to $f(x) = x^{n+1}$ and comparing the calculated error with the exact result.

Example 12–9. Trapezoidal rule

$$\int_0^h f(x)\, dx = \frac{h}{2} (f_0 + f_1) + E,$$

$$f(x) = x^2, f''(x) = 2,$$

$$\int_0^h x^2\, dx = \frac{h^3}{3},$$

$$E = \frac{h^3}{3} - \frac{h}{2} (x_0^2 + x_1^2)$$

$$= \frac{h^3}{3} - \frac{h}{2} (0 + h^2) = \frac{h^3}{3} - \frac{h^3}{2} = -\frac{h^3}{6} = -\frac{h^3}{12} f''(\xi).$$

Example 12–10. Simpson's rule

$$\int_0^{2h} f(x)\, dx = \frac{h}{3} (f_0 + 4f_1 + f_2) + E,$$

$$f(x) = x^3, \qquad f^{(3)}(x) = 6,$$

$$\int_0^{2h} x^3\, dx = 4h^4,$$

$$E = 4h^4 - \frac{h}{3} (0 + 4h^3 + 8h^3) = 4h^4 - 4h^4 = 0.$$

This does *not* mean that the error is zero. It means rather that Simpson's rule, although derived for a quadratic, yields correct integration of a cubic as well.

Table 12–1

Closed Newton-Cotes formulas

$$\int_{x_0}^{x_1} y\, dx = \frac{h}{2}(y_0 + y_1) - \frac{h^3}{12} y^{(2)}(\xi) \qquad \text{(trapezoidal rule)}$$

$$\int_{x_0}^{x_2} y\, dx = \frac{h}{3}(y_0 + 4y_1 + y_2) - \frac{h^5}{90} y^{(4)}(\xi) \qquad \text{(Simpson's one-third rule)}$$

$$\int_{x_0}^{x_3} y\, dx = \frac{3h}{8}(y_0 + 3y_1 + 3y_2 + y_3) - \frac{3h^5}{80} y^{(4)}(\xi) \quad \text{(Simpson's three-eighths rule)}$$

$$\int_{x_0}^{x_4} y\, dx = \frac{2h}{45}(7y_0 + 32y_1 + 12y_2 + 32y_3 + 7y_4) - \frac{8h^7}{945} y^{(6)}(\xi)$$

Open Newton-Cotes formulas

$$\int_{x_0}^{x_2} y\, dx = 2hy_1 + \frac{h^3}{3} y^{(2)}(\xi),$$

$$\int_{x_0}^{x_3} y\, dx = \frac{3h}{2}(y_1 + y_2) + \frac{h^3}{4} y^{(2)}(\xi),$$

$$\int_{x_0}^{x_4} y\, dx = \frac{4h}{3}(2y_1 - y_2 + 2y_3) + \frac{14h^5}{45} y^{(4)}(\xi).$$

Closed Adams formulas

$$\int_{x_0}^{x_1} y\, dx = hy_1 - \frac{h^2}{2} y'(\xi),$$

$$= \frac{h}{2}(y_1 + y_0) - \frac{h^3}{12} y^{(2)}(\xi),$$

$$= \frac{h}{12}(5y_1 + 8y_0 - y_{-1}) - \frac{h^4}{24} y^{(3)}(\xi),$$

$$= \frac{h}{24}(9y_1 + 19y_0 - 5y_{-1} + y_{-2}) - \frac{19}{720} h^5 y^{(4)}(\xi).$$

Open Adams formulas

$$\int_{x_0}^{x_1} y\, dx = hy_0 + \frac{h^2}{2} y'(\xi),$$

$$= \frac{h}{2}(3y_0 - y_{-1}) + \frac{5}{12} h^3 y^{(2)}(\xi),$$

$$= \frac{h}{12}(23y_0 - 16y_{-1} + 5y_{-2}) + \frac{3}{8} h^4 y^{(3)}(\xi).$$

If, instead of a cubic, a quartic is tried, one has

$$f(x) = x^4, \qquad f^{(4)}(x) = 24,$$

$$\int_0^{2h} x^4 \, dx = \frac{32h^5}{5},$$

$$E = \frac{32h^5}{5} - \frac{h}{3}(0 + 4h^4 + 16h^4) = -\frac{4}{15}h^5 = -\frac{h^5}{90}f^{(4)}(\xi).$$

The error terms derived in these examples can be shown by more sophisticated methods to be correct. Note that the error in Simpson's rule represents an increase in two orders of h over that in the trapezoidal rule, although only one more point is used. For the Newton-Cotes formulas, integration over an even number n of panels yields an error in $h^{n+3}f^{(n+2)}(x)$, whereas use of an odd number n of panels yields an error in $h^{n+2}f^{(n+1)}(x)$. As a result, formulas with n even are generally preferred.

Several Adams and Newton-Cotes quadrature formulas are listed with error terms in Table 12–1. By $y^{(i)}(\xi)$ is meant the ith derivative of y evaluated at some point ξ within the range spanned by the values of x corresponding to the ordinates in the formula. Further formulas of these and other families can be found in most numerical analysis textbooks.

Chapter 13

Differential Equations

13–1 ELEMENTARY TECHNIQUES

Instead of the simple equation $y' = f(x)$, solvable by quadrature, consider the more general equation $y' = f(x, y)$, subject to the initial condition $y(x_0) = y_0$. This differential equation defines an integral curve, passing through the point (x_0, y_0), whose behavior depends not only upon the known values of x, but also upon the unknown values of y. A simple approach to the numerical solution of this equation is provided by approximating the integral curve through a given point by a straight line through that point. If the slope of the line through the point (x_j, y_j) is λ_j, a recursion equation is obtained of the form

$$y(x_j + h) = y_j + h\lambda_j. \tag{13–1}$$

Each step determines a new point that, because of error, lies in general on a different integral curve. The next step approximates the new rather than the original integral curve. Error is thus cumulative, and increases more rapidly if the differential equation has a divergent family of integral curves, as in Fig. 13–1(a), than if it has a convergent family, as in Fig. 13–1(b).

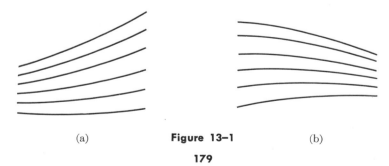

(a) **Figure 13–1** (b)

(a) Euler's Method

The simplest value of λ_j is the known slope y_j' of the integral curve through the point (x_j, y_j). This yields the elementary formula

$$y_{j+1} = y_j + hf(x_j, y_j), \tag{13–2}$$

which is the basis of Euler's method. Figure 13–2 interprets Euler's method geometrically.

Example 13–1

$$y' = x^2 + y^2,$$
$$y(0) = 1,$$
$$h = 0.1,$$
$$y_{j+1} = y_j + h(x_j^2 + y_j^2).$$

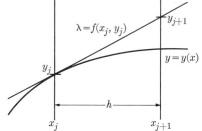

Figure 13–2

j	x_j	y_j	x_j^2	y_j^2	$h(x_j^2 + y_j^2)$	y_{j+1}
0	0.0	1.000	0.000	1.000	0.100	1.100
1	0.1	1.100	0.010	1.210	0.122	1.222
2	0.2	1.222	0.040	1.493	0.153	1.375
3	0.3	1.375				

The accumulation of error is evident from Table 13–1.

Table 13–1

x	y(Euler)	y(True)	Error
0.0	1.000	1.000	0.000
0.1	1.100	1.111	−0.011
0.2	1.222	1.253	−0.031
0.3	1.375	1.440	−0.065

(b) Midpoint Method

It is reasonable to expect a better approximation to be given by the slope of the integral curve near the middle of the panel than by that at one end. The location of the midpoint of the integral curve is not known, of course, but it can be approximated by the location of the midpoint of the line segment defined by Euler's method. This midpoint is $[x_j + h/2, y_j + (h/2)f(x_j, y_j)]$. The resulting formula is therefore

$$y_{j+1} = y_j + hf\left[x_j + \frac{h}{2}, y_j + \frac{h}{2}f(x_j, y_j)\right]. \tag{13–3}$$

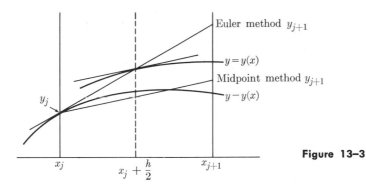

Figure 13–3

Two evaluations of the function $f(x, y)$ are required per panel, but the only value of y needed is the known value y_j. The midpoint method is illustrated in Fig. 13–3. The calculation is organized with the aid of the equations

$$y'_j = f(x_j, y_j),$$

$$y'_m = f\left(x_j + \frac{h}{2}, y_j + \frac{h}{2} y'_j\right),$$

$$y_{j+1} = y_j + hy'_m.$$

Example 13–2

$$y' = x^2 + y^2, \qquad y(0) = 1, \qquad h = 0.1$$

x_j	y_j	y'_j	$(h/2)y'_j + y_j$	$x_j + h/2$	y'_m
0.0	1.0000	1.0000	1.0500	0.05	1.1055
0.1	1.1106	1.2434	1.1728	0.15	1.3980
0.2	1.2504	1.6035	1.3306	0.25	1.8330
0.3	1.4337				

As the solution was extended from $x = 0.0$ to $x = 0.3$, $f(x, y)$ was evaluated 6 times. The same number of evaluations is required by the use of the basic Euler method with $h = 0.05$. For the differential equation of the examples, the midpoint method is superior, as is shown by Table 13–2.

Table 13–2

	True	Midpoint ($h = 0.1$)		Euler ($h = 0.05$)	
x	y	y	ϵ	y	ϵ
0.0	1.0000	1.0000	0.0000	1.0000	0.0000
0.1	1.1115	1.1106	−0.0009	1.1053	−0.0062
0.2	1.2530	1.2504	−0.0026	1.2361	−0.0169
0.3	1.4396	1.4337	−0.0059	1.4040	−0.0356

(c) Modified Euler Method

A more attractive choice for λ_j in Eq. (13–1) is the mean of y'_j and y'_{j+1}. The corresponding formula can be derived formally from the trapezoidal rule for quadrature

$$\int_{x_0}^{x_1} z \, dx = \frac{h}{2} (z_0 + z_1) - \frac{h^3}{12} z''(\xi).$$

Substitution of y' for z yields

$$\int_{x_0}^{x_1} y' \, dx = \frac{h}{2} (y'_0 + y'_1) - \frac{h^3}{12} y'''(\xi).$$

The resulting modified Euler formula is therefore

$$y_{j+1} = y_j + \frac{h}{2} [f(x_j, y_j) + f(x_{j+1}, y_{j+1})]. \tag{13–4}$$

If the differential equation is linear, $y' = f(x, y) = a(x) + b(x)y$, and Eq. (13–4) can be solved explicitly for y_{j+1}.

$$y_{j+1} = y_j + \frac{h}{2} (a_j + b_j y_j + a_{j+1} + b_{j+1} y_{j+1}),$$

$$y_{j+1} = \frac{1}{1 - (h/2)b_{j+1}} \left[y_j \left(1 + \frac{h}{2} b_j \right) + \frac{h}{2} (a_j + a_{j+1}) \right].$$

Here a_j, a_{j+1}, b_j, and b_{j+1} are of course functions of x.

If the differential equation is nonlinear, an initial approximation to y_{j+1} is obtained by any method, such as the unmodified Euler formula, and the modified formula is used to refine the approximation. The process consists of four steps:

(1) predict y_{j+1} by the use of Eq. (13–2);
(2) compute $y'_{j+1} = f(x_{j+1}, y_{j+1})$ from the differential equation;
(3) correct y_{j+1} by the use of Eq. (13–4);
(4) return to step 2 unless adequate convergence has occurred.

The combination of prediction and correction is a common motif in the solution of differential equations.

After the process has converged to a value of y_{j+1}, there will still be an error of $(h^3/12)y'''(\xi)$, where $x_j \leq \xi \leq x_{j+1}$. This error exists whether or not the differential equation is linear.

Example 13–3

$$y' = x^2 + y, \qquad y(0) = 1, \qquad h = 0.1,$$

$$y_1 = y_0 + \frac{h}{2} (x_0^2 + y_0 + x_1^2 + y_1)$$

$$= 1 + 0.05(0 + 1 + 0.01 + y_1)$$

$$= \frac{1 + 0.05(1.01)}{1 - 0.05} = \frac{1.0505}{0.95} = 1.1058.$$

Example 13–4

$$y' = x^2 + y^2, \qquad y(0) = 1, \qquad h = 0.1,$$

$$y_1 = 1 + \frac{h}{2}(y_0' + y_1')$$

$$= 1 + 0.05(1 + y_1') = 1 + 0.05(1.01 + y_1^2).$$

y_1	y_1^2	$1.01 + y_1^2$	$(h/2)(1 + y_1')$
1.100	1.2100	2.2200	0.1100
1.1110	1.2343	2.2443	0.1122
1.1122	1.2370	2.2470	0.1124
1.1124	1.2374	2.2474	0.11237
1.11237	1.23737	2.24737	0.11237
1.11237			

The initial value 1.100 of y_1 was obtained from Example 13–1. The error can be estimated as follows:

$$y' = x^2 + y^2,$$
$$y'' = 2x + 2yy',$$
$$y''' = 2 + 2yy'' + 2(y')^2.$$

$$y'(0) = 1, \qquad y'(0.1) < 1.25,$$
$$y''(0) = 2, \qquad y''(0.1) < 0.2 + 2(1.12)(1.25) < 3,$$
$$y'''(0) = 8, \qquad y'''(0.1) < 2 + 2(1.12)3 + 2(1.25)^2 < 12.$$

Because y and its derivatives are monotonic in the interval $(0.0, 0.1)$, $8 \le y'''(\xi) < 12$ and the error lies between $\frac{2}{3} \cdot 10^{-3}$ and 10^{-3}. Comparison with Table 13–2 shows that the error is actually about 0.0009.

13–2 STARTING THE SOLUTION

Less elementary methods of solution than the foregoing derive greater accuracy from the use of not one, but several points on an integral curve to determine each new point. Such methods are applicable for *continuing* a solution once the first few points have been found. In *starting* the solution, these initial values can be determined by either incremental or series techniques.

(a) Incremental Methods

The modified Euler method previously described is one of many generalizations of Euler's method. It is itself subject to modification, as in the solution of Eq. (13–4) for y_{j+1} even if the differential equation is nonlinear. This can be accomplished, for example, by casting Eq. (13–4) as $F(y_{j+1}) = 0$, and solving it by a Newton-Raphson process.

The prediction of y_{j+1} can be simplified either by making any initial guess, or by using y_j as a first approximation. The poorer the prediction, however, the more iterations of the corrector are required.

Another modification is the substitution for the trapezoidal rule of other quadrature formulas. The three-point closed Adams formulas

$$y_{-1} = y_0 - \frac{h}{12} (5y'_{-1} + 8y'_0 - y'_1),$$

$$y_1 = y_0 + \frac{h}{12} (-y'_{-1} + 8y'_0 + 5y'_1),$$

can be used to determine an additional point on each side of the given one. Substitution of the differential equation yields

$$y_{-1} = y_0 - \frac{h}{12} [5f(x_{-1}, y_{-1}) + 8f(x_0, y_0) - f(x_1, y_1)],$$

$$y_1 = y_0 + \frac{h}{12} [-f(x_{-1}, y_{-1}) + 8f(x_0, y_0) + 5f(x_1, y_1)]. \qquad (13\text{–}5)$$

Initial values, such as $y_{-1} = y_1 = y_0$, are assumed, and the Eqs. (13–5) simultaneously solved iteratively for y_{-1} and y_1. Subsequent use of the five-point closed Adams formula generates two more points. Other formulas can of course be used to yield any number of points on either side or both.

Among the noniterative generalizations of Euler's method are the Runge-Kutta formulas, which are based upon the evaluation of $y' = f(x, y)$ at judiciously selected points. The midpoint method and the trapezoidal rule can both be derived from the second-order Runge-Kutta form

$$y_{j+1} = y_j + ha_0 f(x_j, y_j) + ha_1 f(x_j + bh, y_j + ch). \qquad (13\text{–}6)$$

A popular fourth-order Runge-Kutta formula is

$$y_{j+1} = y_j + \tfrac{1}{6}(k_1 + 2k_2 + 2k_3 + k_4), \qquad (13\text{–}7)$$

where

$$k_1 = hf(x_j, y_j),$$

$$k_2 = hf\left(x_j + \frac{h}{2}, y_j + \frac{k_1}{2}\right),$$

$$k_3 = hf\left(x_j + \frac{h}{2}, y_j + \frac{k_2}{2}\right),$$

$$k_4 = hf(x_j + h, y_j + k_3).$$

The error in formula (13–7) is $0(h^5)$.

Example 13–5 $y' = x^2 + y^2$, $y(0) = 1$, $h = 0.1$.

$$k_1 = 0.1(0^2 + 1^2) = 0.1,$$
$$k_2 = 0.1(0.05^2 + 1.05^2) = 0.1105,$$
$$k_3 = 0.1(0.05^2 + 1.05525^2) = 0.11161,$$
$$k_4 = 0.1(0.1^2 + 1.11161^2) = 0.12457,$$
$$y(0.1) = 1 + \tfrac{1}{6}(0.66879) = 1.11147.$$

The correct value is 1.111463, and the error is indeed comparable to h^5 in magnitude.

(b) Series Methods

The object of series methods of starting the solution of a differential equation is to express the solution as an infinite series in powers of the independent variable. The series, truncated after some finite number of terms, can be evaluated at several points to yield a set of starting values.

The differential equation $y' = f(x, y)$ may be integrated to yield

$$\int_{x_0}^{x} y' \, dx = \int_{x_0}^{x} f(x, y) \, dx$$

$$y(x) = y(x_0) + \int_{x_0}^{x} f(x, y) \, dx. \tag{13–8}$$

Equation (13–8) is the basis of Picard's method of successive approximations. The initial approximation $^0y(x) = y(x_0)$ is substituted in the integrand of Eq. (13–8) to yield a new approximation $^1y(x)$. The recursion formula may be written as

$$^{i+1}y(x) = y(x_0) + \int_{x_0}^{x} f[x, \, ^iy(x)] \, dx. \tag{13–9}$$

A sequence of functions is generated that can be proved under extremely general conditions to converge to the desired solution of the differential equation. Each iteration provides one more term in a series representation of the solution.

Example 13–6 $y' = x - y$, $y(0) = 1$.

Equation (13–9) becomes $^{i+1}y(x) = 1 + \int_0^x (x - \, ^iy) \, dx$. The first few approximations are

$$^1y(x) = 1 + \int_0^x (x - 1) \, dx = 1 - x + \frac{x^2}{2},$$

$$^2y(x) = 1 + \int_0^x \left(x - 1 + x - \frac{x^2}{2} \right) dx = 1 - x + x^2 - \frac{x^3}{6},$$

$$^3y(x) = 1 + \int_0^x \left(x - 1 + x - x^2 + \frac{x^2}{6} \right) dx = 1 - x + x^2 - \frac{x^3}{3} + \frac{x^4}{24}.$$

The first four terms of the solution are therefore

$$y(x) = 1 - x + x^2 - \frac{x^3}{3} + \cdots$$

If $y' = f(x, y)$ is easily differentiated, the Taylor series*

$$y(x) = y(x_0) + (x - x_0)y'(x_0)$$

$$+ \frac{(x - x_0)^2}{2!} y''(x_0) + \frac{(x - x_0)^3}{3!} y'''(x_0) + \cdots \qquad (13\text{–}10)$$

may be used. For the equation of Example 13–6, $y' = x - y$, $y'' = 1 - y'$, and $y''' = -y''$. Substitution of $x_0 = 0$ yields $y'(0) = -1$, $y''(0) = 2$, and $y'''(0) = -2$. The first few terms of the series are therefore given by

$$y(x) = 1 - x + x^2 - \frac{x^3}{3} + \cdots,$$

which agrees with the result of Picard's method.

For the differential equation of Example 13–6, Eqs. (13–9) and (13–10) both yield a series solution. For many differential equations, however, one method or the other fails. The differential equation $y' = \sqrt{x + y}$, $y(0) = 1$, generates, by Picard's method, expressions that resist integration. The differential equation $y' = x^{1/2} + y - 1$, $y(0) = 1$, cannot be solved in a Taylor series because all derivatives are infinite at $x = 0$.

Once a series is obtained, it is necessary to decide how many of its terms to use. If successive terms of a convergent series have opposite signs, the error in truncating this *alternating* series at any point after it has begun to converge can be proved to be less in magnitude than the value of the first term neglected. If the series is not alternating, then the first term neglected may or may not provide a good estimate of the error.

For the differential equation of Example 13–6, use of the first three terms of the series creates an error bounded by $|x^3/3|$. Thus $y(0.1)$ is calculated as $1 - 0.1 + 0.01 = 0.910$, with an error not exceeding $\frac{1}{3}$ in the last place.

13–3 CONTINUING THE SOLUTION

Any starting method can continue the solution, and the Runge-Kutta formulas are often so used. Many continuation methods proper depend on the value of the solution at several previous points, and cannot be used for starting. Attention will be directed here to methods based on ordinates rather than those

---

* The reader unfamiliar with Taylor series can omit this paragraph without loss of continuity.

derived from difference tables. Each method will be illustrated by calculating $y(0.3)$ from the starting points listed in Table 13–3 and comparing with the true value 1.4396.

Table 13–3

x	y	$y' = x^2 + y^2$
-0.1	0.9088	0.8359
0.0	1.0000	1.0000
0.1	1.1115	1.2454
0.2	1.2530	1.6100

(a) Single Derivative Method

One of the simplest methods is related to Euler's. Instead of the Euler formula

$$y_{j+1} = y_j + hy'_j, \tag{13–2}$$

in which the error is $0(h^2)$, the formula

$$y_{j+1} = y_{j-1} + 2hy'_j \tag{13–11}$$

is used. The error in Eq. (13–11) is only $0(h^3)$.

Example 13–7

$$
\begin{aligned}
y(0.3) &= y(0.1) + 2(0.1)y'(0.2) \\
&= 1.1115 + 0.2(1.6100) \\
&= 1.4335, \\
\epsilon &= 1.4335 - 1.4396 = -0.0061.
\end{aligned}
$$

(b) Closed Formula Method

Any closed quadrature formula yields an equation which can be solved, at least in theory, for the ordinate at the endpoint of its range. Thus the substitution of $z = y'$ in Simpson's rule

$$\int_{x_0}^{x_2} z\, dx = \frac{h}{3}(z_0 + 4z_1 + z_2)$$

yields

$$y_2 = y_0 + \frac{h}{3}(y'_0 + 4y'_1 + y'_2). \tag{13–12}$$

The further substitution, from the differential equation, of $y'_2 = f(x_2, y_2)$ for y'_2 yields an equation which can be solved by some method for y_2. This technique is a generalization of the modified Euler method.

Example 13–8

$$y(0.3) = y(0.1) + \frac{0.1}{3} [y'(0.1) + 4y'(0.2) + (0.3)^2 + y^2(0.3)].$$

By setting $\alpha = y(0.3)$, one obtains

$$30\alpha = 30(1.1115) + 1.2454 + 4(1.6100) + 0.09 + \alpha^2,$$
$$\alpha^2 - 30\alpha + 41.1204 = 0,$$
$$\alpha = 1.4398, 28.5602.$$

The error in the first value is 0.0002.

If the differential equation is linear, Eq. (13–12), or one similarly derived, is linear in y_2 and hence solved trivially.

If the differential equation is easily solved for $y = g(x, y')$, it may be more advantageous to substitute in Eq. (13–12) not for y_2', but for y_2. For a differential equation such as $y' = \sqrt{y - x^2}$, this would simplify the calculations. Usually, however, the differential equation is not easily solved for y. Moreover, even when it is, the resulting equation (13–12) is rarely easily solved for y_2'.

(c) Predictor-Corrector Methods

The foregoing drawbacks are circumvented by an iterative method based on the use of both open and closed quadrature formulas. Any open formula can be used as a *predictor;* any closed formula, as a *corrector.* The process, one form of which appeared in Section 13–1(c), consists of four steps:

(1) predict y_k by using the open formula;
(2) compute y_k' from the differential equation;
(3) correct y_k by using the closed formula;
(4) return to step (2) unless the convergence is sufficient.

Example 13–9.   The open and closed three-point Newton-Cotes formulas may be written as

$$y_4 = y_0 + \frac{4h}{3} (2y_1' - y_2' + 2y_3'), \qquad y_4 = y_2 + \frac{h}{3} (y_2' + 4y_3' + y_4'),$$

and the differential equation evaluated as

$$y_4' = x_4^2 + y_4^2.$$

Prediction yields

$$y(0.3) = y(-0.1) + \frac{0.4}{3} [2y'(0.0) - y'(0.1) + 2y'(0.2)]$$

$$= 0.9088 + \frac{0.4}{3} [2(1.0000) - 1.2454 + 2(1.6100)]$$

$$= 1.4387.$$

The error in the predicted value is -0.0009. The corrector,

$$y(0.3) = y(0.1) + \frac{0.1}{3} [y'(0.1) + 4y'(0.2) + y'(0.3)],$$

can be combined with the differential equation to yield

$$y(0.3) = 1.1115 + \frac{0.1}{3} [1.2454 + 4(1.6100) + 0.09 + y^2(0.3)]$$

$$= 1.3707 + \frac{y^2(0.3)}{30}.$$

y	y^2	$y^2/30$
1.4387	2.0699	0.0690
1.4397	2.0727	0.0691
1.4398	2.0730	0.0691

The error in the corrected result is only 0.0002.

References for Part IV

AITKEN, A. C., *Determinants and Matrices*. 9th ed. New York: Interscience, 1956.

GRABBE, E. M., S. RAMO, and D. E. WOOLDRIDGE, eds., *Handbook of Automation, Computation, and Control*. Vol. 1. New York: Wiley, 1958. Chapter 14.

HILDEBRAND, F. B., *Introduction to Numerical Analysis*. New York: McGraw-Hill, 1956.

LOVITT, W. V., *Elementary Theory of Equations*. New York: Prentice-Hall, 1939.

MCCRACKEN, D. D., and W. S. DORN, *Numerical Analysis and FORTRAN Programming*. New York: Wiley, 1964.

MILNE, W. E., *Numerical Calculus*. Princeton: Princeton University Press, 1949. Chapter 1.

MILNE, W. E., *Numerical Solution of Differential Equations*. New York: Wiley, 1953.

RALSTON, A., and H. S. WILF, eds., *Mathematical Methods for Digital Computers*. New York: Wiley, 1960.

USPENSKY, J. V., *Theory of Equations*. New York: McGraw-Hill, 1948. Chapters 2, 3, and 12.

WEISNER, L., *Introduction to the Theory of Equations*. New York: Macmillan, 1949. Chapters 2–4 and 6.

Exercise Set for Part IV

1. Find the zero of $f(x) = 3x - \cos x$ by performing four iterations of each of the following methods. Estimate the accuracy of each result.
   (a) General iteration, $x_0 = 0.5$ (b) False position, $x_0 = 0.5$ and $x_1 = 0.1$
   (c) Constant slope, $x_0 = 0.5$ (d) Newton-Raphson, $x_0 = 0.5$

2. (a) The root of each of the following equations is the reciprocal of the number N:

$$g(x) = Nx - 1 = 0$$

$$h(x) = \frac{1}{x} - N = 0$$

   Derive from each of the two equations a Newton-Raphson formula for improving an approximation to $1/N$. Which one would you use in programming a computer with no division operation? Justify your choice.
   (b) If $\pm N = r \times 10^t$, where $1 \le r < 10$ and t is a positive or negative integer, show that a suitable initial approximation is given by $\pm x_0 = s \times 10^{-t}$, where s is determined only by the most significant digit of r, according to the following table.

Digit	s	Digit	s
1	0.7	6	0.2
2	0.4	7	0.1
3	0.3	8	0.1
4	0.2	9	0.1
5	0.2		

   (c) Program a decimal computer to determine x_0 from N by use of the foregoing table. Suggest an initial approximation of a form more easily evaluated by computer. How would you determine a suitable x_0 in a binary computer?

3. Derive a Newton-Raphson formula for extracting cube roots.

4. Tabulate the errors in the successive approximations of Examples 9–1 through 9–4. Verify the order of convergence of each process.

5. Present an example in which averaging the Newton-Raphson slope with the false-position slope yields faster convergence than a pure Newton-Raphson process.

6. Program a computer to effect Gauss elimination.

7. (a) Determine the sum and products of the matrices

$$\mathbf{A} = \begin{pmatrix} 1 & 3 & 2 \\ -2 & 4 & 5 \\ 2 & -1 & -3 \end{pmatrix} \quad \text{and} \quad \mathbf{B} = \begin{pmatrix} -1 & -4 & 3 \\ 2 & 1 & -5 \\ 4 & 3 & -2 \end{pmatrix}.$$

   (b) How many multiplications are required to obtain $\mathbf{BA}$?
   (c) Program a computer to multiply square matrices of arbitrary order, assuming sufficient capacity in the store.

8. Verify that $\mathbf{A}_r^{-1}$ in Example 10–7 is not a left inverse of $\mathbf{A}$.

9. Prove that if $\mathbf{C} = \mathbf{AB}$, where $\mathbf{A}$ and $\mathbf{B}$ are nonsingular square matrices, then $\mathbf{C}^{-1} = \mathbf{B}^{-1}\mathbf{A}^{-1}$.

10. State and prove for column operations the analogs of Theorems 10–3 through 10–5.

11. Solve the simultaneous linear equations

$$\begin{pmatrix} 3421 & 1234 & 736 & 124 \\ 1202 & 3575 & 874 & 210 \\ 422 & 543 & 3428 & 428 \\ 166 & 256 & 488 & 3627 \end{pmatrix} \begin{pmatrix} w \\ x \\ y \\ z \end{pmatrix} = \begin{pmatrix} 365 \\ 256 \\ 444 \\ 868 \end{pmatrix}.$$

12. Reconcile Theorem 10–6 with Example 10–2.

13. Find the determinant of the system of Example 10–2.

14. Modify the results of Section 10–7 to apply to $\mathbf{Ax} = \mathbf{b}$.

15. (a) Write a computer program to improve an approximate inverse of a matrix of order exactly 5. The matrices $\mathbf{A}$ and $\mathbf{X}_0$ are to be presented as input. The Newton-Raphson process is to be repeated until $|[\mathbf{E}_n]_{ij}| < t$, where t is a preassigned tolerance. The matrix $\mathbf{E}_n$ is never known exactly, of course, but a close approximation to it may be developed either as a byproduct of the computation of $\mathbf{X}_{n+1}$ or as the difference $\mathbf{X}_{n+1} - \mathbf{X}_n$. Show $\mathbf{A}$, $\mathbf{X}_n$, n, $\mathbf{R}_n$, $\mathbf{E}_n$, and t as output.

(b) Explain how your computer program for refining an approximation to the inverse of a matrix of order exactly 5 can be used with matrices of order less than 5.

16. Carry out two iterations of the Newton-Raphson process for inverting

$$\mathbf{A} = \begin{pmatrix} 1 & 2 & 3 \\ 2 & -1 & -3 \\ 4 & 0 & -1 \end{pmatrix},$$

starting with

$$\mathbf{X}_0 = \begin{pmatrix} -0.1 & -0.3 & 0.4 \\ 1.4 & 1.9 & -1.3 \\ -0.6 & -1.1 & 0.7 \end{pmatrix}.$$

17. Program the Seidel process for solving $\mathbf{Ax} = \mathbf{b}$. Incorporate a test for ending the process. How would you guard against divergence?

18. Solve the system

$$\begin{pmatrix} +54.135 & -12.246 & +5.921 \\ -8.294 & -32.589 & +10.437 \\ -2.948 & -18.263 & -67.842 \end{pmatrix} \mathbf{x} = \begin{pmatrix} -45.483 \\ +91.402 \\ -30.651 \end{pmatrix}.$$

(a) Use Gauss elimination to obtain $\mathbf{x}$ to three places beyond the decimal point.

(b) Use the Seidel method to obtain as many more places as your desk calculator can represent. Approximately nine iterations should extend accuracy from 3 to 9 places.

19. Prove that equal polynomials have equal coefficients.

20. Evaluate $P_5(x) = x^5 - 5x^4 + 10x^3 - 10x^2 + 5x - 1$ for $x = 2.4$.

21. Find all the roots of $P_6(x) = x^6 - 3x^5 + 3x^4 + 2x^3 + 2x^2 - 20x$, making use of the fact that one of them is $(3 - i\sqrt{11})/2$.

22. Find all roots of $x^4 + 1.85x^3 - 0.915x^2 - 6.459x - 6.696$.

23. Program the Birge-Vieta process for an automatic computer.

24. Let the matrix

$$\begin{pmatrix} a & b \\ -b & a \end{pmatrix}$$

of real numbers correspond to the complex number $a + ib$.
(a) Show that addition and multiplication of complex numbers correspond to addition and multiplication of matrices so defined.
(b) Using the matrix representation, prove that the complex number $a + ib$ has a reciprocal if and only if it is not zero. *Hint:* Find the condition (in terms of matrices) for the existence of a solution $x + iy$ to the equation

$$(a + ib)(x + iy) = 1 + i0.$$

(c) Prove by use of the matrix representation that if the complex number z is a root of a polynomial with real coefficients, then its complex conjugate $\bar{z}$ is also a root of the polynomial.

25. Find the polynomial of lowest degree that passes through each of the following sets of points:
(a) $(0, -1)$, $(1, -2)$, $(2, -3)$, $(3, 2)$
(b) $(1, 3)$, $(2, 2)$, $(3, 3)$, $(4, 6)$

26. Using the data of Table 11-1, find $f(3.0625)$ and determine x such that $f(x) = 0.334$.

27. (a) Derive a formula for the derivative y_3' in terms of the function values y_j for equally spaced arguments x_1 through x_5.
(b) Derive the five-point closed Newton-Cotes quadrature formula.

28. Using the formulas derived in Exercise 27, calculate $y'(6.10)$ and $\int_{6.06}^{6.14} y(x)\,dx$ from the following table.

x	$y(x)$
6.06	0.15481 76536 49793
6.07	0.15456 66882 16177
6.08	0.15430 03654 53749
6.09	0.15401 87178 38843
6.10	0.15372 17793 63046
6.11	0.15340 95855 29243
6.12	0.15308 21733 47503
6.13	0.15273 95813 30827
6.14	0.15238 18494 90744

29. Consider the three-point open Newton-Cotes formula

$$\int_{x_0}^{x_4} f(x)\ dx = \alpha f_1 + \beta f_2 + \gamma f_3.$$

    (a) Derive the formula by integrating the interpolation polynomial.
    (b) Derive the formula by the method of undetermined coefficients.
    (c) Calculate the error term.

30. Using the method of undetermined coefficients, derive Simpson's three-eighths rule (four-point closed Newton-Cotes formula) for integrating $f(x)$ over three panels. Calculate the error term, on the assumption that it is of the form $E = \alpha h^{k+1} f^{(k)}(\xi)$.

31. Estimate the error in the numerical evaluation by Simpson's one-third rule of $\int_{3.0}^{3.4} (1/x)\ dx$ from the data of Table 11–1.

32. Derive the error term of the four-point open Adams quadrature formula.

33. Using $h = 0.1$, extend in both directions the solution by the midpoint method of $y' = \frac{1}{2}(x^2 - y^2)$, $y(-1) = 1$. Compare with Fig. 6–17.

34. Estimate the error in the value obtained in Example 13–3.

35. Use Eqs. (13–5) with $h = 0.1$ to obtain starting values for the solution of $y' = x^2 + y^2$, $y(0) = 1$.

36. Obtain by Picard's method a series solution of $y' = x^{1/2} + y - 1$, $y(0) = 1$.

37. Start the solution of $y' = x^2 + y$, $y(0) = 1$, for $x = 0(0.1)0.4$ by each of the following methods:
    (a) Use the modified Euler method. Carry 6 significant figures and estimate the error.
    (b) Use the fourth-order Runge-Kutta formula (13–7). Carry 6 significant figures.
    (c) Show that Picard's method yields a Taylor-series solution. Evaluate the series to 6 figures of accuracy and compare with your answers to (a) and (b).

38. Continue to $x = 0.8$ the solution started in Exercise 37.
    (a) Use the single-derivative method.
    (b) Use the closed-formula method.

39. Write an expression for an arbitrary closed quadrature formula in which the integrand is the derivative that appears in a first-order differential equation. Show that, if the differential equation is linear, the formula can be solved explicitly for the ordinate at either end of the range.

40. Solve the differential equation of Exercise 33 for $x = -1(0.1)0$. Start the solution for $x = -1.1, -0.9, -0.8$ by the Runge-Kutta formula (13–7), and continue it with the five-point Newton-Cotes corrector.

41. Program a computer to solve $y' = x^2 + y^2$, $y(0) = 1$, for $x = 0(0.01)1$ by the Runge-Kutta formula (13–7).

42. Program a computer to continue from $x = 0.03$ the solution started by the program of Exercise 41. Use the two-point Adams predictor and the five-point Newton-Cotes corrector.